Barber

P9-BHS-673

The Red Road to Wellbriety

to Healing.

to Recovery

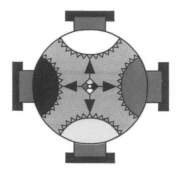

The Red Road to Wellbriety

In the Native American Way

White Bison, Inc.
An American Indian non Profit Organization

Copyright © 2002 White Bison, Inc.

All rights reserved. No portion of this work may be reproduced by any means without written permission from the publisher.

ISBN 0-9719904-0-9

1. Addictions recovery   2. Native American studies

To order books:

White Bison, Inc.
6145 Lehman Drive, Suite 200
Colorado Springs, CO 80918
(719) 548-1000 voice
(719) 548-9407 fax
website:
www.whitebison.org

We dedicate <u>The Red Road to Wellbriety</u> to <u>Handsome Lake</u> (Ganioda'yo), Seneca Nation, for the strength, heart and courage he found to overcome his own struggle with alcohol. Handsome Lake lived in about the year 1800 in the Haudenosaunee (Iroquois) country in what is now upstate New York. We honor him for his active resistance to the disease of alcoholism, and for his dedication to the Good Mind that he understood, so that we may all find sobriety, recovery and Wellbriety.

Opening Prayer

The **Red Road to Wellbriety** is the result of many people's efforts and wisdom all taking place under the sheltering tree of the White Bison, Inc., organization. Some people were directly involved and others lent their words and suggestions through their talks or writing in books, articles, e mails, and in other ways.

We wish to honor the many people who made this book possible.

We also wish to honor the many who gave their personal recovery stories, which are presented here anonymously.

The **Red Road to Wellbriety** is offered to the Great Spirit so that all our relatives may find Sobriety, Recovery, Wellbriety, Healing and Peace.

White Bison, Inc.
Spring, 2002

CONTENTS

CONTENTS

CONTENTS

CONTENTS

Preface

◇ ▱ ◇ ▱ ◇

The Red Road to Wellbriety is a journey of hope and healing for Native Americans seeking recovery from addictions. This is our book to read, to use, and to study as we take our own Red Road journey to sobriety and Wellbriety in a spiritual, emotional, mental, and physical way.

Preface
The Red Road to Wellbriety

The **Red Road to Wellbriety** is a journey of hope and healing for Native Americans seeking recovery from addictions. In this book you will find teaching chapters that provide words of learning about the "Mind Changers" (alcohol and drugs) as they affect our Native people. You will also find many personal recovery stories from Native people who have found sobriety and who are taking the further journey to Wellbriety—*to be both sober and well.* What is this new word *Wellbriety?* We translated it from an Indian word which means a balanced being, a balanced warrior with both a developed male and female side, strongly connected to the principles, laws and values of the universe, someone who walks the Red Road.

This **Red Road to Wellbriety** draws on the philosophies and practices of Alcoholics and Narcotics Anonymous—especially the Twelve Step process. Native Elders say that the Twelve Steps originally compiled by Alcoholics Anonymous have much in common with traditional Native ways—especially if they are viewed in a circle.

But where have we come from and where are we going?

Our Native peoples, families, and those who are different suffered immeasurable loss of life, land, resources, and culture as the European influence started to eradicate our tribal lives. Included in their treatment of indigenous groups was genocide, residential schools, reservations, forced assimilation, and the outlawing of cultural practice, such as

language, spiritual expression and customs. We were left with helplessness, hopelessness, sadness, despair, shame, and anger.

As taught by our Elders, the time would come for us to awaken from our long sleep and search again for the teachings of the Creator through which we would find healing, wisdom, and power. Not power over others, but power over our greatest enemy, ourselves. Many Native people are seeking healing at this time—some because they want to stop inflicting pain on themselves and their loved ones, some to quiet the tears of their children, and some because they want to fill the spiritual emptiness. True healing calls us to ask for the Creator's help. We must learn to cry our tears of sorrow, to confront our shame, to forgive the unforgivable, and to return to the values of our ancestors—love, courage, justice, generosity, respect, humility, gratitude, and acceptance of those who are different.

It is the Good Mind that we seek, the power to see truth, to consult with the Elders again, to seek the counsel of the Creator, to make decisions with the welfare of our children, our families, and our communities to be our first priority. We are each being called to journey the Red Road, to do the healing work that will provide freedom for generations of children to come. We will be free to—

> ❖ **Live life fully with a Good Mind and a loving heart,**
> ❖ **To sing and drum the traditional songs,**
> ❖ **Dream and see visions,**
> ❖ **Perform our sacred ceremonies,**
> ❖ **Seek the wisdom of the Creator,**
> ❖ **Live in peace & harmony with all our relations,**
> ❖ **And to live our lives once again alcohol and drug free.**

Preface

This is our book to read, to use, and to study as we take our own Red Road journey to sobriety and Wellbriety in a spiritual, emotional, mental, and physical way. It is a book to share with our families as we learn to live life fully with a Good Mind and an open heart.

Today, there are thousands of us Native people sober. This book is about how many of our people continue their sobriety, and how we are returning to the Red Road, to help ourselves and all our brothers and sisters to the Path of Recovery.

Introduction

Here the destruction stops.
We will heal ourselves,
We will heal our wounded
relationships,
We will heal our children,
We will heal our Nations.
On this day, our future history
begins

Introduction

All things come full circle. The publication of the *Red Road to Wellbriety* marks a milestone in the history of addiction and recovery among Native peoples in America. It is fitting that the *Red Road to Wellbriety* offers Native interpretations of the Twelve Steps of Alcoholics Anonymous (A.A.) for it was in Native America that the first networks of recovery support groups were formed–nearly 200 years before the founding of A.A.

The history of alcohol problems among Native American tribes is not one of passive destruction, but one of active resistance. Addiction was an alien disease injected into Native cultures, but frameworks of recovery emerged, and have continued to re-emerge, that tap the deepest and most sacred roots of these cultures. There are dark truths in this book that are almost too painful to bear, but rising from the ashes of this pain are liberating truths that burn with the brightness of the sun.

As early as the 1750s, recovery circles grew out of Native American cultural revitalization and religious movements. The beginning of any history of alcoholism recovery in America should be filled with the names of

> ❖ **Wangomend (Assinsink Munsee)**
> ❖ **Papoonan (Unami Delaware)**
> ❖ **Neolin (and the other Delaware Prophets)**
> ❖ **Samson Occom (Mohegan)**
> ❖ **William Apess (Pequot)**
> ❖ **Kenekuk (the Kickapoo Prophet)**

◇ ━ ◆ ━ d ━ ◆ ━ ◇

Introduction

- ❖ Tenskwatawa (the Shawnee Prophet)
- ❖ Kahgegagahbowh (George Copway) (Ojibway)
- ❖ Squ-sacht-un (John Slocum) (Sahewamish)
- ❖ Whe-bul-eht-sah (Mary Thompson) (Sahewamish)
- ❖ Zuanah (Quanah Parker)(Comanche)
- ❖ Ganioda'yo (Handsome Lake) (Seneca)

Zuanah (Quanah Parker) was the central figure in the rise of peyotism and the Native American Church. Squ-sacht-un (John Slocum) and Whe-bul-eht-sah (Mary Thompson) both played pivotal roles in the founding of the Indian Shaker Church. One of the earliest equivalents of A.A.'s Twelve Steps and "Big Book" was the orally-transmitted teachings–the Gai'wiiò ("Good Message") of Ganioda'yo (Handsome Lake) that became known as the Code of Handsome Lake following its introduction in 1799. From the Handsome Lake Movement to the Indian Shaker Church to the Native American Church to the recently emerging Wellbriety Movement, there is an enduring Native tradition of sobriety-based cultural and religious movements.

This publication is dedicated to Handsome Lake and his early efforts in Native American sobriety. It is hoped that this publication will spark interest in Native contributions to the history of alcoholism recovery in America.

What most Native recovery pioneers shared in common was a call for personal sobriety, the use of ancestral teachings to anchor sobriety, and adherence to a code of moral conduct. This way of living has gone by many names, including the "Red Road." The Red Road is a way of achieving sobriety and healing personal and cultural wounds. The Red Road is a way of breaking the cycle of destruction that so often accompanies historical trauma and oppression.

e

Introduction

The *Red Road to Wellbriety* is an invitation to take the Red Road Journey. The term *Wellbriety* is an affirmation that recovery is more than the removal of alcohol and other drugs from an otherwise unchanged life. Wellbriety is a larger change in personal identity and values and a visible change in one's relationship with others. It is about physical, emotional, spiritual, and relational health. Wellbriety is founded on the recognition that we cannot bring one part of our lives under control while other parts are out of control. It is the beginning of a quest for harmony and wholeness within the self, the family and the tribe.

True Wellbriety occurs in the context of community. The *Red Road to Wellbriety* teaches that healthy seeds cannot grow in diseased soil. It teaches that injured seeds need a "Healing Forest." The stories in the *Red Road to Wellbriety* make it clear that the sobriety and healing of the individual are inseparable from the sobriety and healing of the family and the tribe. In these pages are found the connecting tissue between personal sobriety, cultural renewal, nationhood, and sovereignty. (As the *Red Road to Wellbriety* teaches, "There is no sovereignty without sobriety.") The voices that fill these pages reveal how the wounds the individual and community have inflicted on each other can be healed. These voices call for a new relationship between self and community. The Wellbriety of the community creates a healing sanctuary–a culture of recovery–for the wounded individual, just as the growing Wellbriety of the individual feeds the strength of the community. In the Red Road to Wellbriety, the individual, family and community are not separate; they are one. To injure one is to injure all; to heal one is to heal all.

The Wellbriety path does not compete with A.A. or any other pathway of personal recovery, but instead enriches those pathways by embracing them within the web of Native American tribal histories and cultures. In these pages, you will meet people who have committed themselves to live their lives on the Red Road. Here you will meet Native people whose stories embody the living history of Native American recovery. You will hear the details of their addiction and recovery journeys and feel the life

and hope in their words. You will meet a woman of two cultures, a misplaced Indian who found his home, a woman who forgot and then rediscovered who she was, a re-emerging man, and the children and grandchildren who have survived alcoholism. You will learn about A.A. and Al-Anon in the *Red Road to Wellbriety* but you will also learn about Talking Circles, Helping Spirits, the sweat lodge, the Medicine Wheel, sacred dances, smudging rituals, and praying with the eagle feather. You will hear men and women of many tribes and traditions illustrating the diversity of how they came to live sober, meaningful lives.

The tear-stained path of the Red Road leads to recovery, health, wholeness, and dignity, but it is not an easy road to walk. It calls for the power of the Creator, the wisdom of the elder, the courage of the warrior, and the heart of the mother; but like A.A., it is a path of progress, not perfection. Those who contribute their own tears to this path do so as an act of submission and an act of resistance. To walk the Red Road is to offer a silent proclamation:

> **Here the destruction stops.**
> **We will heal ourselves,**
> **We will heal our wounded relationships,**
> **We will heal our children,**
> **We will heal our nation.**
> **On this day, our future history begins.**

The healing from addiction began more than 250 years ago in Native America. The teachings and stories in the *Red Road to Wellbriety* are a call to finish that healing and embark on the journey of Wellbriety. They are a call to open your heart and have faith in where this quest will lead.

Our Native Elders Speak

*We Native people have many names
for this Power that runs the universe.
This book is about what each of our
tribes and traditional ways always
knew. It is about finding this Power
and letting it be in our lives so we
will never have to drink again.*

White Bison

Our Native Elders Speak

In the Big Book of Alcoholics Anonymous, the medical people and the doctors explain the science and the medical understanding of the disease of alcoholism. We believe this chapter in the Big Book is highly accurate and all this knowledge applies to Native People. Here we only want to include some of the insights from our Native Elders, adding to the perspective of the medical model. We want to add a point of view about the spiritual and cultural model.

A long time ago, the Elders told us that a new people (the light skins) would bring four mind changers to our land. These mind changers would place us in a time of being tested as Native people. The Elders told us that the mind changers would have the power to control our thoughts and take over our minds. They would have the power to make us leave our traditional ways. They told us that each of these mind changers had the power to destroy entire tribes. Each had the power to make us turn against one another. They could destroy our families. They said the mind changers had the power to take away all the knowledge we had about ceremonies, raising families, songs, dance, and all we knew about the Mother Earth and her inhabitants—the two-legged, the four-legged, the winged ones, and all the knowledge we had about getting along with each other.

They told us the mind changers would take away our knowledge about how to treat women and how to treat men. The knowledge about the cycle of life and the sacred teachings we gave to our children so they could pass it on to their children. The knowledge about how we were to develop ourselves, to build our character, to ask the Creator to guide our

h

lives and to live in harmony with the earth. All this knowledge was ours at one time. Then the light skins introduced us to the mind changers.

We were told we needed to avoid the mind changers, that if we wrestled with them we would go through a period of being tested. If we failed the test, our people could disappear, our families would crumble, and our world as we once knew it would disappear. They told us the names of the four mind changers. One would be a Liquid, one would be a Black Book, one would be a Song and one would be a Card.

This <u>Red Road to Wellbriety</u> you are reading will deal with the first mind changer, the Liquid. This liquid has many names. It is called alcohol, and in some places it is called "spirits." The Elders said if we drink this spirit, we would be tested, and it would change the minds of many of us.

When our people first started living together, we discovered that nature was a tremendous source of knowledge and wisdom. Because the Creator designed nature, He hid in nature the secrets allowing us to function on this wonderful Mother Earth that we live on. As we observed nature and as we prayed for the Creator to show us its ways, we learned about the spiritual laws, the physical laws, about the stars and about the values that organize the earth. We learned other important information allowing our tribes and people to function.

One of the teachings we learned is that everything travels in a cycle or circle. So we learned about the cycle of life—baby-youth-adult-elder. We learned the four aspects of human development—emotional-mental-physical and spiritual. We knew how to use these elements of growth and how to teach these to our children. We called this knowledge "teachings." These teachings were given to us by the Creator and by nature. They have been passed down for generations by our tribal Elders. We learned that these teachings were meant to guide our thinking. Sometimes we call these teachings and this knowledge the "Good Mind." We learned we do

not own the earth, the earth owns us. We learned to respect all forms of life. Through prayer, clans, tribal societies, and ceremonies we maintained our lives as a people and grew in this way.

Then we were introduced to the mind changer—alcohol. From the very beginning when alcohol was introduced to Indians, there was a noticeable change as soon as it was consumed. It was so powerful the Elders called it a "spirit." They could only see a bottle of liquid, but the Elders said within that liquid was a spirit. This spirit had the power to change our mind, to make us say things and do things that were shocking. Even the settlers knew about its power. They had us drink it before we traded furs and before we signed papers to "give" our land away. They knew it changed our minds and made us foolish.

We have been struggling with this "spirit" ever since. Each generation has tried to pass this test and each generation has failed. Each generation has suffered the results of the mind changer, just as the old people said might happen a long time ago.

But we do have the power to overcome this mind changer. One way is just not to drink it. If you never drink it, you won't have to enter the testing time.

But if you already drank it, then there are other powers that will help you overcome the alcohol spirit so we can straighten out the damage and destruction we have generated. The Elders are very clear—*we must find a Power greater than ourselves and ask it for help*. For some of us, each time we drink an immediate reaction is noticeable. It affects our judgment, it

allows us to be more sociable and friendly, it allows us to hurt the ones we love, it allows us to put ourselves down and feel unworthy.

This battle with alcohol is not a white man's problem. It is not a BIA problem. It is not a government problem. This is an Indian problem. No one is making us take this drink. We are the ones who are drinking it. It is the first drink that makes us drunk. It is the first drink that makes the mind changer show up.

The Elders say that the Mother Earth who gave knowledge to our ancestors is still here with the same knowledge. She will give it to us if we are willing to seek it. But they tell us because we are made with a free will it is *us* who must reach out our hand for help.

There are so many ways available for us to get help and find this Power greater than ourselves. We have the sweat lodge, our eagle feathers, the Elders, ceremonies, going into nature to pray. Many of us have hurt a lot of people, especially the ones we love, and we are ashamed. For many of us, the only way back is to find a contact with the Higher Power.

We must be willing to start the healing and look for ways to help ourselves. When we start to heal after having used the mind changer for a long time, we find out the mind changer still has power over us. It has power over our will, power over our mind, and power over our heart. It has the control—so we need to find a Power that is stronger and bigger than it is. A Power that is interested in our good. A Power that will help us repair our lives and restore ourselves, our families, and our communities.

We Native people have many names for this Power that runs the universe. This book is about what each of our tribes and traditional ways always knew. It is about finding this Power and letting it be in our lives so we will never have to drink again.

As alcoholics, and people wounded by other drugs, each of us is probably able to tell the story of how this Power didn't show up in our lives. Maybe I wasn't raised with a Higher Power in my life. Maybe I attended church but didn't understand the teaching. Maybe I used the drunk's prayer, "God, get me out of this one and I promise I will never do it again..." But He didn't get me out of it. We could tell many stories of something that happened causing us not to accept a Higher Power in our lives. Maybe it was the death of a loved one, a brother or sister, or a mother or father. There are many reasons why we didn't allow this Higher Power in our lives.

Our Elders are very clear that if we have a problem with alcohol or drugs, we need to find this Power and ask it to help us. This is our Elders' opinion.

Chapter 1
One Journey to Wellbriety
A Lakota Elder

I used to be against religion, but after I sobered up I went back to traditional philosophy as my Higher Power. I got the Pipe and had my vision quest. I Sundanced. I went through everything I felt it was necessary for me to do. But I condemned religion wrongly. Religion and faith are OK.

Chapter 1
One Journey to Wellbriety
A Lakota Elder

The principles of Alcoholics Anonymous and traditional Native culture have a lot in common. Traditional culture teaches respect and service to the people. An Elder speaks about his sobriety journey through AA and his Native ways.

I appreciate this opportunity to share some of the knowledge which I've learned over quite a period of years. I started on my own journey on January 1st, 1954. It just happened that I got thrown in jail on New Year's Eve, 1953, and from there I did five months in jail, so I had a good jump on sobriety. I got into AA (Alcoholics Anonymous) at that time and it was my first introduction to it. At that time alcoholism and alcoholics weren't part of our vocabulary as Indian people. We didn't know anything about it and we couldn't care less. That was the start of my journey.

It would be nice if I could say I have been sober for 45 years, but like a lot of us after four years of sobriety I fell off the wagon and had to struggle to keep my journey going. In 1966 I got out of jail again after 47 days in Mira Loma up north of Los Angeles. I got a 60-day sentence and did 47 of them before starting on my sober journey again. It's kind of funny that both of my long periods of sobriety started out by being thrown in jail. That part of my history gave me an opportunity to take another good look at where I was going, what I was doing, and what changes I had to

make to be an acceptable person in the communities in which I was involved.

I had a hard time with the spiritual part of the program and particularly the Third Step: **Made a decision to turn my will and my life over to the care of God as I understood Him.** I read a lot about the genocide that occurred amongst our people. I read about the Minnesota uprising where 38 of our warriors were hung because they rebelled against unjust treatment (Mankato, Minnesota, 1862). I blamed the Christian dominant society. At that time I blamed the people who did all this to us because they were supposed to be a government under God. I couldn't talk about my spiritual program because I couldn't accept the Christian concept of God. I could talk about my life being unmanageable and that I wanted to help somebody else. I was a First and Twelfth stepper. So that's where I had some problems with the total structure of AA.

The guys used to tell me, "If you don't believe in God, you are either an atheist or an agnostic." And I knew that I was neither. I was fortunate enough to have been born in an era where I experienced the love and caring of my grandparents who grew up in the old style, in the old way of life. My grandmother used to talk about fighting the soldiers and running. My grandmother was my grandfather's second woman. His first woman had passed away and left him two sons. My grandmother was quite a lot younger than he was. My grandfather and his old buddies used to talk about "when we killed Custer..." I grew up with those Elders as my mentors, and with people who guided me in my early years. When we got something special to eat, my grandmother would put a piece of it out and give it to the spirits. So I had a spiritual background, a traditional spiritual background.

When I sobered up and got out of jail in Los Angeles, I had a full-time job at a dye factory, and then a part-time job as a Vista coordinator under an OEO (Office of Economic Opportunity) program at the Indian Center. One day while I was sorting through the mail, I ran into a periodical and

found an article called "An Indian's Creed." The first paragraph said, "Although he believed in many lesser gods, he accepted the idea of one Supreme Spirit who was everywhere all the time and whose help was needed continually and could be sought through prayer and sacrifice." I had struggled for many years trying to have a spiritual program, but I think this was my spiritual experience or spiritual awakening. I read the whole article through, and it dealt with a lot of behavioral things—about honesty, respect, the body as a temple of your soul, respect for parents, respect for each other, morality, and all the positive virtues and values that go into being a decent human being. My ancestors believed in this, they believed in a Creator and this was my Higher Power. So I had a higher power. I've been sober ever since. My sobriety birthday is November 22, 1966.

After that, I started to study and learn about the culture. A lot of us of that time were pretty much brain-washed through the boarding school system by being taught that our way of life was not very good. When I came home, I started learning about the Sacred Pipe and about some of our ceremonies. I was familiar with them because of things that I had heard from the medicine people. My spiritual journey began, but I still went to AA. I still go to AA, too.

I've been an alcoholism counselor and a program director. I worked at the VA (Veteran's Administration) hospital in Hot Springs, South Dakota, where a lot of our people came. Sometimes up to 75% of a thirty-bed treatment program was made up of Native people. One time I went to a conference on behavioral science in New Orleans. The treatment program was under the department of psychology. The chief of psychology services took me along to this conference in New Orleans, and I got to

meet the head of all alcohol and drug programs for the Veterans Administration. He was concerned because our people weren't taking advantage of all the benefits, which were ours in the veteran's program.

When I came back to Hot Springs we eventually got an hour a day for our Native people to talk about their issues. I told the guys that part of their commitment as warriors is to help our people—the widows and orphans, the elderly or physically handicapped, or the mentally ill who can't help themselves adequately. And also to bring honor to the Warrior Society. We started to talk about that, and the guys complained, "...there's nothing to do." I said, "there's all kinds of stuff to do. You can work with kids, be on the school board—there's a lot of things that you can do to bring honor to warriors."

I started to do research on warrior societies. I looked into the culture, background and history of why warrior societies were organized and how individuals became members of the society. I felt that I had seen this before. Then all at once it dawned on me. All these principles, all these values, the things that we should do and shouldn't do were also in the AA 12 Steps and 12 Traditions. This is part of our ancestor's way of life. This is something that they followed in order to be who they were. It surprised me that some of the guys were shying away from AA.

We talked about it, and I said we shouldn't have any problems as to the spiritual program. Some said, "I'm not a religious person, I don't go to church." I told them they should have no problem with spirituality because our culture is a spiritually based culture. It's part of our heritage. It's passed down to us. So within us, each one of us as a Native American, whether you are north of the border in this country, or south of the border, has this spirituality flowing through their DNA. It's part of us. We can't get rid of it. It's here. That's what stirs us.

When we hear the drum, we feel like dancing. I've seen guys who have been raised by non-Indian foster parents from the time they were babies

until they became adults, come back into the community, come to the powwows and just fit right in because that's who they are. So we should have no problem going to AA or following our traditional methods to stay sober.

I looked at the 12 Steps of AA and started to compare them to some of the things that we did. I wrote an article about AA and its cultural relevance. I also found information on the Laws of the Lodge—the Laws of how we should treat our guests and the things we are obligated to do as traditional people, Native people. I also found information on our Native American traditional ethics. They are good articles to look at and try to practice because this is the way our ancestors lived. In doing all these studies and research I came to believe, and I firmly believe, that our ancestors were very, very intelligent people.

A lot of the concept of the traditional way of life being comparable to the AA way of life comes up in other places. In our way, we say our children are sacred, we should nurture them, we should love them, we should care for them, because they are like the jewels in our crown. Someone said it takes a whole village to raise a child. It's a catch phrase used by politicians who want to sound good. But our people were doing that before the European ever came over here.

If you dig deep enough into our history, go back into your culture and where you are from, a lot of the concepts that come up as social solutions and resolutions about what our human behavior should be, our people were practicing in some way or another before the European ever came over here. I tell the youngsters who I work with that they are the descendants of a very, very intelligent race of people. As an example, I

asked how many had ever seen a birch bark canoe? And one or two said they had. And then I said, "You didn't see a nail or any metal in that birch bark canoe." I said, "Your ancestors built that without a diagram." I said, "If you want to build a chair, somewhere you'll find a diagram that tells you exactly how to build that chair. But your ancestors took the raw materials and built a canoe that would carry weight, take some bumping on the rocks, and be light enough to carry around the falls, without a single instrument or diagram. It all came out of their heads." Intelligence. That's how smart our ancestors are. I wanted to emphasize the high degree of intelligence, the medicines they used, their belief in the unity of the whole universe.

One person told me years ago that in order to turn things around for yourself you have to have had high ideals and principles instilled in you early in life. I was fortunate enough to have that as a basis of my recovery. It helped me to persevere and to struggle when things were tough. I now know you can also learn good principles and values on the Wellbriety journey.

On one occasion, I spoke at an AA meeting in Rapid City. I spoke about what I had understood about the traditional culture and AA—how they coincided and how our ancestors had thought of this pattern of living before the white man ever came. When I got through with my story they looked at me like I had just committed blasphemy, like I had shot down the concept of AA, which I didn't do. There were a lot of AA hard liners who really believed in AA solidly and who got angry if there was anything negative said about AA.

On another occasion, an article came out in a newspaper, which said at least one-fourth of the prison population in South Dakota is Native American. It talked about sobriety and how the prisoners wouldn't go to AA because it didn't have a cultural orientation. I worked with many people over the years who said they wouldn't go to AA because it was white man's stuff. After I did my research on AA and our traditional way

of life, I talked about using the sweat lodge ceremony. As an example, we can go into the sweat lodge and "admit we are powerless over alcohol and that our lives had become unmanageable." We can ask for help to get our act back together and restore us to sanity in the sweat lodge. We can commit ourselves to our Higher Power, our Creator. We can "Turn our will and our lives over to the care of the Creator, as we understood Him." And we can take our inventory in the lodge. In the Sioux culture we call the sweat lodge a purification ceremony. In purification and prayer ceremonies, you can ask for forgiveness. Or you can "Admit to yourself, to God and to another human being the exact nature of our wrongs." That could be done in the sweat lodge.

The sweat lodge is also a good place to say, "We were entirely ready to have God remove all these defects of character," and "To humbly ask him to remove our shortcomings," and "To make a list of all the persons we had harmed and became willing to make amends to them all." And then there are the maintenance steps of AA: Steps 10, 11 and 12. Those can be done at every sweat lodge ceremony. "Continue to take inventory and when wrong promptly admit it." "Continue to improve our conscious contact with God." "Pray only for knowledge of his will for us and the power to carry that out." You can do that in the sweat lodge. And "Having had a spiritual experience as a result of these Steps, we try to practice these principles in all our affairs." The AA idea of "Principles before Personalities" was always a way of life in our traditional culture.

We have the answers to all of our problems within our culture and within our heritage. We don't have to go outside of our own culture to find solutions to our problems. We just have to look at them honestly and

without bias. The traditional way of life that our ancestors developed was passed on to us as our heritage but we somehow dropped the ball and now are struggling to solve our problems.

I used to be against religion, but after I sobered up I went back to traditional philosophy as my Higher Power. I got the Pipe and had my vision quest. 1 sundanced. I went through everything I felt it was necessary for me to do. But I condemned religion wrongly. Religion and faith are OK. There's nothing wrong with them—if you follow that way as it is presented to the best of your ability, you'll be a good person. All the principles of any world religion—the Old Testament, the Hebrew faith, the New Testament, the Islamic faith, Buddhism, Shintoism, Confucianism—all these are world religions that we should respect. Their basic principles teach us to be a good person. I have no problems with religion any more.

As a people, we have a head start because we are from a basically spiritual culture. In AA, it says our leaders are our trusted servants—they do not govern. In our traditional cultures the headman of any clan, or group, or tribe is a person who was selected not because he was a strong man, not because he was wealthy, but because he was a good role model. Compare it to the European social structure where there was a king or a ruler or an emperor—an upper class and a ruling class of people who had absolute power over their subjects. They could order somebody killed and they would be killed. Our ancestors didn't allow that. We didn't have a caste system. There was no upper class, middle class or lower class, shopkeepers and peons. They knew if you put power in the hands of one person or a small group of people they would abuse that power. They knew people would suffer, so they never allowed that. That, to me, was another indication of a high degree of intelligence. Nobody can convince me that I didn't come from a very intelligent race of people.

Chapter 2
The Solution is in the Culture

There is a solution for us as Native people, and for some of us it is a return to the traditional ceremonies of our Nations. For some of us, it is to <u>seek out an Elder and have him or her help us find the path to the Good Road</u> or to the Red Road as we call it.

Chapter 2
The Solution is in the Culture

A long time ago, our people knew about living in harmony with the Earth Mother. We knew that our Mother Earth was sacred, and all that she produced was sacred, and all things were to be held in respect. When we encountered the European influence and were re-educated through their schools we lost the knowledge of how to think with the Good Mind or how to keep the realization of how we were supposed to conduct ourselves. We started to forget how to be respectful to our children, to our spouses, to our communities, and to nature. The solution for those of us who have this disease of alcoholism or other addictions is to find contact with The Great Mystery, which goes by many other names in each of our own traditions.

This is not about going back and living in teepees. This is about looking back to find out how our ancestors used to think and conduct themselves, and learning how to think like that today in the world in which we live—a world of computers and contemporary life. In our cultural ways are the secrets of how to contact the Higher Power, which will help us to change our lives around and become the responsible people we secretly want to be. When we return to our culture, or to whatever spirituality that works for us, we will grow stronger in self-understanding and self-forgiveness. We will begin to understand our feelings. We will begin to understand why it is that we think our lives are going one way but end up going on a destructive path instead. A path guided by alcohol and drugs. You know the questions we have asked ourselves so many times, "...why is my life so screwed up? What happened to me?"

There Are Solutions

There are solutions for us as Indian people, and for some of us it is a return to the traditional ceremonies of our Nations. For some of us, it is to seek out an Elder and have him or her help us find our path to the Good Road, or to the Red Road as we call it. For many of us it is participation in sobriety sweat lodges. It will require learning our ways of prayer. Many of us are now smudging with sage, cedar, sweetgrass or the other herbs of our Mother Earth. We are forming our Circles of Recovery and we are praying with the Eagle Feather, passing it back and forth to talk to one another when subjects of importance are discussed. Some of us seek a vision in the traditional way, going on the hill with the guidance of our medicine people. And some are revitalizing the old warrior or clan societies after talking with Elders who still remember those ways.

Our communities have suffered from alcohol, domestic violence, dysfunctional families, and now, drug use. It's a cycle that goes through our families. It is called a "cycle of hurt" because our violence and drinking problems are passed down through our families and communities. Generation after generation, through grandpa and grandma, father and mother, on to our own children, and to their children, the hurtful patterns repeat themselves. For some of us, we thought this way of life was normal. Now we need to get our people to a place where we can do our part in breaking this harmful repeating pattern. We have our part to do. The Higher Power working through us does the rest.

Each of our Tribes and Nations are different from one another. We each have our own cultural ways and even our own cultural names for Creator. (See the end of this chapter) Some of us have chosen to follow the ways of a tribe that is different than our own. We do whatever it takes

to <u>find a relationship</u> with the <u>Creator</u> that will help us stop struggling with the alcohol, drugs and violence behaviors.

Many of us are trying to find our way out of this addicted way of life. It is so hard sometimes to find a something we can grasp onto that will help us pull ourselves out of this hell hole. We hope to offer a few suggestions that will help all us Native Americans.

The old people tell us that the frame of reference for our thinking is the Mother Earth and the Universe. When the Creator finished creating the earth, He left all things to function by a set of **Principles, Laws and Values**. The Creator said all creatures, plants, the four legged, the two legged, the Two Spirited, the winged ones—all forms of life—will abide by these laws, sometimes called the Natural Laws. If we live in harmony with these laws, we will know harmony, balance, and peace. If we live out of harmony, we will know chaos. Long ago, our communities were very knowledgeable about how to live in harmony. We passed this information from generation to generation through our clans, societies, songs, dance, ceremonies, Elders, and our teachings. When we stopped passing it on, we started to forget. Today, many of us are searching for this knowledge. When each of us finds it again, we will find the door to the Creator and spirituality. It is then we stop drinking and drugging and we get back on the Red Road. Today, we call this knowledge our teachings.

The Medicine Wheel Teachings
The Medicine Wheel is a circle teaching. It is a way of sharing knowledge, information or concepts that align with the system that the Great Spirit put into place a long time ago. The Medicine Wheel teachings explain that anything growing always grows as **a system of circles and cycles.** Whether it's animals, plants, organizations or anything that's growing,

anything that has life, that being always grows following circular or cyclic principles.

One of these principles is **the four directions: east, south, west and north.** Each of these directions has qualities and powers associated with it. The Medicine Wheel teaches about **a cycle of life.** In the east you have the direction of the baby or infanthood. In the south lies the direction of the youth. In the west would be the direction of the adult. and the north is the direction of the Elder. So, the cycle of life is **baby, youth, adult, and elder.**

There is also a **cycle of seasons: spring, summer, fall, and winter,** associated with the four directions. Springtime is about new beginnings and new possibilities. In Summertime the sun pours down on the land in a time of growth. Fall or the autumn season is the time of the harvest and when bountiful crops come in. Winter is a time of stopping and reflection when the mother earth rests. There are **four directions of human growth—the emotional, the mental, the physical, and the spiritual,** also linked to the four directions. If we want to get to our place of power, if we want to find our place of harmony, then it is by working with ourselves in these four directions that such growth will be achieved. Different colors are often associated with the Medicine Wheel and these may vary from tradition to tradition. In the Wellbriety Movement we use **red for the east, yellow for the south, black for the west and white for the north.** These four colors also symbolize all the races or ethnicities that are coming together at this time and meeting in the circle.

A Medicine Wheel that's connected with breaking the cycle of hurt from alcohol and drugs is one that places the individual in the East, the family in the South, the community in the West and the Nation in the North. This is the **Individual, Family, Community and Nation** Medicine Wheel. To take the Red Road Wellbriety Journey, we always come into this Medicine Wheel through the first door—the individual. When you receive healing yourself, then you can go on and help in healing your

family. When families begin to change or heal, then communities naturally begin to change. As our communities come into wellness, then our Native Nations will heal and become functional.

We were also told that the system the Creator put into place is **a balanced system.** Whether we are talking about the system at the level of an atom, or about life, there always seems to be two roads. It's a balanced system with two polarities—**a polarity-based system.** For example, there is plus-minus, man-woman, here-there, up-down, boy-girl, east-west, north-south and good-bad, just to name a few examples of polarities. The Medicine Wheel teaches about bringing and keeping that system in balance. The natural laws are designed to have us live in balance. If we go out of balance, the natural laws let us know through feedback. We human beings will experience this feedback in some form of tension, anxiety or stress. If we go more out of balance, the stress increases.

The Elders also told us that in the system the Creator put into place there are two worlds that exist—there is a **seen world** and there's also **an unseen world.** The seen world we might call the physical world, and the unseen world today we might call the spiritual world. The unseen world is just as real as the seen world. If we, in building our families or running our organizations, live our lives and direct our thinking to be **in harmony** with all the principles, laws, and values of both the physical and spiritual worlds, we will see positive results in our lives and in our organizations. They also said we have the choice of living **out of harmony**. Should we choose dis-harmony, we will see different results in our lives. We'll see a lot of confusion, a lot of chaos, a lot of fighting, a lot of injustice, a lot of fault-finding, a lot of conflict, a lot of violence between one another—which we are living through today.

The teachings of the Medicine Wheel also tell us that the system that the Creator put into place is an **interconnected system.** All too often we continue to be taught about the separateness of things. We make decisions based on what our eyes can see, we make decisions based on what our ears can hear, we make decisions based on what we can smell or what we can measure. But if we just give that a little thought we are able to come to terms with the fact that there is a world beyond our sight, there is a world beyond our senses. Our Elders told us that the system that we live in is really **interconnected, interdependent,** and all things are in **relationship** with one another. In many of the Native ceremonies you will hear people say "we are related to one another." The Lakota people say, "Mitkuye Oyasin," which means *for all my relations.*

When we look at our families and our organizations, we need to understand and look at things as being integrated, interconnected and related. For example, one of the teachings of the Medicine Wheel says that **The Honor of One is the Honor of All.** And if that is true, then **The Pain of One is the Pain of All.** In an interconnected system, because everything is connected, if there is pain anywhere, then that pain is everyone's pain. If something happens in one side of the system, whatever happens there is always felt through the entire family or organization.

The Medicine Wheel also teaches about the alignment of **spirit and intent**. If my thinking, feelings and decisions are in harmony with the principles, laws, and values of the Medicine Wheel, if my thoughts are aligned with that spirit and intent, you can tell because you and I are connected. Because we're connected, you can also tell if I function out of harmony with spirit and intent. In other words, if I lie or use

manipulative words, or if I function outside of truth, you can tell because we're connected in the unseen world of spirit.

Another thing that the Elders have taught us about this interconnected system is that it is **an evolving system.** "Evolving" means it is designed with a mechanism that is constantly changing. The teachings of the Medicine Wheel say this: that which is built is constantly being destroyed. That which is loose is being used to build new things. For example, if you were to take and build a log cabin out in the woods, and you did nothing to maintain that log cabin, it would be just a matter of time, without anyone doing anything, that it would start to crumble. It would start to return to the mother earth. And then it would just finally be absorbed and you wouldn't even know it had been there.

One consequence of a constantly changing polarity-based system is the reality of **conflict and struggle.** Everything in the universe grows and changes through a process of struggle and conflict. In order for anything to grow or change it must struggle to do so first. Conflict is a natural part of growing. Conflict is a friend, not an enemy. We usually hate it when conflict begins. But the teaching says, "When the struggle starts, get happy." It means a change is starting to occur. **Conflict precedes clarity.**

If there's no struggle, the odds aren't too good that anything of significance is going to occur. Conflict is a guidance system, it's a friend. Did you ever notice how good you feel when you get clarity after a conflict?

These teachings of the Medicine Wheel are what we are seeking in the Medicine Wheel and the 12 steps Way. If I don't have these teachings in my life, then my life is unmanageable.

Some Medicine Wheels

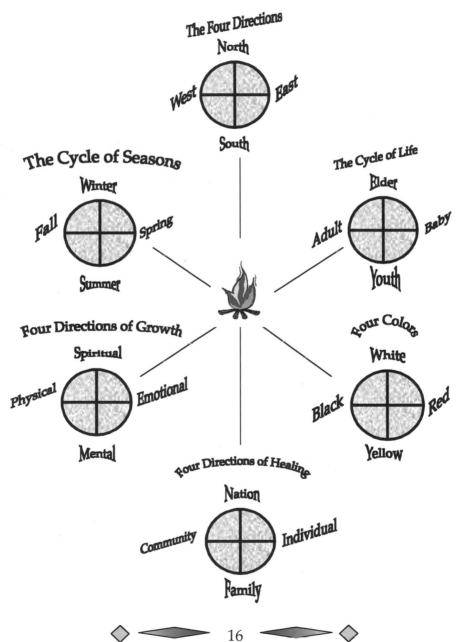

The Four Directions

North

West

East

South

The Cycle of Seasons

Winter

Fall

Spring

Summer

The Cycle of Life

Elder

Adult

Baby

Youth

Four Directions of Growth

Spiritual

Physical

Emotional

Mental

Four Colors

White

Black

Red

Yellow

Four Directions of Healing

Nation

Community

Individual

Family

The Circle

The circle is sacred. When we sit in a circle, we are sitting in the exact design of the universe. The atom is in a circle and Mother earth is in a circle. The moon circles around the earth and the earth circles around the sun. Therefore, when we sit in a circle all the natural laws are designed to support anything that is taking place in a circle. When we recover we form **Circles of Recovery.** We heal in a circle and we talk in a circle. We experience the **power of the circle.** The **Talking Circle** is one of our solutions for addictions recovery as Native Americans.

To meet together in a talking circle, arrange the chairs in a circle in the room where you'll hold your recovery session. Leave a space in the chairs at the eastern door of the circle. At the center of the circle place some of the sacred elements that are of meaning to your Nation or culture. Your Elders will know what these are. At the center of our talking circles, we use cloth of the four colors and four directions—red, yellow, black and white—to signify the four colors of the Medicine Wheel. These colors also signify the **coming together time** in which all races of the earth are meeting each other now. We also have an abalone shell with sage for a smudge, and an eagle wing or feather at the center of the circle.

The facilitator of the talking circle lights the sage and makes a prayer in his or her own way. Then the facilitator takes the smudge of burning sage, or whatever is appropriate in your culture or region, around to each and every person in the circle. The facilitator allows each person to smudge themselves, and may also brush them down with the eagle feather. When the facilitator completes the circle, he or she gives the sage and the feather to someone else so he or she can smudge.

To begin the talking part of the talking circle, the facilitator might speak on a topic to get the circle going, or might just ask people to introduce themselves. A sacred talking object is passed to the first speaker. The talking object or element can be the eagle feather, or it can be anything of meaning to the community. When a person is holding the talking object, only that person should speak without any interruption. Try to speak from the heart. Say what you are feeling. When you are finished, pass the talking element to the next person, or place it back at the center so the next person who decides to speak can pick it up.

The facilitator is not a leader in the sense of someone in control, but rather is a person who allows the circle to take place in a good way. He or she might have to intervene with a particular speaker if there is a time limit on the circle as a whole, in order to keep to some orderly schedule. The facilitator might also intervene if people are talking directly back and forth to one another or becoming disrespectful. Respect is the main guideline for a talking circle. At the conclusion of a talking circle, the facilitator or someone else makes a closing prayer.

The talking circle is one of the solutions available to us as Native people. It is very sacred because people will let go of their difficulties into the circle and become much lighter and freer. There are many **gifts of the circle** waiting for us. When you participate in a talking circle, remember: *What you hear here.... Who you see here.... When you leave here.... Leave it here..*

Values

Our traditional values are another solution for us in the struggle against alcohol, drugs and dysfunctional behaviors. European influence caused us to take on values and attitudes that were not those coming through our families and nations. This conflict in values between our own and

ones coming from a far-off land, created stress, anxiety and frustration in the people who lived here. Returning to our own cultures means returning to some of our traditional values.

Here is a list that compares Traditional Native American Values with today's Euro-American values. Study and think about what you read here. Talk over what the words mean. Discuss the meaning of our traditional values in your recovery talking circles. How can you return to some of the traditional values in your own life and in your families and communities? How can your local school systems and community organizations begin returning to these traditional values? What is the interplay, give-and-take, or possibly struggle that we might feel between our traditional values as Native Americans, and today's contemporary values?

Traditional Native American Values	Euro-American Contemporary Values
Cooperation	Competition
Group Emphasis	Individual Emphasis
Modesty, Humility	Self-Important
Individual Autonomy	Interference/Involvement
Passivity/Calmness	Activity / Restlessness
Generosity	Saving
Patience	Impatience
Non-materialism	Materialism
Work to Meet Need	Puritan Work Ethic
Time--Always With Us	Time--Use Every Minute

Traditional Native American Values (Continued)	Euro-American Contemporary Values
Orientation to Present	Orientation to the Future
Pragmatic, Practical	Theoretical
Respect for Age	Respect for Youth
Right Brain Orientation	Left Brain Orientation
Cooperate with Nature	Control over Nature
Religion--Way of Life	Religion--Segment of Life
Spiritual-Mystical	Skeptical
Personal Caution	Personal Openness
Listening / Observation Skills	Verbal Skills
Indirect Criticism	Direct Criticism
Extended Family	Nuclear Family
Cultural Pluralist	Assimilationist
No Eye to Eye Contact	Eye to Eye Contact Important
Self-Exploratory Child Rearing	Strict Discipline
Restitution	Punishment
Character=Source of Status	Degree=Source of Status
Bilingualism	Monolingualism
Illness=Imbalance(s)	Illness=Physical Issue
Belief in the Unseen	Belief in the Seen /Proven
Respect for Tradition	Progress Oriented

Our Communities

The Four Laws of Change are another solution available to our communities on the Wellbriety journey. The Four Laws were given by a Native American Elder and can take us all the way from individual wellness to the healing of our families, communities, and nations. The Four Laws of Change state:

> *The Four Laws of Change*
>
> 1) **Change is from within**
> 2) **In order for development to occur it must be preceded by a vision**
> 3) **A great learning must occur**
> 4) **You must create a healing forest**

1-Change is from within means that all positive and lasting change begins on the inside of an individual and works its way out. The change that ends our drinking and drugging is <u>a change in our hearts</u>. It's a change in the way we are "leaning," which is what we mean when we say "attitudes." It's not just <u>a change in where we live</u> (the "geographic cure") or a change in jobs or spouses. Something must touch us and get through to us. It can happen in a ceremony. It can happen in a Circle. It can happen when we are alone out on the land. It can happen in so many ways. But it first <u>happens deep inside a person.</u>

2-In order for development to occur it must be preceded by a vision Another way of saying this is "No vision--no development." Our communities must go through a visioning process in which the deep

hopes and dreams of community members come out from inside and are expressed. This community vision is the direction the community wants to take. It can be facilitated by asking the question, "What would our community be like if it were healthy and 'working?'" The answers to this question are the direction that our leadership will take us as the community begins its healing and growth process. The community can't develop economically, educationally, in sovereignty, and in other ways unless there is a clear community dream pointing the way.

3-A great learning must occur means that new information and learning must begin to happen in both individuals and community life. Bringing the Teachings of the Medicine Wheel into the heart is one example of a great learning. Understanding the ways of the **fear-based system** and the **love-based systems** are another. (See chapter 10) Learning about the alcoholic family and Indian Alanon issues is still another. This Third Law also includes school-based education and the skills needed for today's way of life. All four ages in the cycle of life—Baby, Youth, Adult and Elder—must participate in the Learning.

4-You must create a healing forest. Suppose there is a one-hundred acre forest that is very sick. If a few of the trees decide they want to get well they might decide to slip away by night and go to a nearby tree nursery for a thirty-day treatment of de-tox for trees, followed by vitamins and lots of group processes and other recovery activities. But after thirty days those trees might think, "Well, now I'm all better and I want to go back home to my forest." But the forest at home is still sick and pretty soon the trees that went into treatment and felt so good will slowly but surely get sick once again after they go home.

Our communities are like that sick forest. Our family and community members are like sick trees having their roots down in unhealthy soil. The first layer of the soil is a layer of anger. The next layer is a layer of guilt. The layer beneath that is a layer of shame. And the deepest layer of our community and family soil is a layer of fear. How can our communities

heal if everyone is experiencing **anger, guilt, shame and fear**? Some of our "trees" might be alcoholic trees. And some of the trees, if not alcoholic themselves, might be married to the alcoholic trees. Some of the trees are co-dependent trees and some are children of alcoholic trees. Some trees might be domestic violence trees and some might be the men, women or children who are targets of that family violence.

The Fourth Law of Change says our communities heal best if much of the community begins to participate in the healing. We must create a Healing Forest.

Cultural Names for the Sacred

Each of our own Tribal Nations, cultures or Ways has its own word for the Sacred in its own Native language. One of the ways we can return to the culture is to begin to learn and use these special words in our spirituality. Each of these names might have slightly different spellings when they come into English because the English word is trying to imitate the word in our language. Here is a very short listing of some of the names for the Sacred from a few Native cultures. To understand the real meaning of these words we would have to go to the Culture they represent. We encourage you to talk to an Elder or a traditional person in your own Tribe to learn of the name that is right for you. We invite you to add to this list and to use Creator's name in your language in a good and respectful way. [1]

Acaahadadea (Crow) • **Awonawilona** (Zuni) • **Kitche Manito** (Algonquian) • **Maheo** (Cheyenne) • **Nawalak** (Kwakiutl) • **Orenda** (Iroquois) • **Sulia** (Salish) • **Sus-sustinako** (Keres, Tabaldak, or Ktsi) • **Nwaska** (Abenaki) • **Taiowa** (Hopi) • **Tam Apo** (Shoshone) • **Ussen** (Apache) • **Wakan Tanka** (Lakota) • **Yoka** (Cherokee) • **Tunkashila** (Lakota) • **Sila** (Iglulik) • **Hozho** (Dine' or Navajo)
Creator's Name in My Culture: XaLe's

Remembering This Chapter

Teachings of the Medicine Wheel

- Circles and Cycles
- The Cycle of Life
- Four Directions of growth

- Four Directions of Healing
- Balance
- Polarity Based System

- Spirit and Intent
- Conflict Precedes Clarity

- The Four Directions
- The Cycle of Seasons
- Four Colors (Coming Together Time)

- Harmony
- Interconnectedness
- The Seen and the Unseen World

- Evolving System
- The Honor of One Is the Honor of All

- Principles, Laws and Values

Some Solutions For Us

- ❖ Medicine Wheel Teachings
- ❖ Gifts of the Circle
- ❖ Traditional Values and Culture
- ❖ The Four Laws of Change
- ❖ Cultural Names for the Sacred

Chapter 3
Alcoholism
The Hurt of Our Past is the Hurt of Our Present

*"Whiskey is a great and monstrous evil
and has reared a high mound of bones.
You lose your minds, and whiskey causes
it all. So now all must say, 'I will use it
nevermore.'"*

Handsome Lake (**Ganioda'yo**)
Seneca Nation, about 1800

Chapter 3
Alcoholism
The Hurt of Our Past is the Hurt of Our Present

Indian people can benefit from many of the alcohol and other drug recovery programs that are out there today. The Big Book of Alcoholics Anonymous contains a great deal of information about what alcoholism is all about, what alcohol does to us as human beings, and then how we behave in return. But there are some reasons for alcoholism in Indian country that are different than in the wider society and it will be good to think a little about our own history.

Our indigenous peoples of Turtle Island (North America) were not peoples who used alcohol for ceremonial or social purposes before Europeans arrived in the Caribbean in 1492. Other indigenous peoples in other parts of the world may have used alcohol in their traditional past, but our people in this part of the world did not. The Europeans who came to our land had been using alcohol in their societies for thousands of years. Today when archeological digs reveal artifacts from sites in the Near East, the birthplace of European civilization, they almost always discover wine cups and other evidence of alcohol consumption. Europeans had become used to drinking alcohol by the time they arrived on our shores, but the Indigenous people of Turtle Island had no natural physical defense or mental understanding of alcohol.

Words From The People

Our Elders and leaders struggled with what they saw happening to their people as a result of alcohol consumption long before the United States became a Nation. In 1722 Mohican Chief Aupaumut, in what is now the Hudson Valley of New York, spoke to the European leaders in his region in an attempt to stem the flow of alcohol to his people. He said, *"When our people come from hunting to the town or plantations and acquaint the traders and people that we want powder and shot and clothing, they first give us a large cup of rum. And after we get the taste of it, crave for more so that all the beaver and peltry we have hunted goes for drink, and we are left destitute either of clothing or ammunition. Therefore we desire our father to order the tap to be shut and to prohibit selling of rum; for as long as the Christians will sell rum, our people will drink it."* [1]

Many of our historic chiefs felt the same way. In 1763, Odawa chief Pontiac, in the woodland country of what is now Michigan, Minnesota, Wisconsin and southern Canada, saw the loss of cultural ways as the result of alcohol on his Odawa people. His words were recorded and they said, *"My children, you have forgotten the customs and traditions of your forefathers. Why do you not clothe yourselves in skins, as they did, use bows and arrows and the stone pointed lances, which they used? You have bought guns, knives, kettles, and blankets from the white man until you can no longer do without them; and what is worse you have drunk the poison firewater, which turns you into fools. Fling all these things away; live as your forefathers did before you."* [2]

Shawnee leader Tecumseh tried with only small success to unite the Native people from the south all the way to Canada in a confederacy to resist the encroachments of American settlers. He saw that some of the people's strength was being lost to alcohol. His words of warning in 1800 come down to us as *"Touch not the poisonous firewater that makes wise men turn to fools and robs the spirit of its vision."* [3]

Tecumseh's brother Tenskwautawa was a spiritual leader of his Shawnee people. He, too, saw what alcohol was doing and was one of the first to recognize that alcohol may have been good for Europeans, but was an enemy to Indian people. He also saw that the two cultural ways were different and that the European way was weakening his people. *"I told my people that the way they were in was not good, and they ought to abandon it,"* he said in 1808. *"I told them that we should consider ourselves as one man,"* he went on, *"that we ought to live agreeable to our several customs--the red man after their mode, and the white people after theirs; particularly, they should not drink whiskey; that it was not made for them, and that it is the cause of all the mischiefs the Indians suffer."* [4]

The Seneca Tribal leader Handsome Lake began the first great sobriety movement among Native people about the year 1800 in the Six Nations country of New York State. Handsome Lake saw what was happening to his people. He said, *"Whiskey is a great and monstrous evil and has reared a high mound of bones. You lose your minds, and whiskey causes it all. So now all must say, 'I will use it nevermore.'"* [5]

According to the Iroquois " Good Message" the Gaihwiyoh, Handsome Lake was sick on and off for over a year. In 1799 Handsome Lake went into a coma-like state. Handsome Lake looked as if he were dead and his family dressed him in his finest clothes to be buried. During this time Handsome Lake received a vision and was met by three spiritual messengers. This message was timely, since many people had fallen victim of the ravages of alcohol and were no longer paying attention to their own traditions. At one point the spirit of the corn touched his shoulder with her leaf and told him that she wanted to leave the earth. That she was no longer seeing the thanksgiving ceremonies in her honor. Handsome Lake new that this would cause great trauma to his people and many would starve. He begged her to stay and said he would remind the people to continue with the ceremonies in her honor. The messengers took him on a journey where they showed him many vignettes or scenes.

Some were prophetic and some were lessons as to how the people should treat one another. One of these lessons given by the Spiritual messengers was about the consumption of alcohol and any "mind changer" that the people would encounter. After he was awake and able to speak once again, he told his family and friends what he learned from the messengers.

"What you call (alcohol) is what the messengers call the 'mind changer' and was not given to (our people)," Handsome Lake told his listeners. *"It was given only to our white brothers in a form of medicine. It was meant for them to use, as they will be laboring from morning to night and will need this alcohol. It was to be used only for our white brothers as medicine, but they have abused it and it will now be the cause for many minds to split and many will die from it. For (our people) it will bring great misery and hardship. When you have touched the firewater called (alcohol) you will like it. You must remember what will result from drinking it. Anyone who has drunk the firewater will know it as the 'mind changer.' They must reaffirm their faith and renewal to (our Creator) and pledge never to touch it again."* [6]

Sometimes there is conversation about whether Indian people are more physically susceptible to alcohol than others. It is certainly true that if there is an alcohol problem with the mom or dad or with the grandparents in a particular family there is a high chance, probably higher than in other cultures, that once it runs in the family it will be rare if a person is not affected by it. Sooner or later all family members are affected by it, but no one is sure, or understands why that is. We just know that it is. At this time, there is no final understanding about this. There are studies that indicate it is a community issue, some are saying it

is an environmental issue, some say there is nothing else to do for fun but drink in Indian communities, so people just end up drinking. The Wellbriety movement treats it like a myth and tells Indian people that they are not more physically susceptible to alcohol than non-Indians. We tell them that no physical genetic disposition to alcohol has been documented in scientific studies to date.

It is important for us as Indian people to educate ourselves about what happened to us as Nations and communities since the Europeans arrived. Since about 1970, more accurate and honest accounts of our cultures have begun to appear in books, films, and videos. Our own people have become historians, archeologists, and scholars telling the truth about our people. One part of every Indian person's recovery from alcohol could be the reading or viewing of books and films that tell the true story of the oppression and historical trauma that our people experienced, as well as the greatness of our traditional knowledge and cultures. Making a study like this will reveal that a great deal of hardship and despair have followed us since contact with European cultures. This may well be a root of our alcoholism that is different from the wider society. One of the forms of oppression that has been unique to Indian people of Turtle Island is the Indian boarding school or residential school.

Boarding Schools or Residential Schools

Starting in 1860, Indian boarding schools were set up to educate us in ways similar to those of Europeans, with the goal that we would forget our culture and become assimilated into Euro-American society. Our children were often forcibly taken away from their families and homes and made to live far away from their parents or loved ones. They were made to cut their hair short and were punished if they spoke Indian languages. One of the most famous residential schools was the Carlisle Indian School in Carlisle, Pennsylvania, established by Henry Pratt in

1879. The motto of Carlisle was "Kill the Indian and Save the Man." As the 20th Century began, the government set up many other boarding schools around the country. One of the mottoes for the government boarding schools was "Tradition is the Enemy of Progress."

Indian people were not opposed to European education in the period when the boarding schools were established. We saw what wonders education opened up in the world and hoped they would be made available to our people. The great chief Sitting Bull recognized the value of education when, in 1883, he spoke to the youth of his day. *"In the future your business dealings with the whites are going to be very hard, and it behooves you to learn well what you are taught,"* he said. *"But that is not all. We older people need you. In our dealings with the white men, we are just the same as blind men, because we do not understand them. We need you to help us understand what the white men are up to. My grandchildren, be good. Try and make a mark for yourselves. Learn all you can."* [7] Many of our great, great grandparents would have welcomed learning the new ways if they could have also kept their culture and religion. But cultural oppression and education were inseparable in the days of the boarding schools.

The forced boarding school is now a thing of the past but the harmful effects of the boarding schools, from 1860 until the early 1970's, have been handed down through the family. If a grandpa or grandma had a bad experience at boarding school, it was probably handed down all the way to the children of today. We now know that many of the causes for alcoholism for Indian people today had their beginnings in the boarding school experiences of our people. What are some of the boarding school experiences? How have those experiences, handed down from generation to generation, impacted ourselves, or even our parents, who never went to boarding schools? What is their connection to Indian alcoholism?

The Carlisle Indian School is an example. It was run in a military fashion. Students were marched from their quarters to breakfast, they marched to

lunch and they <u>marched</u> to supper. They received little affection from the staff at the school. They longed for the affection that a parent would have given them when they were of an age when affection is so important. They were told many times that their people's ways were evil and that their people would die out. They were not allowed to speak their Native language or conduct ceremony, such as smudging. Our religion was disrespected and its practice was prohibited. In 1890, as the boarding School era was getting into full swing, Sitting Bull observed how Euro-American society disliked our religious beliefs and ways when he said, *"You should say nothing against our religion, for we said nothing against yours. You pray to God. So do all of us Indians, as well as the whites. We both pray to only one God, who made us all."* [8] But our leaders and Elders were powerless to protect the younger people during those earlier days of educational trauma.

What Happened In The Boarding Schools?

Shame, and shaming behavior on the part of the staff, was one of the most hurtful kinds of emotional abuse experienced by Indian people in the historic boarding schools. Shame is the feeling that comes from being disgraced, embarrassed, dishonored or humiliated. Shame was encountered on many levels. We were shamed for being Native people. We felt shame from being sexually abused, either directly from the boarding schools, or by relatives affected by boarding schools. We were shamed by being verbally abused and physically abused. <u>As a result, rage and anger, unexpressed toward the boarding school staff, fell on the children of boarding school survivors.</u>

We also hold anger and rage from having our families killed, tortured, cheated and pushed out of their spacious homelands to small tracts of land, or to none at all. Rage and anger continued to be a characteristic of

the children of the survivors, and lateral violence in our families continues to this day as a result of that original abuse. Lateral violence refers to violence we do to one another, in contrast to violent acts against non-Native society.

Our lives are wonderful today because more individuals are beginning to understand that they have the power to *purposely* heal the effects we inherited from boarding schools. It is refreshing to understand that our shame isn't all ours. There was good reason for the feelings we carried-- for the anger and hurt. It wasn't all our fault that our grandparents refused to teach us our language. When we understand how they were treated, our understanding of what happened to them increases and shame lessens. It also helps to realize that stifled anger never goes away. It lingers in the background ready to show up to add to your next angry moment. Once that old anger is expressed in a safe place, we release it from storage and it is no longer there to add dangerous emotion to our lives. The road to recovery is difficult and doesn't happen overnight, but it is well worth regaining the healthy and loving family and communities that we deserve.

To summarize, here are some of the harmful effects the boarding schools had on our people, which were then passed down through our families through the process called "intergenerational trauma." These effects set up an emotionally dysfunctional environment where escape from pain was an overriding need and alcohol was an affordable self-medication.

- ❖ **Shame of being Native, leading to low self-esteem**
- ❖ **Belief that our people would die out**
- ❖ **Loss of Native language and a loss of spirituality**
- ❖ **Loss of parenting skills because of not being adequately parented ourselves**
- ❖ **Anger towards authority figures and all white people**

- ❖ **Loss of respect for women**
- ❖ **A history of verbal and emotional abuse**
- ❖ **A history of physical and sexual abuse**
- ❖ **A feeling of being disconnected from our communities**
- ❖ **Hatred towards education**
- ❖ **Feelings of being powerless to affect the very school systems that educate our youth**

It is also important to say here that not every Native American in our parent's and grandparent's generation had a completely negative experience in the boarding schools. Stories and books are coming out now by some of us whose ancestors were given opportunities through the boarding school experience that went on to enrich their lives.

Thanks to the many people who were able to save and continue our ceremonies and to preserve our languages and cultures, somehow we have managed to survive. Of those of us who managed to survive the effects of the boarding schools, some of us have found ways to heal and recover. Others are still dealing with the ill effects of the boarding schools. Our cultures are strong and we are very resilient. We are learning the lessons of intergenerational trauma and healing, and we are able now to help others on their journey to healing.

A few years ago we were blaming other people because of our alcoholism. It was the white man's fault, the government's fault, the BIA's fault, etcetera. But part of the power of this Wellbriety movement is the realization that we, as Native people, have to make this journey ourselves. The journey away from blaming, to wellness, is ours. Since about 1970, our people have fought hard for tribal rights and sovereignty. We have won many legal battles and have begun to protect those very rights that were denied to us in the historical period of the boarding

schools and even before that. Now we accept that alcohol is a symptom of some of our problems and not a cause. We are becoming free to learn that negative patterns in our thinking processes are some of the many reasons behind our alcoholism and drug use today. When we work on healing the hurt in our thoughts and feelings, we can begin to eliminate some of the deeper roots of drug and alcohol abuse, domestic violence, and dysfunctional families. We will let go of our need to blame others or find excuses for our drug abuse.

The chapters to come talk about some of the negative and harmful thinking we do as alcoholics, drug abusers, and people who have grown up around these addictions. With the help of the Creator, some understanding of our history, culture and mental processes will begin to set us free.

Chapter 4
Many Paths to the Creator

We may have misplaced our Native
spirituality or sense of the sacred,
but we can't say it's lost because
we have ancestors within. Inside
of us are grandmas and grandpas.
When we start to come back to the
culture they wake up, and we find
that there are helpers both inside
and outside.

White
Bison

Chapter 4
Many Paths to the Creator

"Did you ever see an agnostic Indian?" a friend said one day. I thought about it and realized right away that among our people, agnosticism was not much of a concern. We have a lot of issues bothering us in Indian country, but agnosticism and atheism are probably not high on the list.

The chapter "We Agnostics" in the Big Book of Alcoholics Anonymous has a lot to say to people who wonder whether there is a Great Spirit in the first place. An agnostic is a person who believes that nothing can be known about the existence or nature of God or of anything beyond the material world. In other words, an agnostic is someone who doesn't know if there is an unseen world of spirituality. The chapter "We Agnostics" was also written for people who think of themselves as atheists. Atheists don't believe that God exists. We Indian people might say that atheists feel that there is no Great Mystery behind and underneath everything we see, think, or feel.

The chapter "We Agnostics" works hard to give faith back to a struggling alcoholic. The writers of the Big Book discovered that many alcoholics had become estranged or alienated from their own Judeo-Christian religions. Many had become anti-religious, or the word "God" brought up an idea of God that didn't make sense to an individual. Even though they were brought up in their own religions, they had no personal feeling that a creative intelligence exists in the universe. They didn't have a

relationship with God. So the great gift of the Big Book was to tell suffering alcoholics that he or she didn't have to believe in a God the way their own religions taught or other people spoke. All they had to do was to allow the fact that a power greater than themselves existed and might be able to help them with their alcoholism if it were asked in any manner that made sense to the individual. All they had to do was open up to a Higher Power any way that they could, separate from whatever had gone wrong in their own religious backgrounds. All they had to do was to welcome a power greater than themselves into their lives and they would have help in healing from alcoholism.

Many of our Indian people have found sobriety and fellowship by working the program of Alcoholics Anonymous in our own ways. Some of the recovery stories in this book you are now reading are about Indian people who found freedom from alcohol and drugs by working the AA programs of the wider society or by working Indian AA programs. Many of us have read every word in the Big Book of Alcoholics Anonymous. The Big Book is a gift from the Creator, which made a difference in our life and death struggle with alcohol. Maybe we knew that the Big Book drew from the experiences of white men in the 1930's who were struggling with alcohol just as we are now. Maybe we knew that the Big Book came from a doctor and a business man with Judeo-Christian roots who were speaking in the culture of white society. But did it matter? If we could be helped to find sobriety by thinking about what it said in the Big Book, did it matter who wrote the Big Book or where it came from?

We feel that the words on recovery from alcoholism in the Big Book are truly inspired. We feel that they come straight from the Great Spirit, through the pens and stories of a few men and women and into the book that has saved so many lives. The Big Book has helped many people from different cultures or ethnic backgrounds recover from alcoholism because first and foremost our problem is alcohol, not our cultural backgrounds. But sometimes as Indian people we need to hear certain teachings and ideas spoken in ways that are familiar and comfortable to us. Sometimes

we need to hear that some of our problems, which lead us to use drinking for escape, are a little bit different than the wider society. The Big Book is culturally specific to white society out of which it evolved. Sometimes we need to hear what a recovery book might have to say in our own cultural terms.

What Happened to Us?

Many of us are now coming to understand that alcoholism and other serious chemical dependencies are troubles that sometimes come to Indians through the loss of spirituality in our lives, oppression and historical trauma. The loss of our spirituality is like having a weakened immune system. If our spiritual immune system is weak, the disease of alcoholism can take root. Might it also be that the addictions epidemic in the wider society has come about because of the loss of spirituality in the everyday life of the world? As Indian people we know that this is true. We know that modern society has lost track of the Creator and has forgotten its Maker. But what about us as Indian people? We never denied the Great Spirit, as atheists or agnostics do. However, we stopped living our spirituality.

As Euro-American society began to dominate and spread over Turtle Island beginning in the 1500's, we were increasingly forbidden to live our cultures and practice our spiritual ways. Not only was the spirituality and way of life of the visitors different than our ways, but the conquerors denounced our tribal ways as inferior and "pagan." Using their own standards of sin, heaven and hell and a punishing God, they denounced our ways as evil. They said our ways came from the devil, an idea that none of us had heard before. As the visitors spread across our homelands, they punished us just as they thought their own God must punish them. We lost our culture and our spirituality because our ways were overpowered and even declared illegal. When we lost our spirituality

through means like genocide, oppression, and assimilation, then alcohol, violence, and other addictions naturally followed, just as they have now arisen on such a large scale in society. By genocide we mean that Native Americans were systematically killed as Euro-American society settled the Western Hemisphere.

A miracle occurred for Indian people in the late 1960's and the early 1970's. The miracle was that the federal governments of the United States and Canada began to take a second look at how the indigenous people of Turtle Island had been oppressed. They began to do this because the hearts of the people who make up the wider society began to change in a good way as Native Americans fought for their rights as individuals and as a people. Both governments began to protect the very cultures and Indian religions that they had marked for extinction for hundreds upon hundreds of years. Making this miracle a reality took the hard work and sacrifice of many good Indian and non-Indian people. The work has been for tribal sovereignty, the end of racism, economic and educational opportunities for native peoples, and recovery from addictions. Some lost their lives in this struggle. Now we are freer than ever to revitalize our native cultures and reawaken our traditional spiritualities in any manner that works for us at this time in history. We are free to have a relationship with the sacred in our own traditional ways or in any blending with other religions that makes sense to an individual or group of Indian people.

There Are Many Ways

Many of us were raised in the Christian faith and have a connection with Christianity. Our Pueblo brothers and sisters in the Southwest have been Christians for over 400 years, blending their own traditional ways with the Catholic church of the Spaniards since the 1500's. On the northern Plains, Lakota Elder Frank Fool's Crow was both a devout Catholic and a traditionalist. Most of our reservations have Protestant, Catholic or

Mormon churches, which were established by missionaries many years ago. Most of the Christian churches in our communities now bring some part of the local tribal traditions into the Service or Mass. Many of us have a heart connection with Jesus as the Higher Power we need to help us through alcoholic recovery. Others of us do not.

Some of us found healing through the Christian God, found the Lord and became a Christian even though we didn't have that connection before. Some of us were completely delivered from alcoholism by Christianity. True healing comes from the Creator, his miracles, and his power to heal us. God wants us to be whole and if we are still using drugs and alcohol, breaking our bodies down, that's far from wholeness. If we would allow God, in any way we understand him or her, to come in and do the miracle that he or she would like to do, then that's a way to find our sobriety. As we begin to return to our own cultures and traditional spirituality, we may do so by blending with the religions of society.

We will also have to think about our relationship to a punishing God. Ours was never a punishing God. The Great Spirit of our traditions never sought to quell evil forces. It did not punish the animals and the birds, and likewise did not punish the people. Many of our children were punished in boarding schools simply for being Indian. The justification for their punishment was that God punished sinners and to be an Indian was to be a sinner. Among many people now, the kinds of harming attitudes and behaviors once attributed to God are now being looked at and revised in this healing time that we are all living through together.

The good healing ways of the 12 Steps can be blended with our traditions in many different activities. For example, in the Steps it says turn your life over to God. We can do that in our own way by smoking the Sacred Pipe. Or if the Step says to pray and meditate, we can undertake a traditional vision quest by fasting and following traditional practices under the guidance of our medicine people. Most world religions encourage a person to look at their character defects and shortcomings and to confess

their sins. We can do this in a sweat lodge in the traditional way. Is there a difference between a church and a sweat lodge because the lodge is a rounded hut? Do you have to have a building with a furnace in it or can you have a hut that is heated by many glowing grandfathers (stones) in the center? We can take our character defects and failures in life into the lodge and let them go up in the prayers and sage smoke we find there. Or we can put them into a tobacco prayer tie, take them into the lodge, and turn them over to God in that way. What's the difference? In the sweat lodge today you never hear anybody asking what religion you are. Whatever you are, you are allowed to come in and pray.

There are many, many religions and different kinds of spirituality meeting one another now in the coming together time that the world is experiencing. Each of the sacred ways may have different beliefs and different practices, but they all go to the same place. If you want to get to that place you can take the journey offered by organized religions of many different kinds. You can take the road of the Native American Church that uses peyote Medicine, you can follow your own traditional spirituality, or you can walk the Red Road that all can share. The Creator made different paths for different people to come find Him/Her. All those roads are good, although they are different from each other. Most of them know there is a "there" that you are trying to get to. The difference is how do we get there? Every human being knows that there is a "there" where we can each meet the Creator. We know of Native people who are following Christianity, Hinduism, Bahai, Buddhism, and other paths while at the same time exploring a return to their own cultures. If you are an Indian person on any of these roads we encourage you to just keep going.

What We Believe...

Our Indian people come from many, many different traditions and hundreds upon hundreds of different tribes throughout Turtle Island. We are a very diverse people, and there is no such thing as a single Indian spirituality. But most of our traditional ways do have some features in common that people of different tribes would recognize. What do we recognize among ourselves?

---

1 All Native cultures believe in a *Supreme Being*

2 We believe there is a natural order running the universe

3- We believe the *Elders* are our guiding force

4- Tribal nations are different from each other

5 Our traditional ways were knowledgeable about the natural order

6- Alcohol is destroying us and we want to stop using it

7 We believe a spiritual person is one who may make mistakes every day but keeps coming back to the Creator

8 We believe those who walk this good road will find that their thoughts must change to the way *Warriors* think.

As we begin to return to our traditional ways we will understand that culture offers the greatest prevention for chemical addictions, violence and all the other dysfunctional behaviors that the world is full of today. But how do we embrace our cultural ways again and the understanding of sacredness that we find there? What many of us have to do is go back to the Elders and say, "I'm looking for God, will you help me?" We may have misplaced our Native spirituality or sense of the sacred, but we can't

say it's lost because we have ancestors within. Inside of us are grandmas and grandpas. These are our ancestors within. When we start to come back to the culture they wake up, and we find that there are helpers both inside and outside.

Our inside helpers are a sense of wholeness and interconnectedness that we didn't even know we had. Our ancestors within held those gifts for us until we were ready. When we hear the drum, something inside of us becomes alert. When we smell the sage, cedar, or sweetgrass, something from a long time ago begins to stir. When we handle the eagle feather, we suddenly know how to do it and what it's telling us.

Our outside helpers might be people who come into our lives holding a tiny bit of the culture that means something to us. It might be someone who teaches us a traditional song. It might be an invitation to come sit at the drum. It might be a community project that you are asked to lend a hand at. It might be an alcohol recovery circle that is using cultural ways. Go sit with your brothers and sisters and everybody will become stronger.

Glancing Backward to Go Forward

In this chapter we have said that as Indian people we don't have many agnostics and atheists, but we have misplaced our spirituality and are looking to get it back. Returning to our culture and spirituality, even if they are blended with healthy aspects of other religions, is part of the journey into Wellbriety. We might be able to find sobriety or abstention from alcohol, drugs and other dysfunctional behaviors, but to become balanced and well as human beings we must begin to live a life of spirituality because that is our unique gift as Native people.

Occasionally we can consult our Elders by going to books. Ohiyesa, or Dr. Charles A Eastman, was one of the first of our people to be educated as a medical doctor around the turn of the 20th century. A Santee Sioux, he was raised in the old ways but made the journey to North American society just as many of us are doing today. He served his people as a doctor and as a writer of books. In 1911 he talked about his traditional spirituality.

"The worship of the Great Mystery was silent, solitary, free from all self-seeking," said Dr. Eastman. *"It was silent because all speech is of necessity feeble and imperfect. It was solitary, because Indian people believed that He is nearer to us in Solitude, and there were no priests authorized to come between a man and his Maker. None might exhort or confuse or in any way meddle with the religious experience of another. Among us, all men were created sons of God and stood erect, as conscious of their divinity."* [1]

His words reach out from our traditional past to say even more about what Native spirituality meant to our grandfathers and grandmothers.

"The first American mingled with his pride a singular humility," Dr. Eastman continues. *"Spiritual arrogance was foreign to his nature and teaching. He never claimed that the power of articulate speech was proof of his superiority over the dumb creation; on the other hand, it is to him a perilous gift. He believes profoundly in silence--the sound of perfect equilibrium. Silence is the absolute poise and balance of body, mind, and spirit. The man who preserves his selfhood is ever calm and unshaken by the storms of existence. His, in the mind of the unlettered sage, is the ideal attitude and conduct of life. If you ask him, 'What is silence?' he will answer, 'It is the Great Mystery! The holy silence is His voice!' If you ask, 'What are the fruits of silence?' he will say, 'they are self-control, true*

courage or endurance, patience, dignity, and reverence. Silence *is the cornerstone of character.'"* [2]

We may have misplaced our spirituality, but in this new coming together time we will get it back. Sometimes when we are new in recovery there are many personal tests and challenges. There may be personal conflict and it might seem that we are losing a lot. But conflict always precedes clarity, and at times all we can do is get down on the Mother Earth in order to realize that when all is gone, there is still something left that is more than enough. We can hold some of the hairs of the good Mother Earth in our hand, hold the grasses which cover the land, and pray:

God, thank you for what you've given me,
Creator, thank you for what you've taken from me,
God, thank you for what you've left me,
Creator, thank you for letting me be in recovery,
And feeling proud to be a recovering Indian person.

Chapter 5
The Healing Steps of the Red Road

Time and again our Elders have said that the 12 Steps of AA are just the same as the principles that our ancestors lived by, with only one change. When we place the 12 Steps in a circle then they come into alignment with the circle teachings that we know from many of our Tribal ways.

Chapter 5
The Healing Steps of the Red Road

We, **as Native people, stand at the dawn of a new spring time.** For the first time in over five hundred years, our Tribal Nations are starting to come back to their traditions, languages, and ceremonies. We are coming back to the principles, laws, and values that we once knew. We are fighting for our sovereignty in the courts, and we are winning. We are becoming bicultural people, full citizens of both mainstream society and our own ancestral ways.

To enjoy sovereignty as proud Nations, we must also achieve sovereignty over ourselves as individuals. This journey on the Red Road may not be an easy one. We need to go to many addictions recovery meetings on a regular basis. We need to learn to live one day at a time. We may have many problems to overcome. It might be that our family has fallen apart, we have financial problems, job problems, bad reputations, low self esteem, feel bad about ourselves, experience guilt and shame, and have no known plan as to how we are going to pull our lives together. For many of us, we will come to realize that we have grown up in communities or families that are very negative or toxic. So often the support we need may not be there when we need it. But recovery and Wellbriety is still possible because this is an individual and internal journey.

When we reach the turning point of being "Sick and Tired of Being Sick and Tired," when we reach the point of being willing to "Let Go and Let God," when we are willing to "Surrender to Win," remarkable things start

to happen. We will come to realize the 12 Steps are a program that will work for all people--red, yellow, black and white. When we realize that most of our problems are of our own making, then we can see that most of the solutions we need to find, with the Creator's help, will be attracted to our lives as we walk the Red Road. We can see that alcohol and drugs are ruining our lives, that we are powerless over alcohol, that it is even stronger than our own will, and stronger than all the vows we make when we are in trouble—such as... "God, get me out of this one and I will never drink again..." Or, "I will quit tomorrow..." When we are able to fully admit to ourselves that we are REAL alcoholics, this is the first step and the first footprint on the Red Road.

The name of this chapter says it all. *The Healing Steps of the Red Road.* There are steps we must take in order to do this. This means devoting time--time dedicated to healing ourselves and being a part of this Wellbriety journey. Today there are thousands of Native People in recovery who had the same problems you may now have when they first came into recovery.

Things to Think About

The Elders say there are two states of mind that we can be in. One state of mind is called the state of **"I don't know what I don't know."** Often when we come into recovery we don't know the truth from the false. When we are willing and become *teachable*, we will move from the state of mind of "I don't know what I don't know," to **"Now I know what I don't know."** This means that I am willing to listen to the experience, strength, and hope of another alcoholic. As we listen to their stories, we can start to have an understanding of the affects of alcohol. We can see that alcohol is a symptom of what we need to work on. We will come to see that most of the time when we got in trouble we were under the influence of alcohol. The effects of alcohol will eventually touch and ruin every area of our lives. When we stop drinking alcohol, then our lives begin to change.

It is the first drink that gets us drunk. We must come to realize we don't have the power, on our own, to not take that first drink. We cannot get the right thoughts or vow to not take that first drink--that kind of willpower won't work. We do not have the power to leave the drink alone. The power we need to overcome our addictions must come from the Creator. Only by daily prayer, sometimes minute by minute, we ask the Creator to help us. Only moment by moment will we ever permanently, one day at a time, overcome alcohol and other addictions. We must bring our lives into harmony and heal from the alcohol and drugs which have threatened to take away everything we love.

Our Lakota Elder Frank Fools Crow once said that **alcohol and jealousy** are the two biggest enemies that Indian people have. We have a longing and a yearning to walk the Red Road, but these two enemies are a road of difficulty for us. Yet when you read some of the sobriety stories at the back of this book, you'll see that many of our people have been sober and clean for ten, twenty and thirty years or more. You'll also see that they are more than sober. Many of our people have become both sober and well—and that's what we mean by Wellbriety.

When you read the stories in the back of this book, and if you have a committed connection with the AA program and the 12 Steps of AA, you'll see that both our people and people of the non-Indian society have found peace by working and living through the 12 Steps. Many of our people have found the Red Road by going to both regular AA and Indian AA. Yet some of us are not comfortable with AA or its 12 Steps. We need to take a look at our own prejudices about the 12 steps. Some of us say this is a white man's program. Some of us reach this conclusion by only attending a few meetings. Many of us will find recovery through the Native American Church or other teachings. None of these ways should be criticized. We should accept whatever way works for us to overcome alcohol. This book is written for those who choose to use the 12 Steps in a circle and the teachings the Elders have given to us.

We've already said that AA came about in the 1930's from the work of two white men who found sobriety by first finding that if they helped each other, they started to stay sober. As they started to stay sober, then the third drunk showed up. And this person stayed sober! Eventually the Big Book was written by the first 100 people, sharing their experiences about how they made this journey. Our culture says the same thing. We live in an interconnected system and pieces of interconnected systems need each other. We don't necessarily need to *like* each other, but we need each other to stay sober and function.

If you've read the Big Book or worked the AA program, you know that, without a doubt, the Great Spirit is behind all that's there. But AA and the 12 Steps often come across in cultural ways that are strange to us. The words used might not be our words, and the feelings might not be exactly the spiritual feelings of our families, relatives, and communities.

But time and again our Elders have said that the 12 Steps of AA are just the same as the principles that our ancestors lived by, with only one change. When we place the 12 Steps in a circle then they come into alignment with the circle teachings that we know from many of our tribal ways. When we think of them in a circle and use them a little differently, then the words will be more familiar to us.

There is really only one question: do you want to become sober and clean? Do you want to become free of the alcohol spirit that is just as cunning, baffling and powerful to us as it is to our non-Native brothers and sisters? Do you want to let go of the painful spirit of drug addiction, which now captures more and more of our people?

We can't go half way with this. We must make a commitment. We must ask the Great Spirit's help to become free from the effects of alcohol. We must also do our part: we can choose to accept the gift and hard work of **the 12 Steps and 12 Principles** stated here. On the next page is a journey that we may now choose as a road to sobriety, recovery, and happiness:

Twelve Steps and Twelve Principles

An Alternate Wording of the 12 Steps for Native Americans
STEPS 1-6

FACE THE EAST—Finding the Creator

STEP 1   Honesty
We admitted we were powerless over alcohol—that we had lost control of our lives.

STEP 2   Hope
We came to believe that a Power greater than ourselves could help us regain control.

STEP 3   Faith
We made a decision to ask for help from a Higher Power and others who understand.

←——→

FACE THE SOUTH—Finding Ourselves

STEP 4   Courage
We stopped and thought about our strengths and our weaknesses and thought about ourselves.

STEP 5   Integrity
We admitted to the Great Spirit, to ourselves, and to another person the things we thought were wrong about ourselves.

STEP 6   Willingness
We are ready, with the help of the Great Spirit, to change.

STEPS 7-12
(Continued)

FACE THE WEST—Finding our Relatives

STEP 7   Humility
We humbly ask a Higher Power and our friends to help us to change.

STEP 8   Forgiveness
We made a list of people who were hurt by our drinking and want to make up for these hurts.

STEP 9   Justice
We are making up to those people whenever we can, except when to do so would hurt them more.

FACE THE NORTH—Finding the Elders' Wisdom

STEP 10   Perseverance
We continue to think about our strengths and weaknesses and when we are wrong we say so.

STEP 11   Spiritual Awareness
We pray and think about ourselves, praying only for the strength to do what is right.

STEP 12   Service
We try to help other alcoholics and to practice these principles in everything we do.

How is it for you now? Are you suffering from the effects of alcohol? Do you have drugs in your system? Perhaps you have been clean and sober but had a relapse? Or have you been walking the good Red Road for some time? This is a good day to begin the journey or to renew the journey to sobriety and Wellbriety. It is a good day to pick up the eagle feather or another sacred object. If you have a cleansing smudge of sage, cedar, sweetgrass or something else you consider to be sacred, brush yourself down with the feather and let yourself be cleansed by the sacred smoke. Quiet your heart and mind and let the Creator enter. It's a good day to start, or to re-commit to wellness.

IT'S A GOOD DAY TO LIVE!!

The Steps in a Circle

To work the 12 Steps in our Indian way, we place **Steps 1, 2 and 3 in the East.** This is the direction of **Finding a Relationship with the Creator.** Each of the directions has Powers. We sometimes call these Powers the Grandfathers or the Grandmothers. When the sun comes up in the east, the flowers wake up, the birds start singing, the dew melts, the sky turns from darkness to light. When this Power happens, all of nature responds. A Power force touches all of nature, including we humans. As we experience the darkness of alcohol and drugs we turn to ask this Power for help. We ask it to cause an awakening inside of us. We ask this Power to bring us from darkness to light. To enlighten our insides so we can see the path of the Red Road. The Power of the first three steps is from the East.

Placing the 12 Steps in a circle, we next understand **Steps 4, 5 and 6 to lie in the South.** This is the direction in which we **Find Ourselves.** This is

the direction when the sun is spreading its warmth and powers to help each bird and plant to personally grow. These Powers come from the South. A long time ago, when we became lost and we went to the Elders, they would take us down by a small quiet pond. They would brush the leaves away. They would have you bend over and look at your reflection in the still water. They would ask you if you like the person you see in the pond. It was always a natural cultural way for us Native people to build our character. The respect in our communities was not from our education or how many degrees we had. The focus was on character building. When we were respectful, caring, trustworthy and committed, when our word was good, courageous, honest, fearless, strong, prayerful, loving, and kind, this is what every traditional person tried to achieve.

If we were angry, treated women with disrespect, gossiped, were abusive to our mates, hurt our children, were disrespectful to property, stole from our neighbors, this was looked down upon. The Powers from the South and the three steps, 4,5,6 help restore us to have a sound character. They find out the blockages and the fears that are in the way of us being the type of man, woman, child, grandpa or grandma, that the Creator wants us to be. We need to find the answer to the question… **"who am I?"**

Steps 7, 8 and 9 are located in the West, which is the direction of the sunset. This is the direction of **Finding our relatives,** the direction of forgiveness. In order for us to quit drinking, we need to set ourselves "right" with every person we hurt while we were drinking. In our traditional culture, forgiveness was a very strong part of our culture. No human can be right with the Creator when we are harboring resentment and hurt between ourselves and any other human being. We live in an interconnected system, so if we are out of harmony with one, we are out

of harmony with all. This is true because we are all connected to each other. If we are out of harmony with each other, then we are out of harmony with the Creator. This is true because we are all children of the Creator. So when we come to the Red Road, we must make amends to our brothers and sisters so we find harmony with the Great One. When we do this, we will not need to drink again. The Powers of the West help us to do this part of our recovery.

Steps 10, 11 and 12 are the direction of the Elders' Wisdom. Once we have found the Creator and have Him/Her working in our lives, once we have looked at our strengths and weaknesses and admitted them to ourselves, another human being, and to our Creator, and once we have found out who we are and have made amends to our brothers and sisters, we then turn to the North—the direction of the **Elders' wisdom.** We need this wisdom for us to be able to live on life's terms, with life's setbacks and all the challenges of life. To walk the Red Road is not always easy. Actually, sometimes it is lonely because other people in our communities may not be walking the Red Road or seeking Wellbriety. This is where we need wisdom and spiritual guidance. This is the Power and the gifts from the north, the words and actions we need to interface with all types of people. This is also the wisdom to know there are things and people we cannot change. There is courage to change what we can, and wisdom to know the difference.

Placing the 12 Steps in a circle also helps us to realize that all 12 of these great principles for recovery are interrelated and interconnected. Think of the 12 Steps placed around the outside circle of a **dream catcher.**

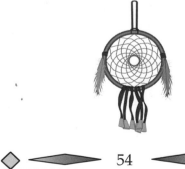

Do you have a dream catcher hanging in your home? Perhaps one is hanging over the baby's crib. Look at the web of interconnection on the inside of the dream catcher circle. Imagine that this web connects each of the 12 Steps that are spaced around the outside of the circle. So even though we will work the Steps one at a time, we will always be aware of, and use some of the Powers of the other Steps. For example, we might already have prayers that we do. So even while we are being honest about our drug and alcohol use in Step 1, we still pray each and every morning and night—which is part of Step 11. The dream catcher connects the Indian 12 Steps and helps us relate to them in wholeness.

The Two Thought Systems
Polarity teachings from the Medicine Wheel

The universe is run by a set of principles, laws, and values. If we live in harmony with these principles, laws, and values, the natural laws put certain consequences in our lives. If our thoughts are in harmony with the principles, laws and values, we will have certain results in our lives. If our thoughts are out of harmony with the principles, laws and values, the natural laws will cause us to have other consequences. These we call unmanageability in Step 1. They are the confusion, fear, guilt, anger, control issues, misery and all the other things that cause us to drink.

Therefore, our thinking will be in only one of two thought systems. One we call **Love** and the other we call **Fear.** The system called Love is where the American Indian culture was developed. This is where our ceremonies were born, where our songs developed, and where we learned to 'pray. Here are some examples of characteristics in these systems:

Love-Based Thought System
(Positive Warrior)

Unity
Love-seeker   Balance
Respect   Honor
Responsible   Forgiveness
Honest   Justice
Understanding   Integrity
Patience   "Power-with..."
Acceptance   (people, places and things)

Fear-Based Thought System
(Negative Warrior)

Conflict
Fault finder   Sarcasm
Disrespect   Belittling
Irresponsible   Anger
Dishonest   Control
Shame   Malicious teasing
Impatience   "Power-over..."
Guilt   (people, places and things)

The fear-based thought system of negative warriors is one that has caused endless unhappiness to ourselves and those close to us. When we drink and drug we are negative warriors living in a fear-based thought system.

The fear-based thought system is also called an **ego thought system.** "Ego" is a word that means "I" in a negative sense. It means "too much 'me.'" It means that I am self-centered and acting as if no one else exists. It means I am selfish and full of anger and fear. All of us are that way when we are drinking and drugging. We may also feel that way in the early days of our recovery.

As **negative warriors** we tend to be attackers, fault finders and judgmental people. We feel guilty and will use words of guilt to shame other people. Our words will be sarcastic and belittling. We are always concerned with looking good in the eyes of others and being Mr. or Ms. "Right." Being in the ego or fear system, we are constantly seeking power over people, places and things. We must be in control. And we probably thrive on excitement and chaos. If you recognize yourself in this description, it might mean you have the honesty to work these Steps. Steps four and five will help us face the fear-based thought system with courage and integrity. This is the way to begin to enter the love-based thought system of the Creator.

Positive warriors are grounded in the love-based thought system. Our traditional societies were deeply rooted in positive warriorship. That doesn't mean that they were all saints or perfect people. It just means that when individuals got off center, the People as a whole were a role model to bring them back. Positive warriors feel a great deal of unity, harmony, and balance in their lives. They feel a great deal of respect and are able to forgive when injustices are done to them. They are men and women of honor and integrity.

The Cycle of Healing

There is another teaching to help us understand the 12 Steps in a circle so that we can work them in a cultural way. This teaching is called the **Cycle of Healing** and includes the four directions of **Recognize**, **Acknowledge**, **Forgive**, and **Change**, grouped around the Steps in a Circle like this:

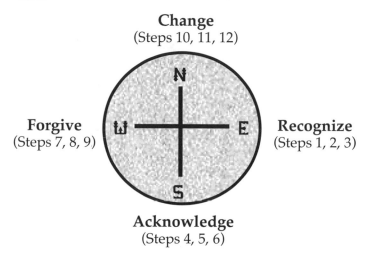

Change
(Steps 10, 11, 12)

Forgive
(Steps 7, 8, 9)

Recognize
(Steps 1, 2, 3)

Acknowledge
(Steps 4, 5, 6)

Recognize means I finally accept the fact that I am powerless or helpless over my addiction and my life is unmanageable. It means I see that I have been dishonest, irresponsible and self-centered. It means that I finally see the need for a Higher Power in my life and am ready to ask for help.

Acknowledge means I am ready to do the hard personal work to allow what I recognized to actually come in and change me. It means I say, "Yes, that's me. Dishonest, irresponsible, self-centered, and full of untruths." When I acknowledge, then I am ready to *do the work.*

Forgive means to finally take off the backpack full of harms and hurt that I have been carrying around. It means first and foremost to forgive myself. I forgive myself by making myself right with the Higher Power and learning how to make amends. I forgive by letting go of past behavior and walking the Red Road.

Change means that I stop doing all the negative behaviors that were associated with my drinking and drugging. Steps 10, 11 and 12 in the North are sometimes called the Maintenance Steps because to keep changing in a good way I have to persevere with spiritual awareness and service to others. I take the changes the Creator gave to me and begin to give back to others in Step 12. As people who are suffering from drugs and alcohol, we can learn to live as positive warriors through the Love-Based System. It all begins with honesty. It begins with Step 1.

Remembering This Chapter

Turning Point
> Sick and Tired of Being Sick and Tired
> Let Go and Let God
> Surrender to Win

The two states of mind
> I don't know what I don't know
> Now I know what I don't know

The Steps in a Circle
> 12 Steps and 12 Principles

The Two Thought Systems
> Love-based (Positive warrior)
> Fear-based (Negative warrior)

The Cycle of Healing
> Recognize, Acknowledge, Forgive, Change

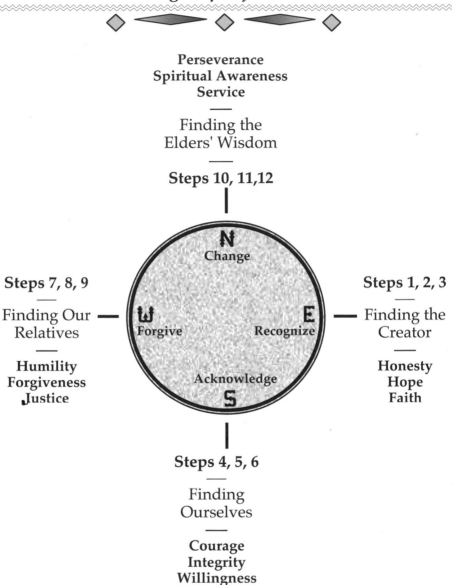

Perseverance
Spiritual Awareness
Service

Finding the
Elders' Wisdom

Steps 10, 11, 12

N
Change

Steps 7, 8, 9

Finding Our
Relatives

Humility
Forgiveness
Justice

W Forgive

E Recognize

Acknowledge
S

Steps 1, 2, 3

Finding the
Creator

Honesty
Hope
Faith

Steps 4, 5, 6

Finding
Ourselves

Courage
Integrity
Willingness

The Steps in a Circle

Chapter 6
Interconnectedness
of the *12 Steps*

The Elders tell us the Steps are interconnected and are numbered in a natural order, which helps the human put their lives back in harmony with natural order. The Steps are a way for us to take all the things we have done out of harmony, and start a process of natural order to get ourselves back in order.

White Bison

Chapter 6
Interconnectedness of the 12 Steps

The Medicine Wheel and other Native teachings tell us that everything is interconnected. When we make changes and untangle our lives we need to do so with the understanding of **interconnectedness and natural order.** The Elders tell us the Steps are interconnected and are numbered in a natural order, which helps the human put their lives back in harmony with natural order. The first steps to get this process going are for us to be **honest**, to have **hope** and to have **faith.** These are the first steps to get the natural order going. When we begin our recovery process by being honest, having hope, and finding faith, we place our self in alignment with the natural order of things. We first need to recognize what is unmanageable in our lives by being honest.

The Steps are connected to each other. The Steps are a way for us to take all the things we have done *out of harmony* and start a process of natural order to get ourselves *back in order.* Here is a diagram showing how the Steps are interconnected in their natural order. This diagram labels the Step number "from the ground up" in the order that we need to work them. After each Step (in brackets) you'll find the main idea, principle, or issue that the Step is associated with.

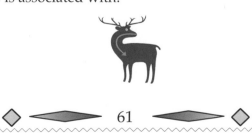

The Foundation of Recovery

Step 12	Give the program to other alcoholics and addictions sufferers so they can recover too {Service}
Step 11	Do morning and evening prayer and meditation {Spiritual Awareness}
Step 10	Take corrective daily actions about my behavior as needed {Perseverance}
Step 9	Make amends to each person who was hurt by me {Justice}
Step 8	Make a list of names of people to whom I owe amends {Forgiveness}
Step 7	Become willing to turn defects and shortcomings over to the Creator {Humility}
Step 6	Create a list of character defects from the Step 4 & 5 inventories {Willingness}
Step 5	Admit my wrongs to myself, to another person, and to the Creator {Integrity}
Step 4	Inventories {Courage}
	Resentments / Fear / Sex
Step 3	Turn my will and life over to the Creator {Faith}
Step 2	Use the 9 areas from Step 1 to create 9 areas of a vision for Step 2 {Hope}
Step 1	Admit, recognize being Powerless over alcohol/drugs Work on 9 areas of unmanageability {Honesty}

Interconnectedness of the 12 Steps

Overview of the 12 Steps

For details about actually working the Steps in the way suggested by the summary that follows please see Chapters 7 and 8 of this book and the White Bison workbooks for the Medicine Wheel and the 12 Steps Program. [1]

Powers of the East

Step 1

Step 1 has two parts: **First**, to take an honest look at what alcohol and/or drugs has done to our lives. **Second**, to honestly admit and take a look at **9 areas** of our lives. In these 9 areas we admit how we are behaving, what we are doing, and how we are treating people, *honestly*. We admit where our emotions are out of control and we admit that we don't know how to handle life without hurting others and ourselves My actions, and how I am managing, are causing great problems that often lead me to more drinking, drugging, or dysfunctional behaviors. There is an interconnectedness between my problems and alcohol. When we can admit this, then we take this information to Step 2. Step 1 and 2 are interconnected and are a part of the natural order.

Step 2

In Step 2, we bring the information from Step 1 and use this information to make **a vision in 9 areas** of our lives. The vision that is created here becomes the spiritual awakening in Step 12. This Step gives us HOPE. The steps are interconnected. When we finish this vision, we now can see the advantage of turning our will over to the care of the Creator. We can see what our life was like when **we** were managing it, and we can see what it would look like if *the Creator* were managing it. We now ask the Creator to help, just like our ancestors did in the old days. We are now ready for Step 3.

Step 3

The instructions in the Big Book of AA are so clear for Step 3 and we encourage you to look there for some help. The only thing that will be added is a brief explanation of the **natural order of change,** and how this fits into the Medicine Wheel Teachings. The natural order of change is the chain of events that takes place in us, giving rise to the results or outcomes in our lives. This natural order begins with our intent and leads to results. Here is the progression:

NATURAL ORDER OF CHANGE

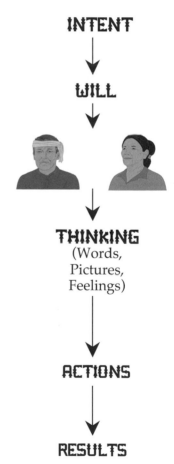

INTENT

↓

WILL

↓

THINKING
(Words,
Pictures,
Feelings)

↓

ACTIONS

↓

RESULTS

In order for the human to change, we must consider the will because the Creator designed us to have a free will. Nothing changes unless the will is considered. If I say, "I WILL NOT!!!!" then nothing happens. If I say, "I Ain't Gonna," then nothing happens. If I say, "I can't... " then nothing happens. If I say, "Not now, maybe later," then nothing happens. These are all expressions of the will. The thinking or feelings will not change if they are against our will.

If I say, "I am willing to be willing," then change starts to happen. Thinking starts to change, so actions change and results start to change. If I choose to have the Creator guide and direct my will, then change starts to happen. If I say, "I am willing to find the teachings and live my life by them," change starts to happen. The teachings were given to us by the Creator, so when I say, "I will follow the teachings, I will start to develop the Good Mind," then change starts to happen. If I want to be a good person and I look at Step 2, even though it may look impossible, the Creator makes all things possible. I *can* return to the person that the Creator intended for me to be. This decision to turn my will and life over to the Creator puts me solidly on the Red Road.

Powers of the South

Step Four

Step 4 is our inventory in three areas: Resentment, Fear and Sex. The resentment inventory is done in 5 columns, the fear inventory is 4 columns, and the sex inventory is 9 columns. Please see the White Bison work book for the Medicine Wheel and the 12 Steps for information about how to do these inventories for yourself. [1]

Step Five

When the inventories of Step 4 are complete, the next step is to make an appointment with a mentor, sponsor or Medicine person and be willing

to admit to yourself, to another human being, and to the Creator that what you wrote on the paper is true. The instructions in the Big Book of AA are quite clear on how to do this. Often a Native person will attend a sweat lodge at this time. In this manner, we now know our strengths and weakness.

Step Six
In the fourth column of the resentment inventory from Step 4 you will have a list of character defects. There will be another list in column 1 of the fear inventory. And there will be more character defects in the sex inventory. This is the information that is needed for Step 6 and for Step 7. It is in this way that the Steps are interconnected. Please see the Workbook [1] for more information.

Powers of the West
When we make amends to the people we hurt, we find we will discover a new relationship to the Creator. When we are "right" with our brother and sisters, we find our Relatives and become strongly connected to the Creator. We will know a new freedom and a new happiness. We will know peace. We will be strongly on the Red Road. The need to drink or drug will leave us. We will know *inside* that the Creator is directing our thinking.

Step 7
The list of character defects from step 6 is the list in which you use to ask the Creator to remove the defects of character. A prayer is said to do this. Please see Chapter 8 of this book.

Step 8
The fifth column of the resentment inventory, and the column "who did we hurt" from the sex inventory, is the list of names we use to make

amends. Step 8 is the place where we become willing to make amends to them all.

Step Nine

This is the Step where amends are made, except when to do so would hurt someone more.

Powers of the North

Step Ten

During the day we watch out for resentment, fear, selfishness and dishonesty.

Step Eleven

In the morning we start the day with prayer, and in the evening we do a review. The instructions for the morning prayer and the evening review are outlined in the Big Book of AA and in Chapter 8 of this book.

Step Twelve

This is the Step in which we recognize our spiritual awakening from Step 2. We practice the 12 Principles in our lives and we help other alcoholics and addictions sufferers by sharing the experience of how we found the Red Road to Recovery

Chapter 7
Steps 1-6 in the Native Way

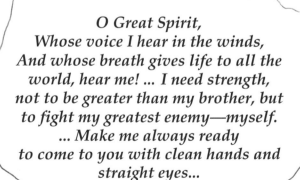

O Great Spirit,
Whose voice I hear in the winds,
And whose breath gives life to all the
world, hear me! ... I need strength,
not to be greater than my brother, but
to fight my greatest enemy—myself.
... Make me always ready
to come to you with clean hands and
straight eyes...

White
Bison

Chapter 7
Steps 1-6 in the Native Way

Some of our Native traditions contain teachings about the Eagle and the Mouse. The Eagle flies high and sees the earth's big picture. He gets an overview of what's going on down on the ground. The little mouse lives down on the ground among the pine cones, stones and grasses. The mouse sees the detail of all that's going on in his or her world. We would like to take an eagle's view of the 12 Steps now, talking some more about the Steps with just a few examples of the actual detail, or the mouse's view of how you can take this journey to become a positive warrior in the Great Spirit's system.

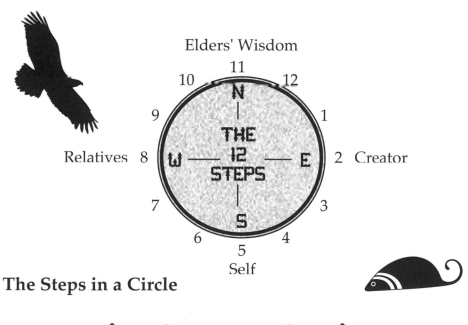

The Steps in a Circle

To actually work the Steps in a way that is in alignment with Native American culture, we suggest that you obtain the White Bison **Medicine Wheel and the 12 Steps program.**[1] There you will find all the detail and examples you need to take the Journey of the 12 Steps. In Chapters 7 and 8 of this book we hope to inspire you to take the Journey by placing the Steps in a Native context or environment to help you start your Journey on the Red Road.

Step 1   Honesty
We admitted we were powerless over alcohol—that we had lost control of our lives.

"control?
dealing?"

Step 1 is about being honest. "Yes, I've really got a problem. My alcohol or drug use is killing me." You can't con yourself with this and just say the words. You have to admit it to yourself inside.

Why? Because change must come from within. We must know the symptoms of any sickness in order to prescribe the right medicine. Alcoholism and abuse of other drugs has a specific set of symptoms. We must know if we have these symptoms and then take the right medicine. Admitting these things may be the first bittersweet spoon of medicine we take. Step 1 has two parts.

Part 1:   We admitted we were powerless over our alcohol and/or drug use.
have control now
Part 2:   Because of that, we had lost control of our lives.

To take Step 1, we are facing the East and seeking to find the Creator in our lives. If your own tradition has a special ceremony to prepare you for a spiritual journey you can perform it now. Or you can simply brush

down with the sage or cedar. Think about Part 1 and Part 2 as you smudge.

Now begin to make a **Mind Map** for Part 1: **I am powerless over my alcohol or drug use.** To make a mind map, draw a circle in the center of a piece of paper. Inside that circle write, "Powerless over Drugs or Alcohol." Now begin a brainstorming session with yourself. Think about everything that losing your power and dignity to alcohol or drugs means to you. Each time you think of something, write it down in a few words on one of the branches leading from the mind map. Each time you think of something that goes deeper into one of the thoughts written on a branch, make a second branch coming off the first like crow's feet, and write that new thought or feeling down. This is how you make a mind map.

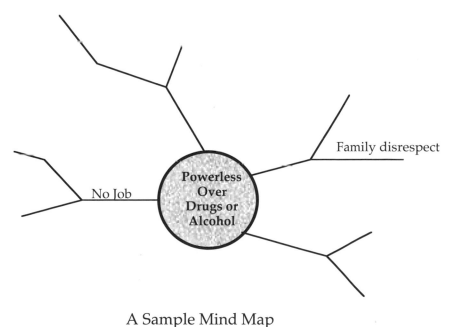

A Sample Mind Map

When the mind map is complete for Part 1, take a break and then later on begin a mind map for Part 2: **Because of my use of alcohol and drugs my life is out of my control**. What is happening to you because you are drinking or using? What is happening to those around you? What is happening to your loved ones? Build this mind map in the same way as you did for the map for Part 1. Take time with this. Pray to the Great Spirit or God as you understand Him to be honest in getting all this out on paper. Don't be dishonest with yourself. This is to save your life.

The "admit" we are talking about in Step 1 is deep admission. "Admit" is often in the head. "Accept" is a bridge from head to the stomach. "Surrender" is feeling it in your gut. Step 1 is about all three.

When you are satisfied with the first two mind maps, begin to think about the following 9 questions. These are the **9 areas of unmanageability** that will become a vision in Step 2, and the content of your spiritual awakening in Step 12.

9 Areas

1	Trouble with my personal relationships?
2	Cannot control my personal nature?
3	Prey to misery?
4	Prey to depression?
5	Can't make a living?
6	Feelings of uselessness?
7	Full of fear?
8	Am I unhappy?
9	Can I not be of real help to other people?

Then, one at a time, make a mind map for each of these questions. Take your time. Be honest with yourself. These **nine mind maps** are what is wrong with your life because of drugs and alcohol. How can you fix something if you don't know exactly what's broken?

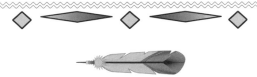

Step 2   Hope
We came to believe that a Power greater than ourselves could help us regain control.

Step 2 is about realizing that there is hope, no matter how miserable we are. God can help us, but we have got to do our part. We have got to do the work.

Our thinking controls the course of our lives. The Creator has gifted us the power of choice and we live by what we practice thinking. Placing our thinking in line with long-term goals will help us live out our short-term goals. You are what you think.

One of our sobriety Elders says, "We move towards and become like that which we think about, Isn't it time to begin thinking about what we are thinking about?"

Each of the mind maps of the **9 areas** of Step 1 expresses a problem or a disharmony in your life. It's what's broken in your life. But now for each mind map from Step 1 ask yourself, "What would it look like if my life were not broken in those areas? What would it look, feel, and sound like if my life were run by the Creator?"

Now make **nine more mind maps,** visioning what your life would look like in each of the nine areas if a power greater than yourself were in your life. Take your time, keep facing East, smudge and pray as much as you need to. Consider this to be a ceremony. The Vision, as expressed by the nine mind maps, becomes the spiritual awakening in Step 12.

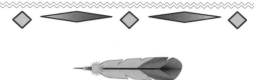

Step 3   Faith
We made a decision to ask for help from a Higher Power and others who understand.

Step 3 is about deciding to ask for help. Most of us don't like to ask for help because our ego won't let us. Maybe we don't actually know how to ask for help, but somehow we are going to do it. When we turn the will over to the Higher Power that's what allows the Natural Order of things to function (see page 64) and our lives to change. Abandon yourself to the Creator. That's faith.

The Elders say if you're going to do something, do it the best you can. Many of us pursued alcohol and drugs with commitment and consistency. When we begin to walk the Red Road with the Creator's guidance we must have that same commitment and consistency, but in a good way.

> *My Creator, please lean close and hear my commitment that I may begin the process of healing. My Creator, I am hurting so bad. Oh Great Spirit, accept the pact I make with you today. I am a spiritual seed. On my own, I don't know how to grow and be happy. Plant me near you that I may grow under your power and wisdom. Great Spirit, alone I don't know how to do this. Creator, mold and shape me into a spiritual warrior. Oh Great Mystery, please hear me...*

Part of Step 3 is to seek help and guidance from an Elder, a Medicine person, a sobriety sponsor, a mentor or a spiritual friend. How can you find a person like that? Keep your eyes, ears and heart open. You'll know who to ask.

To take Step 3, reflect on your relationship with a Higher Power. What would you like that to be like? Now **make a mind map describing your desired relationship with a Higher Power.** When you are ready to take the Third Step, go to that friend, Medicine person, spiritual leader, Pipe Carrier or Elder to help you take this Step. Some of us smoke the Pipe to turn our lives over to the Higher Power in Step 3. Keep facing East. The East is the place of new beginnings. Your new beginning begins today. Turning your life over to the Creator is the most important thing you can do.

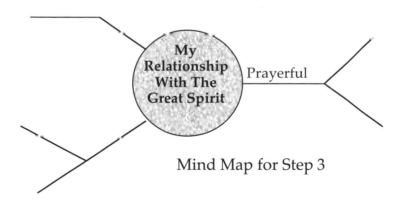

Mind Map for Step 3

On the next page is a **Third Step Prayer** that you can use when you turn your life over to God.

Prayer to the Great Spirit

O Great Spirit,
Whose voice I hear in the winds,
And whose breath gives life to all the world, hear me!

I am small and weak.
I need your strength and wisdom.
Let me walk in beauty and make my eyes ever behold
the red and purple sunset.

Make my hands respect the things you have made
and my ears sharp to hear your voice.

Make me wise so that I may understand
the things you have taught my people.

Let me hear the lessons you have hidden
in every leaf and rock.

I need strength,
not to be greater than my brother,
but to fight my greatest enemy——myself.

Make me always ready
to come to you with clean hands and straight eyes.
So when life fades, as the fading sunset,
My spirit may come to you without shame.
A—ho!

The Prayer to the Great Spirit and the smoke from the Sacred Pipe have now marked a turning point. We turn to the **South** in order to work Steps 4, 5 and 6. We face the South so that we may find ourselves.

Step 4   Courage
We stopped and thought about our strengths and our weaknesses and thought about ourselves.

Step 4 is about looking at ME. Self-examination has always been part of Native culture. Our cultural definition of success is centered on building character. But how can we build character until we know the defects, shortcomings, or weaknesses of the character we have?

[handwritten margin notes: laziness, Julian, Brenna, jealousy, me-smallness]

When we know the problem is within us then we can set out on a quest to learn how to live under the Creator's guidance. But the guidance must be accepted first in order to find the root of the problem. Real self-examination takes a warrior's courage. If you look in the dictionary you'll see that to have courage is to have heart. Step 4 is about beginning to find your heart.

> *Creator, protect me from my worst enemy—myself. I ask that you guide me into the badlands of self, that I may know you better. Please protect my spirit as I relive the past in order to recover. Great Spirit, guide me as I face the self-examination of the South.*

Our people traditionally have many ways to look at ourselves with the help of the Great Spirit. Today we have the solitude of the Vision Quest, which goes by many different names in our different traditions. We have

sobriety sweat lodges where Step 4 prayer and reflection can be done. We can go by ourselves, often out on the land, so that we can see ourselves more clearly in the spirit of Step 4. Some of us spend a night in a Tipi with our brothers and sisters and with the Medicine of the Native American Church. Sometimes a natural self-examination in the spirit of Step 4 happens there. We can participate in sobriety powwows to find indirect cultural support for the Step 4 journey. Nowadays we have the many methods of Step 4 inventory that are utilized by AA, NA and other 12 Step Programs. [2]

As the heart of Step 4, we recommend three central inventories: a **resentment inventory**, a **fear inventory** and a **sex inventory**. You can find charts and diagrams for working Step 4 in this way in the White Bison Medicine Wheel and the 12 Steps workbook. [3]

As you work Step 4, you'll begin to see your problem areas. Problem areas are usually called **character defects.** As you work Step 4, no matter which way you work it, no matter how you decide to a look at yourself, one list you'll keep is called Character Defects or Out of Harmony Behavior. (**Weaknesses or Shortcomings List**) Some people will also make a list of strengths called In-Harmony Behavior. (**Strengths List**). You will discover many things that are wrong about you as you work Step 4. But you can also keep track of what's right with you provided you don't avoid the hard work of naming your defects of character.

As you work this Step, understand each self-discovery in a positive way. Be brave. Never "beat yourself up" by thinking you are unworthy. You are worthy to do this hard work! Say the Prayer to the Great Spirit as much as you need to as you work Step 4. You can write, "God, help me to be honest. Grant me the courage to do this inventory" on every page.

Step 5 (Integrity)
We admitted to the Great Spirit, to ourselves and to another person the things we thought were wrong about ourselves.

Step 5 is about disclosing our secrets. Spiritual sickness lies as deep as the secrets we keep. When we reveal these secrets to ourselves, to another human being, and to the Creator, the heaviness is lifted and we begin to see with our heart, just as the eagle sees Love in everything.

In Step 3 we began a relationship with the Great Spirit. Now our connection will deepen when we reveal to another person what we uncovered about ourselves in Step 4. If your own tradition has a name for the Great Spirit that you are comfortable with, then use it. Honoring the Lakota Way, sometimes we call the Great Spirit *Tunkashila*. For example, undertake Step 5 with Tunkashila and the person who you will pick to stand with you.

Pick the person to do Step 5 with you carefully. It could be the Medicine person or sobriety mentor or sponsor with whom you already connected in Step 3. Pick a person who understands the journey you are on but will not be hurt or personally affected by what you reveal.

You can undertake Step 5 in a sweat lodge while holding an eagle feather. Go into the lodge with Tunkashila and your spiritual guide who is there to witness your heart. Be sure to smudge with sage, cedar, or sweetgrass and face the South during the process. Whether you take Step 5 in the lodge or in another place, be sure you reveal what you discovered about yourself to the sponsor or trusted person who is sitting next to you or

across from you. Think of or refer to your three inventories (resentment, fear, and sex) and the lists from Step 4 as you speak.

As you disclose your heart to Tunkashila, to yourself, and another person, the things that strangle your spirit will begin to loosen their grip. ✗ Your good, hard work from Step 4 now allows you to cast the tyrant within you to the Four Directions. You are becoming lighter by the minute as your backpack of woes is emptied out. You begin to feel good about the wholeness you suddenly feel as you reveal your heart. You are becoming a man or woman of integrity. You begin to hear a Fifth Step Prayer faintly on the wind: *Great Spirit, take my secrets on the four winds and purify them that I may use them in a good way.*

When your Fifth Step is complete, go by yourself for a little while and sit quietly, thinking about what you have done. Thank Tunkashila once again. It is a good, good day.

Step 6   Willingness
We are ready, with the help of the Great Spirit, to change.

Step 6 consolidates and rounds out the process of finding yourself by facing South in the 12 Step Journey. We did some hard inner work in Steps 4 and 5. We learned many things about ourselves with the help of the Creator and a human guide.

But there are many natural laws that we live by. For example, when you place your hand in a fire it will burn. Once we learn this we avoid doing it again. The same principle applies to our character defects. Now that they have burned us, why would we want to hang on to them? Are we willing, are we entirely ready to release our weaknesses to God?

too overwhelming.

From all that you learned about your character defects in Steps 4 and 5, now make a **master list of all defects** that you are asking God to remove. There will be little ones and big ones. Once you have a clear understanding of each major defect then it is time to go back to the mind maps, just as you did in Step 2. Get some sheets of paper and on each sheet **make a mind map of what your life would look, feel and sound like if you did not have each major character defect.** In the center of each circle write "My life without (name of character defect)" This set of mind maps becomes another vision for your future.

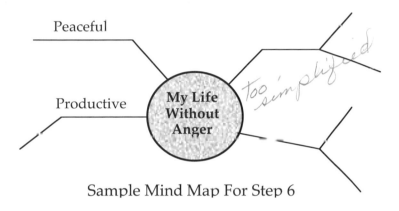

Peaceful

Productive

My Life Without Anger

too simplified

Sample Mind Map For Step 6

The Self-Talk Cycle

Our **willingness** to release or let go of our shortcomings to the Great Mystery may be strong, but it usually requires some skills on our part to make it happen. One of the skills that helps is knowledge of the **self-talk cycle.** The self-talk cycle is the constant conversation we have with ourselves about what is happening to us and around us. However, we don't store and record the "truth." We store and record the "truth" as we see it. So if we decide to change or grow, this self-image becomes our major barrier to change. Then when we make mistakes, as we all do, we don't stop there. We continue to beat ourselves with our self-talk about the mistake, which makes that cycle even stronger the next time.

Three basic principles that apply to the self-talk cycle are:

1- As I think, I am
2- We move toward and become like that which we think about ... Jesus.
3- My present thoughts determine my future

Negative self-talk is like a predator that wants to eat you from the inside. We must become aware of our negative and self-destructive self-talk habits and "reprogram" ourselves with loving, kind and positive intentions or desires. Become aware of how you talk to yourself. Don't talk badly to yourself. Always build yourself up. Speak very well about yourself in your self-talk.

Step six may be completed ceremonially by going into the sweat lodge. Consider making tobacco prayer ties for each of the major character defects from the mind maps you made in this Step. Then, with the support of the others who will sweat with you, offer the prayer ties one by one to the fire, which is heating up the grandfathers (stones) for the lodge. You begin to hear a Sixth Step Prayer: ***Creator, I stand ready for the winds of change to carry on its healing process.***

Chapter 8
Steps 7-12 in the Native Way

• *We are familiar with carrying backpacks of anger, hate and resentment. The spiritual warrior carries a backpack filled with solutions, a love-based thought system, and values that move us toward a life of harmony and balance. Others will want to join this walk, strengthening the Healing Forest that we all share together.*

Chapter 8
Steps 7-12 in the Native Way

We faced and met ourselves as we walked in the South. Steps 4, 5 and 6— what a challenging, good Journey! Now it is time to leave the ways of the youth behind and turn to the **West**—to the direction of the adult in the Medicine Wheel. Steps 7, 8 and 9 carry principles that a mature adult would live by. But how many of us have ever practiced or lived by these principles? Alcohol and drugs stop the journey of inner human growth. Because of our good work this far in recovery we are facing the direction of **finding our relationship with others**--the West.

Step 7   Humility
We humbly ask a Higher Power and our friends to help us to change.

In Step 7 we finally have the knowledge, desire and allies to change. The knowledge we have is the self-knowledge gained from the inventories and lists we made while facing South. Our allies are the sobriety Elders and the Red Road brothers and sisters we've been sitting with in our sobriety circles and healing circles. Creator is an ally who we are finally walking with. In Step 7 we will really begin to change from a negative to a positive warrior.

There is no greater ill than being spiritually sick! When we realize the Great Spirit is the only solution to our insanity, we must give in to our Higher Power. In an act of rebirth our Mother Earth floods everything, from the sickened forest to the beautiful meadow, until all is back in balance. We, too, must start over in every area of our lives.

Humility is an attitude that will help us start fresh in everything we do. Humility helps us face life with a beginner's mind or a learner's mind. Some of us have bad memories of being humbled or humiliated in a negative way, but that's not the humility we are talking about here. To be humble is to drop our arrogance or the attitude that "I know" about everything. Humility is about learning to watch or to listen more in everyday situations so we can approach them freshly. If you look in the dictionary you'll see that "humble" is connected with "humus," which is a special kind of earth. To be humble is to get down on the Mother Earth and ask the Higher Power for help on a regular basis.

There are ways of thinking we can cultivate to help us change. We all have a self-regulator inside of us whose purpose is to keep us inside a **"comfort zone."** This is like standing around a fire. If we are too close to the fire, we are too hot. Step a few paces away and we are too cold. But there's a ring where we are comfortable. When we get outside of our emotional comfort zone, we might find ourselves getting irritable and edgy. That's a dangerous place for recovering alcoholics and addicts. We can increase the size of our comfort zones by changing our self-images, or how we think of ourselves. This is what the Medicine Wheel and the 12 Steps Program teaches. [1] The practice of writing **affirmations** is one way to change our ways of thinking, decrease negative self-images, and widen the comfort zone. There are books and videos that will teach about affirmations. [2] Please see the next page for a few examples.

If certain character defects come up again and again, you may put them into a tobacco tie and offer them to the fire just before you go into a sobriety sweat lodge. This is another way of asking for help from the Higher Power.

Affirmations

I am walking the Red Road Journey of Wellbriety!
I am proud of my own Native heritage.
I will heal and develop myself so that I may be a
role model for the children.
I can do this!   I *am* doing this!
• It's a Good Day to Live!
(Your Turn...)

Thank you for helping me love and serve you this day.

Here is a Seventh Step Prayer that you can say as you work the Seventh Step, or as a regular part of the day no matter what Step you are working:

My creator—I am now willing that you should have all of me—good and bad. I pray that you now remove from me every single defect of character that stands in the way of my usefulness to you and my fellows. Grant me strength, as I go out from here, to do your bidding. A-Ho! [3]

Step 8   Forgiveness
We made a list of people who were hurt by our drinking and want to make up for these hurts.

Step 8 helps us start to mend the wreckage and debris of our relationships with other people, which resulted from our drinking and drugging. In Step 8 we acknowledge in a good way that we hurt people while we were drinking or drugging. We come to this on our own. No one can force us to be willing to make amends or it will create further harm. In Step 8 we prepare the ground to actually make amends in Step 9.

We are connected to all things. When we accept that truth instead of the comfort of denial, we become willing to look at our part in the creation of harm. Each person who has wronged us or who we have wronged is treated like a ceremony—carefully respected and held in high honor. The honor of one is the honor of all, and the dishonor of one is also the dishonor of all.

If we truly want to make up for the hurts we caused, then we pray for forgiveness to be present in the amends we will do with each person. Others may or may not forgive us for what we have done—that's none of

our business. It's in the Creator's hands. But through our desire to make amends we open the door so that the blockages of anger, resentment and hate can be put aside on all sides. No matter what method is chosen to make amends, the amends process usually has two parts:

Part 1: Apologizing for our own hurtful behavior
Part 2: Asking what we can do to restore harmony and balance

Some amends might only involve words, but others might involve action--such as child support or other tangible help.

To work Step 8, use your inventories and lists from Step 4 and any further names that may come out of Steps 5 and 6 to identify those people to whom you owe an amends. We can also get some clarity about the amends process by spending a little **quiet time with the land.** The land has always been an integral part of Native American spirituality. If you can, go by a stream or lake, take a walk, go to a park, or just look up at the sky with the intention to find guidance in the all-important amends steps. The purpose of connecting with land is to get our spirit and intent right so that we don't have a hurtful attitude as we plan to make amends. Step 8 is about doing the work inside us in the unseen world, which will pave the way to actual, active amends in Step 9.

Here is an Eighth Step prayer to help in the sincerity of forgiveness:

Creator, help me meditate on each instance of my past that I may see the truth. Creator, I pray for each and every relation I must approach at this time. Great Spirit, my Sacred Hoop is broken. Please guide me in healing other Hoops that I have broken. Creator, help me to focus on my part in these weakest links of my life.

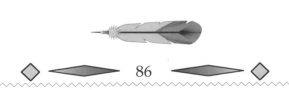

Step 9   Justice

We are making up to those people whenever we can, except when to do so would hurt them more.

Step 8 took the eagle's view of the necessity of forgiveness to make up to the people we hurt while we drank and/or did drugs. Now in Step 9 the mouse gets very busy with the details of how to make amends. There is no better place to hear about some of the ins and outs of making amends than in the Big Book of Alcoholics Anonymous,[4] pages 76 to 84. But also, many of our own tribal traditions have ways to help restore justice between people who have hurt each other. If this is so in your particular case, you can talk to Elders or others who know how restitution for harm is done in your own reservation or Nation.

As we walk the path of forgiveness and justice we stay focused on the things WE have done wrong. We don't focus on argument or "making our case." Even if we think the other person might owe us an amends, we must drop this resentment or we cannot do our own amends. We are on this path to get right with the Creator and with others.

We should always get the help of our sponsor or sobriety counselor before making amends to various people on the list. Talk over each possibility with your mentor to see who might be hurt even more by this process. You can rehearse what you are going to say to a person on your list with your sponsor or counselor. Make your amends as quickly as possible. It may be enough to apologize for specific harms you know you have done and ask how you may make further restitution. Sometimes an amends can be made one-on-one, and sometimes it might be right to have a family member or friend with you. In our traditions, sometimes a mutual helper can arrange a meeting between two families to allow the individual who has created the harm to make his or her amends in the family circle. Some of our cultures have the tradition of offering a pipe at the time of apology.

Some amends can be done by letter or by telephone. In this case many of the same guidelines as mentioned above will still be true. When writing a letter of amends or doing an amends by telephone, you can hold an eagle feather to remain in good spirit and intent.

If you decide that an amends can't be done because it would harm a person more, or if it is not possible to do an amends because a person is not available or has died, an amends can be done by prayer in the unseen world of the spirit. Talk to a Medicine Elder about how to do this.

God is the Love that lets me forgive others and others forgive me. Creator, guide me in finding the greatest peace, fellowship, and justice with all women and men.

Now we come to face the northern direction of the Medicine Wheel. The **North** is the direction of the Elders' wisdom. It is the direction of spirituality and the centering power of solitude, which are our special gifts as Native people. Steps 10, 11 and 12 are also called the maintenance steps in the AA program. Once we have begun to learn how to remove the pain and resentment that blocked us from the Creator's gifts by working the other Steps, we must stay in good spiritual shape or we have the chance of relapse. Steps 10, 11, and 12 help us live our lives from the heart day by day.

Step 10   Perseverance   *yes. Love never gives up.*
We continue to think about our strengths and weaknesses and when we are wrong we say so.

of the heart

Step 10 is about moment-to-moment inner alertness and offering "instant amends" when and if necessary. Steps 4 through 9 taught us about the way we harm other people, and ourselves as well, because of our shortcomings and character defects. We are now in healing and recovery from our own *un-self-love* and our addictions backgrounds. It may take many, many years for the wounds to heal. But we now have the tools and skills to notice when we have created a harm, and then to offer an apology very soon after the disharmony occurs.

The only way to change old habits is to create new habits. We can't just simply turn off who we are. As we practice being a positive warrior, the negative warrior tries to prevail. If we are consistent and diligent we will soon make our new life as positive warriors into a habit.

re: the food things stingy & shut down on kids

Positive warriors might keep a **regular daily written inventory** to check themselves about their behavior and their spirit and intent in the course of a day. Some might write a daily inventory in the evening before bed. Some might even carry a **"Step 10 notebook"** around to jot down out-of-harmony behavior as it comes up. You can usually take a minute to make a note about what's coming up for you and think about it later.

If you catch yourself being out of harmony with another person in the course of a day, you can apologize on the spot. Or if you don't realize it until later, you can approach that person or even make a phone call that begins, "I'm calling because I wanted to offer an apology for…" It may be appropriate to invite that person to take a walk or have tea in order to admit you were wrong about something.

As we face North, we seek to remain at the center of our personal Medicine Wheel. The center includes the gifts of **compassion, love, peace of mind, vision, a positive outlook, trust, forgiveness, acceptance, abundance, empowerment, healing,** and **solutions.** Working the Tenth Step and participating in sobriety sweat lodges and recovery circles helps us stay close to our center. This is a life-long journey that requires perseverance, stick-with-it, and never-give-up. If we have a rough day, we get back up on the horse and keep going.

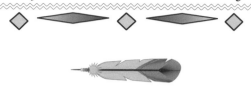

Step 11   Spiritual Awareness
We pray and think about ourselves, praying only for the strength to do what is right.

We have always been a People of prayer. In our old ways, we prayed when the sun came up, we prayed when we picked the herbs that became our medicine, we prayed for a good harvest, and we prayed when the buffalo or deer was taken so our people might live. We are still a People of prayer. Something inside of us becomes alert when an Elder prays before a gathering. At home, there is prayer before a basketball game or a graduation. Step 11 is about re-awakening our gift of prayer and using it for sobriety, recovery and especially on the Wellbriety journey that will last our whole life.

Many of us view a path as a narrow trail. But a spiritual path is unlimited. Prayer and meditation can widen and remove obstacles in our daily walk. When we seek something bigger than our ego-self then we find self-esteem. Our self-esteem as proud Indian people will come back when we look beyond people, places and things for the roots of our wellness, while never giving up on ourselves, families, friends or Nations. The deep root of our wellness is our relationship with the Great Mystery.

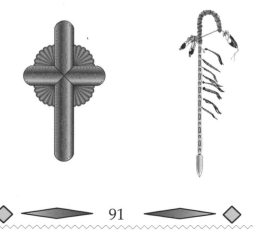

We encourage our people seeking sobriety and living a life of Wellbriety to pray regularly every morning and evening. We have talked the talk, but this is one of the ways we walk the walk. Some of us smudge down with the sage smoke every morning. Many of us have a place in our homes where the sacred elements of our religion or culture are kept. Our morning and evening prayers may be whatever works for us and touches our hearts. We pray to Jesus and the sacred element of the Cross if we are following any of the Christian religions. Sometimes we go outside and listen to the sounds of morning, the birds, and a new day, because the natural world of the land is deep in our DNA, especially as Native people. Prayer and meditation help keep our spiritual awareness of the unseen world of spirit very close.

Here are some guidelines for morning and evening prayer and meditation:

Morning Prayer and Meditation
8 Directives to Follow

1. Ask the Creator to direct my thinking today
2. Ask Him to keep me from feeling self-pity
3. Ask Him to keep me from being dishonest with myself
4. Ask Him to keep me from having self-seeking motives
5. Ask the Creator for inspiration when I am faced with indecision
6. Do not ask for anything for myself, unless others will be helped.
7. Pray that I will be shown what the next step will be.
8. During the day when I become doubtful, ask for the right thought or action.

Evening Prayer and Meditation
13 Questions to Ask Myself

1   Was I resentful?
2   Was I selfish?
3   Was I dishonest?
4   Was I afraid?
5   Do I owe anyone an apology?
6   Do I need to discuss anything with anyone?
    Something that I have been holding inside?
7   Was I kind to everyone?
8   Was I loving to all?
9   Could I have done anything better today?
10 Was I thinking only of myself today?
11 Was I thinking of what I could do for others today?
12 Did I ask the Creator's forgiveness?
13 Did I ask what I can do to make amends

Step 12   Service
We try to help other alcoholics and to practice these principles in everything we do.

Once there was a forest of many trees, bushes, plants and animals. It was a very diverse forest that was once beautiful and plentiful. It had become a sick forest. One night under the cover of darkness, a few of the trees left the forest to go to a nursery where they hoped to get well from the

sickness that was all over the forest. They were given vitamins and medicines of all kinds. They recovered and soon went back to the forest because it was their home. But before long, no matter how hard they tried, they became sick once again. They took on the sickness of the forest once again.

As Indian people, we know we have to heal the forest as well as individual trees. Step 12 is about creating a **Healing Forest** where the community-at-large undergoes healing as well as individuals. This is the story of the Healing Forest, which we will tell again and again. Our culture knows that the individual, the human community, and the land are so completely interconnected that for wellness or Wellbriety, each must participate in the healing journey.

As spiritually-sick people we are familiar with carrying backpacks of anger, hate and resentment. The spiritual warrior carries a backpack filled with solutions, a love-based thought system, and values that move us toward a life of harmony and balance. Others will want to join this walk, strengthening the Healing Forest that we all share together.

As individuals, we can help our brothers and sisters who are suffering from drug and alcohol abuse one-on-one. We can talk to them about what our lives were like when we were addicted, about the Journey we took to heal ourselves, about what we are like now, and our vision for the future. There is excellent advice about working with individuals who are still suffering in Chapter 7 of the AA Big Book, pages 89 to 103. Something good happened to us as we began to walk the Red Road by blending the Medicine Wheel Teachings of our traditions with the 12 Steps of Alcoholics Anonymous. We had many spiritual experiences and we found that **the vision we created through our mind maps in Step 2 was now coming true in Step 12.** We discovered for ourselves that these 12 Steps in a circle are interconnected like the dream catcher that hangs in our baby's bedroom.

We must create a Healing Forest if our cultures are going to survive, grow and thrive as part of the wider society of Turtle Island. Part of our Step 12 work as Indians is to serve our families, communities, Nations, and Indian organizations. This should be no problem for us because our cultures were always about giving back to the people and the Mother Earth. As soon as we are able in our recovery, we will find joyous service by

- ❖ **Helping to conduct our sobriety circles,**
- ❖ **Assisting at our traditional gatherings,**
- ❖ **Becoming involved in community Wellbriety activities,**
- ❖ **Carrying the message of culturally based healing to all who are still suffering.**

But we also have to be very careful that our involvements don't get ahead of our own recovery and sobriety. The Elders say, **"You can't keep what you don't give away, and you can't give away what you don't have."**

Remembering the Medicine Wheel and 12 Steps approach

In Chapters 7 and 8, the eagle and the mouse have helped each other give both a big view and a detailed picture of a sobriety and recovery journey in the Indian way. If this is your first time through the Steps you are probably on the road to recovery. Many of us work a complete set of Steps this way every year. Each time you go through a cycle you will feel more healing recovery from chemical addiction and get a better glimpse of what Welbriety means to us as Native people. Remember that the 12 Steps are an interconnected system. So at any time during the day, the Medicine or principle of a particular Step may come up for you no matter what Step you are working in the yearly cycle. You can use that Medicine to stay in the love-based system.

Here are some of the ideas and methods we talked about to work the Medicine Wheel and the 12 Steps

❖ **The Eagle (big picture) and the Mouse (details)**
❖ **Mind maps**
❖ **The 9 Areas of Unmanageability (Step 1)**
❖ **The 9 Areas of Vision (Step 2)**
❖ **Third Step Prayer**
❖ **Resentment, Fear, and Sex Inventories (Step 4)**
❖ **Cultural ways of Step 4 Inventory**
❖ **The Self-Talk Cycle**
❖ **The Comfort Zone**
❖ **Affirmations**
❖ **Taking quiet time with the land**
❖ **Restoring justice and harmony (amends)**
❖ **Writing regular daily written inventory**
❖ **Keeping a Step 10 notebook**
❖ **Practicing daily prayer and meditation**
❖ **Step 12 Healing Forest**

Chapter 9
To Those Who Walk By Our Sides

As friends, spouses, companions or colleagues of alcoholic or chemically dependent people, the Creator gives us a unique opportunity to undertake our own journey toward Wellbriety as we stand in relationship with our unhappy brothers and sisters who are drinking or drugging. How can we set off on our own healing journey as loved ones of chemically dependent people?

Alanon -
Coda -
ACoA -

Chapter 9
To Those Who Walk By Our Sides

Our Indian communities are slowly recovering from the disease of alcoholism. Nowadays there are thousands of Indians sober. We know of people who have been sober for 8, 10, 12, 14 and 20 years. We know Indian people who have been sober for 45 and 49 years. We also know there are now many young people who have never tasted alcohol or used drugs. This means we can do it. As Native Americans we can take the Wellbriety journey into sobriety and wellness and into a happy future for our people. But there is still a lot of work to be done.

Our Dysfunctional Forest

Most of our communities are still like a sick forest. Remember that forest we talked about in Step 12 of the 12 Steps in Chapter 8, where a few of the trees left to go to a nursery far away from the forest so they could heal from the disease of the forest? They had some healing, but then they came back and got sick once again. Our communities are like that sick forest. Why does the sickness keep coming back generation after generation? One of the reasons is that we have suffered historical trauma and oppression directed at us as Native people. We were forbidden to practice our cultures, which blocked the source of healing for us. In the days after military defeat of our peoples, returning to our culture for healing was not an option as it is now. Alcoholism, dysfunctional families, and domestic violence were some of the results. Now we have discovered that

the roots of the trees in that forest go down into earth that is full of **anger, guilt, shame and fear.** If the soil is full of anger, guilt, shame and fear, how can we expect the trees, which are our people, to be healthy?

The "trees" in our dysfunctional forest are **alcoholic trees, ACOA trees, codependent trees, family violence trees, suicide trees, sexual abuse trees, depression trees, trees with drug abuse problems, trees who are married, related or close to these other trees, and of course, "normal" trees.** You can probably name a few more. All these "trees" live in the seen world of our communities but their roots go down into the unseen world of anger, guilt, shame and fear.

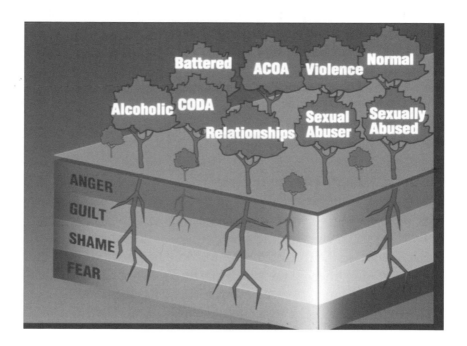

The Community Forest

ACOA Behavior

This story of the forest is just another way of saying that when we, as Indians, start recovering from alcoholism and the effects of historical trauma, we have to dig deep in our past to see the symptoms that we are passing from generation to generation. The trauma many of our people went through during the boarding school era, and the various government policies that followed, created conditions that we started passing on to the children, and they to their children. Our people started to drink to escape the pain, and a lot of alcoholic behavior began poisoning the soil of our future generations. Even if some of us didn't become alcoholic we became **Adult Children of Alcoholics** or ACOA's.

As Native Americans, not only did most of us grow up in alcoholic families, but we grew up in alcoholic communities. The nutrients around our roots were full of many different human poisons leading to what is called ACOA behavior. ACOA behavior encompasses many different dysfunctional ways of relating to one another and coping, such as codependency. Some of those poisons in our growing-up soil included **resentment, distrust, loneliness, sadness and numbness.** Many of us had to numb out so that we could stand the firestorm going on in our families and communities due to drinking, drugging, and being denied acceptance into society as the Indigenous people who we are.

Now, as adults, we might notice lots of ACOA behavior going on inside us even though we ourselves perhaps didn't become alcoholic. Do any of the following describe your own behavior or way through life?

ACOA Behavior

1   I need to be in control of people and situations or I just don't feel comfortable.

2   I have trouble fitting in. I feel like an outsider, whether I am in my Indian community or in the non-Indian world.

3   I don't know how to have fun. I'm very serious all the time and life isn't enjoyable.

4   I'm overly responsible about everything except when I'm irresponsible. There's no happy medium for me.

5   I have difficulty in following a project through from beginning to the end.

6   I have trouble with intimacy and relationships because I'm afraid of rejection or abandonment.

7   Life is an ongoing crisis. When it is not a crisis, I'm wondering what will go wrong next.

8   I feel like I've been abandoned by those close to me, or somebody is about to abandon me.

9   Sexuality is no longer a sacred, pleasurable experience as the Creator intended it to be. It's become a real problem.

10 Sometimes I can't think straight. My thoughts are often confused and muddled. Sometimes I become paralyzed and unable to act.

ACOA Behavior
(Continued)

11 I am extremely loyal, even in the face of evidence the loyalty is underserved.

12 I judge myself without mercy and think I am responsible for anything that goes wrong.

13 I constantly seek approval and affirmation from others.

14 I'm smoking a lot, have an eating disorder, and see signs that I could become alcoholic or chemically dependent, too.

15 I lie when it would be easier to tell the truth.

16 I don't know what "normal" is. I guess at what is normal

So what Are We To Do?

This chapter is about what happens to us if someone close to us is an alcoholic or **is** chemically dependent. That someone could be a spouse, partner, significant other, life companion, family member or friend, child or co-worker. Sometimes it happens slowly and gradually. We loved or enjoyed our relationship with that special someone for a long time but something changed in our friend. He or she started drinking or using drugs. Or maybe it was always that way but we just began to see it. Maybe violence began and we started getting slapped around or beaten up. For some of us, it came on slowly and we compensated and pretended that nothing was wrong. Maybe we put up with it for the children. Maybe we said to ourselves, "I will stay until the children are grown." But pretty soon our own behavior began to change. It's because we were sucked into the environment around drinking or drugging even

though we ourselves weren't using. It's as though we caught the disease from someone close to us.

We now know that, as you live with an alcoholic and/or chemically dependent person who is living out of harmony with the Great Spirit, it will most likely cause you to start living out of harmony too. There will be a tendency for you to feel like a victim and to feel a lot of your own self-pity. "Oh why did this happen to me? My life is not worth living any more..." There is a tendency to blame the other person for all the disharmonious, unhappy thoughts and feelings that are coming up in you as a result of his or her drinking and drugging. You might come up with numerous plans to change that person or you might try many plans to change your life situation. Often times you will feel like you are crazy or insane. You will cry and go through embarrassing times. Your friends will give you all sorts of advice....try this...leave him/her... And still you stay.

Please listen carefully. Sometimes, the person living with an alcoholic can be sicker or as sick as the alcoholic. So, what can be done?

In groups that support family and friends of alcoholics and addicts, you will learn that the alcoholic or addict is not the problem you need to work on. You need to work on yourself. You are your problem. You will also learn about the, "Yeah but, you don't understand..." thing that you might say to rebuff this. You will learn there is a solution for YOU.

You will learn it's about working on yourself. It is about realizing that you might exhibit codependency and other ACOA behaviors because, as an Indian person, you likely grew up in a dysfunctional family or

community that you didn't even know is dysfunctional. Maybe you even thought it was "normal." You can find support groups for those close to troubled people where participants will share their experience, strength and hope. You will learn that the way you are thinking and feeling is what is causing the problems you are having in you life. You might be shocked to discover that you yourself are filled with anger, guilt, shame and fear. We are a proud people with ancestors who were positive and loving warriors. We are a people with a value system that tends toward harmony, and not to conflict and hurt. We are a people of integrity, intelligence and honor, having much to offer the troubled societies of today. But if we are to be that proud Indian Nation, the healing we need to undergo all begins with you and me.

As friends, spouses, companions or colleagues of alcoholic or chemically dependent people, the Creator gives us a unique opportunity to undertake our own journey toward sobriety, recovery and Wellbriety as we stand in relationship with our unhappy brothers and sisters who are drinking or drugging. If we don't choose to take this journey we will probably fall prey to our own background as people who grew up in a forest of alcoholism. We might take a difficult road and become addicted or very unhappy ourselves. How can we set off on our own healing journey as spouses, relatives, friends, or loved ones of chemically dependent people? There are a number of ways.

Solutions

First, we can educate ourselves about codependency and the dysfunctional family system. There has been a lot written and taught about these subjects by our non-Native brothers and sisters because society in general is also suffering from the effects of drug and alcohol abuse.[1] We can take what works of these teachings for us as Indians and change them as needed to fit our own cultural ways. And just like those

who suffer from alcoholism and drug addiction, we can also work the 12 Steps in our own lives. We can participate in the Al-Anon program, which is especially for those close to alcoholics and drug users. [2] We can help to establish Indian Al-Anon meetings in the communities we live in. We can travel to Indian AA and Indian Al-Anon conventions, which are taking place now as part of regular AA and Al-Anon events. [3]

When we as co-alcoholics work the Medicine Wheel and the 12 Steps program, we will begin to learn how to draw boundaries defining who *we* are. We will find our own self-worth and self-esteem, separate from the chemically dependent person in our lives. We will learn how to live our own cycle-of-life in a good way. We will learn how we ourselves are immature and can change. You can't change other people who are drinking and drugging. You've just got to work on you.

To work the 12 Steps as a non-alcoholic, you change the wording of Step 1 and follow the entire path set out in the previous chapters of this book. It will be best to work these Steps in an Indian Al-Anon framework with others like yourself who are related to alcoholics or other drug users. Indian Al-Anon is just beginning to come together as a culture-specific group. In this way we will co-create Indian Al-Anon together!

How do you change the wording of the First Step to work the Steps as an ACOA or somebody related, or close to an alcoholic or chemically dependent person?

Step 1 for those close to a chemically-dependent person--
We admitted we were powerless over our spouse's (relative's, friends, etc.) alcoholism or drug addiction—that we had lost control of our own life.

The principle of Step One is still **Honesty.** "Yes, our family has been going to pieces. My own life is going in a negative direction. There are ugly thoughts, feelings, moods and behaviors coming up in me. I want to regain my own dignity and live the life of a positive warrior." Then, you begin looking at yourself by working the Steps with the support of other people like yourself.

When we say "You work on you" is the way to deal with the addiction of one close to you, we don't mean you should stay in harm's way. Sometimes you have to separate if a person is abusing you in some way that can't be resolved. You may have to take the children to a safe place. No one has the right to commit violence or perpetrate verbal abuse on you or your children. If you work in a business or other organizational situation, you may have to consider legal action or even termination if there is absolutely nothing you can do about your colleague's or the organization's dysfunctional behavior. It is good if this can be done in a non-blaming way. To be non-blaming and forgiving is an internal attitude that helps you to work on <u>you</u> and not get diverted by finger-pointing. Positive warriors are non-blaming and forgiving, even as they clearly see who is accountable for unwell behavior. But it may be necessary to separate from a troubled person or situation—in a loving way if you can.

Roles in the Dysfunctional Family System

Let's return now to educating ourselves about codependency and the dysfunctional family system. We grew up as ACOA's with our roots embedded in family, community, and Reservation anger, guilt, shame and fear. As a result of that, both our families and the community at large adopted some dysfunctional behavior in order to cope and survive. Each family member is like a piece hanging on a **mobile,** those hanging sculptures or decorations whose parts are balanced to move in response to air currents. The purpose of a mobile is to stay in balance and to look beautiful as it floats in the breeze. Our families and communities tried to stay in balance while alcohol was present.

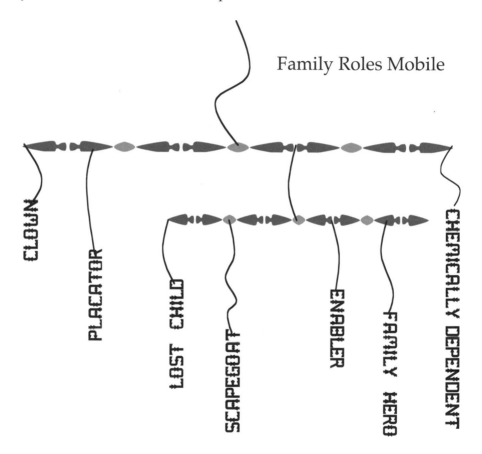

Family Roles Mobile

CLOWN PLACATOR LOST CHILD SCAPEGOAT ENABLER FAMILY HERO CHEMICALLY DEPENDENT

Let's introduce ourselves to the cast of characters in a chemically dependent family system. This family system "mobile" can be either your growing-up family, or your family now, or both. These pieces on the mobile are working so hard to stay in balance and "make it work." Where do you find yourself here?

Family Roles

The **Alcoholic/Chemically Dependent Person** has the drinking or drugging problem and seems to be the sick one in the family or community. In our extended families there is probably more than one chemically dependent person. This person or persons can be male or female, old or young.

The **Enabler** prevents the alcoholic or drug user from experiencing the consequences of his or her addictive behavior and helps the alcoholic stay sick. This person suffers from the disease of codependency.

The **Family Hero** tries to make the family or community look good by achieving success in school, work, or other kinds of activities. The hero over-achieves to make the family proud. This can happen as a child, teenager, or adult. You can become the Family Hero by taking on the job of "parent" at a very young age. Often, later on you will be the workaholic.

The **Scapegoat** diverts attention from the family's problems by constantly getting into trouble. He or she provides a distraction from the family's or community's disharmony. This family member will act out the family dysfunction.

The **Lost Child** hides out, tries not to make waves, becomes remote and invisible. This role is also called the invisible child. The Lost Child will have the hardest time as an adult because this child did not learn any social skills.

The **Clown** lessens tensions in the family or community by being funny and cute. The clown provides fun and humor in the system. The behavior is used to avoid conflict.

The **Placator** also tries to reduce conflict in the family or community by smoothing things over. He or she downplays the seriousness of the troubles the system faces.

Where do you find yourself here? This is important to know because we will not succeed until the disease of codependency and ACOA behavior is also healed in our families and communities. When addiction is present, everyone in our "mobile" example inherits the diseases of codependency and its counterpart "counterdependency," in some form or another.

Codependent Behavior

Codependents are outwardly weak and insecure, seeking to lose themselves in others. They feel themselves to be dependent on another person and not really able to function on their own. Members of a codependent couple each feels themselves to be half a person and can't live without the other person. People can be codependent to spouses, friends, brothers and sisters, organizations and other entities of all kinds. Codependents tend to be the **enablers** in unwell situations like chemical dependency. Because they don't want to lose the other person, they make it easy for the addict or alcoholic to keep on using or drinking. Codependency is an emotional, psychological, behavioral and spiritual condition that develops as a result of long term exposure to a set of oppressive rules. What kinds of oppressive rules did you experience in your family or community?

Here are some of the characteristics or behavior patterns of codependent people:

Codependent Characteristics

1- Relationship Addiction—codependents tend to treat love, work, or community relationships as an addiction.

2 Lack of Boundaries—codependents don't know where they stop and others begin. They often take responsibility for others because they are not sure of who *they* really are themselves.

3 Impression Management—codependents tend to fake how they present themselves to others. They don't know how to have clear, straight interactions with others. Their "outside" appearance is more important than their "inside" feelings, intuition, and stability.

4 Caretaking—codependents must always be taking care of somebody or something.

5 Physical Illness—codependents live under such relationship stress that they often get sick

6 Control Issues—codependents are supreme controllers. They have to be on top of every situation. Being in control provides a sense of security.

7 Distorted Feelings—codependents don't deal with feelings in a healthy way. They change their feelings to keep their image of themselves intact. For example, if something happens that brings up anger, it may be expressed as a smile, which is a distorted feeling.

Codependent Characteristics
(Continued)

8   Thinking Disorders—codependents are often confused in their thinking, falling prey to either excessive or compulsive thinking patterns. For example, they can be obsessed by their work, leading to workaholism. Or there can be such involvement with a social cause that other parts of a person's life are neglected.

9   Manipulation--codependents vacillate between pity and blame. They play all the roles of rescuer, victim, and persecutor.

10   Perfectionism--Codependents place unrealistic demands on themselves and others. When these demands are not met, they place blame.

11   Depression and Negativity—codependents can be chronically unhappy and see the dark, negative side of everything.

12   Too Much Empathy—codependents feel for others and take on their problems in a way that is not quite "true." They are men or women who love too much.

13   Inferiority/Low self-worth—codependents feel inferior and worthless as they interact and live in the world.

14   Loss of Spirituality--Codependent dishonesty not only leads to mistrust in oneself and others, but also to a lack of faith in a Higher Power.

The Counterdependent Person

People usually view a codependent as a weak person who enables the chemically dependent person. He or she is one of the pair that keeps the unwell family or community going on in its sickness. The other one is the addict or alcoholic. The addict or alcoholic often comes across as an outwardly strong, secure and "on-top-of-it" person. This person is called a **counterdependent.** He or she is the other half of the unwell relationship. In the case of spouses, the AA Big Book said, *The rocks in her head matched the holes in his.* The counterdependent is grandiose, confident, seemingly strong and invulnerable. Counterdependents are the macho man and super woman. We are not talking about well people here. We are talking about people who present themselves as strong and confident but are really suffering underneath.

Counterdependents and codependents often share a number of interlocking traits. There are four of them. A counterdependent has grandiosity and a codependent has insecurity. The counterdependent is extremely independent on the surface. The codependent is extremely dependent on the surface. The counterdependent is self-centered. The codependent is other-centered. The counterdependent is intrusive and interfering. The codependent is receptive. This is a dance many of us know all too well.

Suppose a codependent and a counterdependent person were having a conversation. This is what they might say:

Counterdependent: I'm important, strong and capable. Look how grandiose I am!

Codependent: Oh good! I'm insecure and can't handle things on my own.

Counterdependent: I'm self-centered. The world revolves around me-- and you do too...

Codependent: That's OK, 'cause I'm really other-centered and very involved in your life. You are my whole world...

Remembering This Chapter

This is a chapter about what we, as non-addicted family or community members, can do to begin healing ourselves, our families, our communities, and our Tribal nations. When people heal from their codependency, addictions do not get the support they need to continue. When we as codependents and others having ACOA behavior go into treatment for our part of the family and community disease, the grandmas and grandpas inside us begin to wake up and offer us the culture in support of our healing. The road to being a positive warrior in the love-based system of the Creator begins when we "own our own" roles in dysfunctional families and communities, (take responsibility for them) even though we are not the chemically dependent ones. We "own our own stuff" when we begin to take a look at ourselves in a good way, returning to the principles, laws and values that our ancestors in our traditional cultures lived by.

Here are some of the topics that came up in chapter 9:

The dysfunctional community forest
Roots in Anger, guilt, shame, and fear
ACOA behavior
You must work on YOU
Indian Al-Anon
The 12 Steps for a non-alcoholic or non-addict
Family roles
Codependent behavior
Counterdependent behavior

Chapter 10
Strengthening Our Families

The Wellbriety journey begins once we, as individuals, have some sobriety and seek to find a greater wellness in our lives. In order to strengthen our families, there are certain principles, laws and values that we must know about to keep the family harmonious and resilient.

Chapter 10
Strengthening Our Families
Healing Native American Families in Recovery

Were want to talk a little about how our families can thrive once recovery is taking place with individuals in the family. Suppose the adults in the family are in recovery. It could be that the mom and dad, or the grandparents, have been walking the Red Road of sobriety for some time. How can the whole family become involved in that Red Road journey?

When the adults are working the Medicine Wheel and the 12 Steps in their own lives, the family will enjoy the benefit from their healing. In fact, because "You can't keep it unless you give it away," it will help everybody if the Red Road journey is shared with the family as a whole. How can we do this? The family can come together on a regular basis in a special talking circle we'll call a Family Circle. A Family Circle provides a regular focus of communication and sharing that will allow Wellbriety to take place in the family. There are a few ideas or principles about how families or relationships work that we should know before we talk more about the family circle.

Connectedness
First let's remember one of the principles of the Medicine Wheel: **the seen and the unseen world.** The Medicine Wheel teaches that there is a seen and an unseen world. The seen world includes all the visible things

around us, such as the trees, people, cars, traffic lights and so on. But there is also an unseen world that unites or connects all the things of the every day seen world. There are principals, laws and values in the unseen world that are like a connecting fiber knitting together the seen world. If we ignore the principles, laws and values of the unseen world of human relationships, then our families won't experience harmony or love. So when we come together in a Family Circle, it's good to know something about the principles of connectedness.

We use a red cloth in the center of a Family Circle to remind us that this is a sacred area and that our coming together is a sacred event. On top of the red cloth we place four colors of cloth—red in the east, yellow in the south, black in the west, and white in the north—to represent the whole human race. In the center of this ceremonial area we will place a sea shell in which we'll burn sage, cedar or some other herb sacred to the region you live in. The shell attracts the heartbeat of the earth. It's a little like a satellite dish that the Elders invented a long time ago to help keep our communities and families in real connection with each other. This ceremonial area helps our Family Circle become connected in the unseen world of relationships. There are actually eight levels of connectedness that can take place in the unseen world. We'll talk about three.

The first level happens when you look at someone and your eyes connect. The next level is described by a word in the Mohican language called **Natashnayah.** After your eyes connect with someone, a feeling may go across that connection. That sudden feeling is called Natashnayah, or touch-love in English. It is more than when your eyes just connect. In the third level of connectedness you might feel pulled or drawn to another person. That's called **Iwashtanay.** We have to trust that there are other

forces available to help us. These experiences in the unseen world represent those other forces and are available to make our families or relationships real and loving.

The Wellbriety journey begins once we as individuals have some sobriety and seek to find a greater wellness in our lives. In order to strengthen our families, there are certain principles, laws and values that we must know about to keep the family harmonious and resilient. The human being has the ability to choose to live in harmony with the principles, laws and values, or not. If we choose to live out of harmony we will be faced with certain conflict. Conflict does not happen when you live in harmony. Conflict is a feedback system to tell you you're off track. What are some of these principles, laws and values?

In our families and relationships, we have the ability to treat each other with **respect** or with **disrespect.** I can be either **responsible** or **irresponsible. Functional** or **dysfunctional. Honest** or **dishonest.** There will be consequences to each of these behaviors determined by natural laws.

Every relationship should have a **vision.** It shouldn't be an accident. Every family should have a vision of what it is going to work towards. One of the laws is that as human beings we are created to be visionary people. The picture that a vision creates inside ourselves is very, very powerful because it activates a principle: *we move towards and become like that which we think about.*

In this chapter we will talk about some of the principles, laws and values that function in the unseen world to help us live in alignment with the Creator's way. We will also give a few practical methods or techniques to strengthen the family.

Traditional Ways of Child Rearing

Each of our tribal traditions had a special way to relate to the birth of a child. There might be naming ceremonies or commitment ceremonies to place that child into the community. If you have a feeling for your own traditional values, it is still possible to learn how our grandmas and grandpas welcomed a newborn baby into the world. In the Mohican tradition from the Stockbridge-Munsee country in Wisconsin, one of the jobs of the Turtle Clan was to insure that every child knew the story of life. The story of life was hidden in the designs of the turtle's shell. The people knew that a child grew up in a cycle that consisted of four, four-year cycles. The first was until age four, corresponding to springtime, or the east. The next was until age eight and corresponded to summertime in the south. The next was until age 12—fall, in the west. And the final four-year segment of growing up in the traditional ways was the puberty cycle until age 16, corresponding to winter time, in the north.

After a child was born it was first given to the mom and dad to hold. Then it was given to a female Elder of the Turtle Clan who would hold the child and tell it the story of life for the first three cycles, or twelve years. She talked to it as though it were an adult. When she was done she transferred it to a male Elder who took the story from the fourth cycle all the way up to the time of changing worlds at the end of our life. It then became the responsibility of the parents to tell a little bit of the story on the next succeeding days. The child was constantly being told how he or she was supposed to behave and function, what ceremonies to look forward to, and so on. In our traditional ways, we never punished or yelled at children the way it's done today. We would always retell the story of life when children got out of line.

Child Rearing

There were a lot of things that the old people knew about child rearing which were preventers of conflict. You didn't have to go through the conflict to the degree we do today if the beliefs were built correctly in the first place. Every one adhered to the story of life. We've gotten away from the story of life and these traditional ways of child rearing because a different social system with different values dominates our lives today. But perhaps you, the new moms, dads and grandparents can find some way to combine or blend the best of the two social systems with the goal of creating happier individuals, families, communities and Nations.

Principles of Conflict Resolution

Our relationships and families will go through conflicts and struggles because it is natural to do so. Conflict is a guidance system and a message carrier. It tells us which way to go in order to restore harmony to our lives. We talked earlier (Chapter 5) about the fact that we can be in one of two kinds of thought systems: a **fear-based system**, or a **love-based system**. Black Elk [1] called a fear-based system of constant conflict and strife a *black road*. This is a traditional Native idea that refers to a direction of difficulty, not to a race or ethnic identity. But as positive warriors on a Red Road journey we must always focus on a love-based thought system that thrives in a positive mind. There are three negative ways to handle conflict in a fear-based system. These ways always lead to more conflict and unhappiness. There is a fourth and more constructive way to relate to conflict on the love-based Red Road, which has very different results for our families.

Attack

The first unhealthy way to handle conflict is to **attack** one another. This way of attack uses fault finding and fixing of blame. Sometimes you'll hear it said, "If at first you do not succeed, fix the blame fast!" The consequence of any attack is to create more conflict.

Denial

The next unhealthy way to relate to conflict is through **denial**. Just pretend it's not going on. Look the other way. Tune out. Sometimes the ego can build a good case for why a criticism is not true. But this could be just a fancy form of denial. Denial is a dysfunctional way of handling conflict.

Witholding

The third unhealthy way for handling conflict is to **withhold**. You can withhold the keys to the car, money that is requested, your voice or your presence, all just to get your way. And worst of all, you can withhold love. Withholding is just another strategy of conflict avoidance, which never resolves a conflict.

Embrace

The healthy or functional way to resolve a conflict is to **embrace** it. To "embrace" means to work through the conflict, to relate to it, *to lean into it*. We also have a choice to work through a conflict with **love** or with **fear**. We can use tools from the love-based thought system or from the fear-based thought system. The moment we choose to embrace a conflict we should choose to embrace it with **love**.

"Embrace a conflict" means don't run away from it. If you and your companion have had words, you may go off by yourself for a while. You may feel hurt and your mind may be racing with all kinds of thoughts. But as soon as you've cooled off and an opportunity presents itself, why not go to your spouse, partner or friend and say, "I would like to talk about what happened when..." It takes courage, and neither person

should shame the other person when a peace overture like this is made. Keep the love-based system in mind and be sure to listen as much as you talk. You might decide to pass an eagle feather or some other sacred object back and forth when you do this, following the rules for a talking circle. (see Chapter 2) The Creator is there with you. This is one example of "embracing," or leaning into conflict.

Sometimes a companion or a family member might confront us about our words or behavior. Because we love and trust them, we can make the instantaneous choice to engage or embrace what they perceive and resolve it. Align your spirit and intent and embrace the conflict. Healthy relationships are actually built with conflict resolution. They are not built on expecting the absence of conflict. The real basis of conflict resolution is changing yourself. Gandhi said *you must be the change you wish to see in the community.* You must be the change you wish to see at work. You must be the change you wish to see in the family. You must be the change you wish to see in your relationships. This is how we walk our talk on the good Red Road.

The Eight Stages or Feelings of Development

When we are conceived, we first experience life in the womb. It's like being in a cocoon. We feel protected and safe. The womb water surrounds us. We feel connected, wanted and absolutely worthy of all. Then we are born into the physical world. Our first important experience once we are out of the womb is for us to feel safe. We still believe we are in the cocoon. In order to maintain this spiritual cocoon, we need to develop **eight feelings** as we grow up. These feelings are given to us by our parents, family and community. If we get these eight feelings, then we are able to live in an interconnected world and live from the heart in life's challenges.

Traditionally, each of these eight feelings will produce a pattern of thought as we grow up. The human runs its entire life on about eight thought patterns. If these patterns are generated by having the eight feelings, then we will grow up to be mentally healthy human beings. If we don't develop these eight feelings, then WE will grow out of harmony and have dysfunctional thinking. This type of thinking may be a part of why some of us need to drink. In the 12 steps and the Medicine Wheel Teachings, we will learn to get these eight feelings back. Then we can develop a Good Mind and walk the Red Road.

In the 1950's, the psychologist Erik Erikson taught about eight stages of development the human being needs to experience in order to live life in a happy way. [2] If we experience these stages, we are in-harmony with our needs. If we fail to experience these stages, we find ourselves out-of-harmony. Erik Erikson learned of these eight stages or feelings when he lived with both the Sioux people of the Dakotas, and the Yurok people of Northern California in the 1930's and 1940's. So these are **Teachings from our own Native people** about how the cycle-of-life works.

It is important to know what the eight feelings are as we sit in our family circles and work through our own relationships. This knowledge will give us a different insight about how to look at people in conflict and to help them to harmony.

8- INTEGRITY

7- GENERATIVITY

1- TRUST

6- INTIMACY

Stages
of
Development

2- AUTONOMY

5- IDENTITY

3- INITIATIVE

4- ACCOMPLISHMENT

The Eight Feelings

Eight Stages or Feelings

1-Trust

The first is **Trust** and it is the feeling an infant must have during its <u>**first**</u> <u>**year**</u> in order to have a healthy development. Trust includes tender loving care and bodily contact. The infant must know that people are good and trustworthy and that the world is a good place that he or she can trust. But if trust is missing, then there is an out-of-harmony, unhealthy development of **mistrust**. Mistrust may lead to family breakup or

parental rejection or withdrawal later in life. There will be the strong feeling that the world is not safe. Mistrust leaves us unable to develop close relationships.

2-Autonomy/Independence

The second is **autonomy** or **independence,** and for in-harmony, healthy development, a baby must experience INDEPENDENCE during the <u>second year</u> of its life. The feeling of independence says, "I love this world and want all it offers." The child must be encouraged to become its own being through exploration and independence. It must not be over controlled by its parents. If autonomy is missing, then the out-of-harmony development leads to **shame and doubt**. In later life, they may be fearful or ashamed of themselves. They may become an over controlling parent because they were over controlled by their parents. Having this feeling allows us to make healthy decisions and choices. If we have not developed this feeling, we will be wishy-washy. We will tend to let other people make our decisions.

3-Initiative

The third stage takes place between <u>3-7 years</u> and it is a time when **Initiative** must be encouraged for healthy development to take place. Initiative supports active imagination, role playing and pretending, and a healthy testing of the boundaries between imagination and reality. If the third feeling of Initiative doesn't take place properly, then an out-of harmony-condition of **guilt** will take hold in the child. A guilty person has often been told, "...don't be silly, and grow up." They feel foolish for using their imagination and may live in fantasy and daydreams in later life. They have been shamed, and it has a negative effect on how they are in later life.

4-Accomplishment

The fourth stage takes place when a person is between <u>**8-11 years**</u> old and it is called **Accomplishment.** In order for accomplishment to take place, a young person must learn to feel good for something, and good at doing something. They need to receive praise and recognition for their accomplishments. If someone growing up doesn't get the feeling or stage of accomplishment, they will take on the unhealthy developmental state of **low self-esteem**. They might later be an overly critical parent and go on to lack self-confidence.

5-Identity

The fifth stage is called **Identity** and takes place in the age group of <u>**12-18 years**</u> of age. To have in-harmony identity behaviors, a young person must learn to belong and to be somebody while in this age group. They need to get attention and praise for things done well. It is in this age group that they will begin to develop answers to the three questions, **Who am I?, Why am I here?, Where am I Going?** If there is unhealthy development in this age group, then the out-of-harmony condition of **inferiority** takes place. Inferiority brings lack of self worth, low self esteem, with possible depression, suicide attempts and addictions.

6-Intimacy

The sixth stage takes place in the young adult in the age group of <u>**19-30 years**</u> of age. It is called **Intimacy.** In order to have healthy intimacy in life, a person must learn to share ideas with friends, as well as openly sharing his or her innermost thoughts and feelings. Healthy, in-harmony development at this stage also means that you are not worried too much about what others think of you. If we miss this stage, then the out-of-harmony condition of **isolation** takes place. Isolation is a cold place with

the inability to share thoughts and feelings. This unhealthy development causes you to be unable to form and maintain close relationships, and to exhibit unreasonable fears of openness and disclosure.

7-Generativity

The seventh stage of development takes place in the age group of **30-40 years** of age and is called **Generativity.** Generativity means that a person is able to participate in unselfish giving and sharing with others. He or she can give to and guide others without looking for "what's in it for me?" The ability to be of service to others develops at this time. Generativity includes the ability to mentor people who will replace you. If a person misses this stage of development, **stagnation** then develops. A stagnant person is self-centered and self-seeking. They take from others and are overly materialistic.

8-Integrity

The Eighth stage of development takes place for the **remainder of a person's life** and is called **Integrity.** To achieve and experience integrity, a person must become a mentally healthy adult. He or she must break away from parents and relate to them on an adult-to-adult level. In-harmony behavior at this stage involves seeing order and "worthwhileness," or value in the world. A person in this stage has a sense of his or her own values, rules and code of life. If integrity doesn't take place, then a person falls into **despair** and is plagued with fear and being judgmental. They feel the world is a bad place and may lack good values and conscience. They may feel fear and hopelessness. They may feel, "If only this had happened, then I would be..."

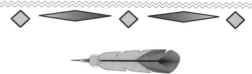

Reclaiming the Eight Stages or Feelings

We can get back the strength of the eight feelings even if we missed them growing up. The traditional ceremonies were designed to awaken these eight feelings in tribal members. Our Circles of Recovery and Wellbriety can also help us get these feelings back. Returning to some of our traditional values (See Chapter 2) can also help. Sharing an intimate relationship, while keeping our spirit and intent aligned with the Red Road and the teachings of the Medicine Wheel and the 12 Steps, is another way. You can probably think of others.

How does knowing about the Eight Stages help? Here is an example. If a person doesn't have a particular Feeling, you'll see troublesome behavioral issues take place later on. In conflict resolution, we'll often see that what people say the conflict is about, is not really it. It might be they can't *feel* in one of these eight ways.

So, for example, suppose I have trouble with my close personal relationships. Suppose I can get just so close in a relationship before serious conflicts of different kinds break out, and I notice that this happens over and over for me. Sticking to the "facts" of the conflict in conflict resolution sessions might not help because the problem could be that I never got the feeling of Intimacy quite right in my own cycle-of-life and growing up. Perhaps the feeling of Intimacy is lacking because the basic feeling of Trust was stunted. **But the feelings of Trust and Intimacy can be re-learned when we're older by participating in our traditional Circles.** If you have a regular recovery circle going, you'll notice that you're learning the gifts of Trust and Intimacy as time goes on. This is also true for other feelings that we didn't get while growing up.

The main idea is that many of us in Indian country didn't grow up with these eight positive feelings. We grew up with them out-of-harmony, more like the eight negative feelings described. But the neat thing about

the human being is that even though we grew up in this way, we were designed with the ability to change and to choose the positive feeling later in life. It doesn't matter whether we were raped, beaten up, addicted, or dysfunctional—there's nothing in the whole world, with the Great Spirit's help, that cannot be healed in order for us to come back and live with these eight positive feelings, and then to pass them on to our children. Our traditional Circles can help us regain any of the missing eight developmental stages. It's very healthy as we work through family conflict to understand the cycle of life in this way.

How to Conduct a Family Circle

We've talked a lot about the many principles and ideas that go into making a successful Family Circle. But what about the actual Family Circle? A Family Circle should meet once a week at a regular time when all members can participate. Each member should be serious about the commitment to attend. The circle can start out formally like the talking circle described in Chapter 2. Arrange a circle of chairs and leave a space at the Eastern door. Begin the circle with a smudge and a prayer that everyone can share. If there are any other traditions special to your region or to your family, they can be incorporated into the ceremonial portion of the circle. Then let every one check in, being sure not to interrupt when someone is speaking. When everyone has been heard, the facilitator can talk about the subject for that evening, or family members can bring their concerns to the Circle. The facilitator can be a grandma or grandpa, mom or dad, auntie, uncle, or cousin. A young person can sometimes facilitate if that seems appropriate in your case.

This form of talking circle can go on for as long as seems right on a particular day. But as the circle begins to wind down, you might want to change the format into a respectful discussion mode in which people can speak directly to one another. Over a period of time the circle will give

you all eight of those feelings. Experiment to see what works best for your family and never force anyone to participate.

Measuring the Eight Feelings

How can we now take some of the ideas we've discussed and use them as exercises in our Family Circles? Think about the eight feelings of the life cycle. First, can you rate yourself as an individual in each of the eight feelings? Lets create a scale of one to ten for each feeling. *One* means we have low or none of whatever it is we are measuring. *Five* is a medium rating, and *ten* is high or perfect. So let's start with **Trust.** How do you rate yourself as a trusting person? Do you feel at home in this world? Study some of the guidelines for Trust in this chapter and then go on to **Independence, Initiative, Accomplishment** and so on. Even younger people can rate themselves in the older categories. Try it.

Rate Yourself

Once the Family Circle is meeting on a regular basis, and once these eight feelings have been discussed in the circle, then we can do the same exercise for the family as a whole. It will take some discussion among the family to come to a consensus. Is it a Trusting family? Is the family as a whole Independent? Is it a family that can take Initiative and Accomplish things? What rating would you give the family in all of these? Once you measure these eight areas, you then ask a question: "Where would you like to take Trust to?" If the Trust rating for a family is a *four*, then set a reasonable goal of *seven* or *eight*. Get some ideas about how to increase

the Trust rating. Make a plan. Talk about what you need to do to increase your Trust rating as a family.

Making the Family Vision

Another project for the Family Circle is to create a family vision. This can also be done by an individual or by a couple in a relationship. The family vision is done by drawing one or more mind maps, just like in Chapter 7. The vision is a dream or a goal that you would like to move toward. One family vision mind map consists of a circle with the words "Our Family Vision" written within the circle. Then, draw branches out from this central circle, naming all the important issues of your family. From the end of each of these branches, begin to brainstorm where you see your family going in each of these areas. There are other kinds of mind maps you can create for the family vision. Experiment until you find one that works for you. The important thing is to work together to dream a future everybody can believe in.

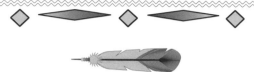

A family Needs and Fears Analysis

Another good family exercise is the Needs and Fears analysis. Divide a piece of paper into two columns. Label one column "Needs" and the second column "Fears." In one column write what you or the subject of the analysis *needs* in order to be happy. In the other column write what you or the subject *is afraid of* and is blocking happiness.

In one variation of the Needs and Fears exercise, parents can list what they think are the needs and fears of each individual child. Then the children can do the same for their parents. What do mom and dad need? What about grandma and grandpa? What are they afraid of? When that is complete, each parent or grandparent can do it for his or her companion.

When these columns are filled out, talk about each one. It's in the lively discussion that the family will come together and experience **Natashnayah** and **Iwashtanay.** Remember, too, that each person can do a Needs and Fears analysis for him or herself and then share it with the family.

Needs	Fears
1	1
2	2
3	3

A Vision

Sooner or later on the Wellbriety journey every human being realizes that our real purpose here is to serve the Creator and help our brothers and sisters. Our *inside purpose* isn't about the car, the house, the boat, and all of that. But if we find harmony with our inside purpose, then those things find their rightful place.

When the drinking and drugging is finally done, we can strengthen and enjoy our families, building up our communities and Nations by using these ideas and tools to help us walk the Red Road.

We have **three mottoes** that might help with the Red Road journey in family healing. Here they are:

You Work On You

❖

Lean Into The Conflict

❖

Be the Change You Wish to See in Your Family

Remembering This Chapter

> ❖ Ceremony for a Family Circle
> ❖ Connecting: Natashnayah and Iwashtanay
> ❖ Conflict is a guidance system
> ❖ Traditional child rearing
> ❖ Eight feelings of development
> ❖ Reclaiming the eight feelings
> ❖ Conducting the Family Circle
> ❖ Measuring the eight feelings
> ❖ The family vision
> ❖ Family needs and fears analysis
> ❖ Three mottoes

Chapter 11
In The Workplace

♦ ◆ ♦ ◆ ♦

*Our stereotypes and attitudes tend to cloud
our ability to treat one another as
individuals first, rather than as members of
a certain race. As employers and human
resource professionals, we can overcome
these stereotypes. We can help ensure that
Native Americans in recovery can succeed
in the workplace by understanding that
recovery takes different forms depending on
the individual and their cultural context.*

Chapter 11
In The Workplace
An HR Manager learns about Native American addictions recovery

W hen John, the company Human Resources (HR) manager, reviewed Dusty's job application, the red flags automatically went up. The box asking if Dusty had been convicted of a felony was checked. In addition, there was a gap of two years between Dusty's last job as a diesel mechanic for the Bureau of Indian Affairs (BIA), and as a car repairman for a local car dealership. Gaps between jobs usually mean an applicant was in trouble. Still, Dusty met the job qualifications and John had gotten a favorable reference on Dusty from a mutual friend in AA. John decided to call Dusty in for an interview.

Dusty's Story
"I got fired from the dealership because of my drinking," said Dusty, who added that he had been sober for the last four years. "While I was out of work, I racked up my third DUI and I ended up getting thrown in prison." Dusty went on to explain that during his time in jail, his best friend was killed in a car accident. According to the police report, his car rolled over an embankment and pinned his body between a tree and the driver's side door. On the seat next to him was a near-empty six pack. Dusty said he was certain that, had he not been in prison, he would have been out riding around that night drinking with his best friend. The

incident had a jarring impact on Dusty. He vowed not to touch another drop of alcohol in memory of his best friend.

To meet this commitment, Dusty immersed himself in the prison's Native American traditional group. He joined the drumming group and went into the group's weekly sweat lodge, where he learned how to pray. Even though Dusty had been raised on the reservation, his prison experience was one of the few times Dusty experienced Native ceremonies first hand. Dusty's father was an alcoholic and not around much. His mother, while she spoke fluent Paiute, never spoke the Indian language at home. She had never forgotten the shame she felt starting grade school and not being able to speak a word of English. Wanting her kids to have a better life, she always encouraged Dusty and his two sisters to get off the reservation, go to school, move away and get a good job. None of them did, choosing instead the security of the reservation to hang out with friends, cruise around, snag, and of course, to party.

Once released from prison, Dusty continued drumming and going to ceremonies on the reservation. He also volunteered his time at the community rehab center where he gathered wood and rocks for the sweat lodge, helped with the group talking circles, and met up with some of the local AA members off the Rez, one of whom offered to be a reference for Dusty. It was that reference which got him an interview with John, who was still trying to decipher whether Dusty's unconventional method for dealing with his addiction was legitimate and effective. John's own recovery experience as a non-Indian didn't include some of things that Dusty did for his recovery. What was Dusty's recovery method, anyway?

John's Deliberation
An experienced HR manager, John knew that an applicant's previous history of alcoholism was a good indicator of whether he or she was

likely to be a future liability to the company regardless of how talented or hard working the employee might be. John wanted to assess Dusty's formula of staying sober since his skills as a mechanic would enable him to hit the ground running with minimal training expense. John was wary how anything but the tried and true methods of counseling and AA meetings could help those unable to control their drinking.

In his own recovery, John almost lost his job, as well as his marriage, to Jack Daniel's five years prior. At the time, John was traveling frequently to job fairs and university campuses to recruit engineers for the company. These recruiting trips meant he was frequently alone in the evenings in unfamiliar cities. To pass the time, John would head down to the hotel bar to socialize and drink. It wasn't long before the bar beckoned on every trip out of town and "JD with a splash of water" called to him after work. His wife threatened to leave him after discovering that he had been having an affair with someone he met at a bar. His boss had also gotten word of John's excessive drinking.

The last straw came when an engineering student contacted the company to say that, during a recent career fair, John had invited her to a bar for an "interview" and implied that she would get an internship if she had sex with him. To retain his job, John was forced to sign an Employee Rehabilitation Agreement, promising he would complete the treatment program recommended by the company's Employee Assistance Program (EAP). It was through the EAP counseling sessions that John recognized that his need for control, and feelings of guilt, contributed to his excessive drinking. By completing the sessions and continuing on with regular AA meetings, John had been able to remain sober and to keep his job and

marriage intact. John understood the approach he had taken to his own recovery--but what about Dusty's?

"I've been sober for five years too," John confided to Dusty during the interview. From alcoholic to alcoholic, John felt comfortable disclosing his addiction to Dusty and expressing his sympathy for the loss of Dusty's best friend from alcohol. John had seen the problem from both sides, both as someone who nearly lost his job and marriage to alcohol, and as someone aware of the tremendous toll that substance abuse takes on an employers' ability to stay in business. John decided it was time to have a talk with a Native American HR colleague at another company who *did* understand about the cultural part of Indian recovery. Here is what he learned.

What John Learned
Many Native Americans grow up carrying what, in clinical terms, is known as "inter-generational trauma" resulting from the massive upheaval in the Native American way of life in just the past 100-150 years. The trauma gets carried from one generation to the next because it is so painful or atrocious that it doesn't get acknowledged and addressed. For many families, the root of the trauma began with the sexual abuse of Indian children at turn-of–the-century Indian boarding schools. The abuse of Indian children at the hands of inept government and church-run boarding school teachers is well documented in both the U.S. and Canada. And while it is widely recognized in Indian communities that this abuse occurred, it has only been in recent years that the Elders who were victims of this abuse have been willing to talk about what happened. It is a touchy subject because many of those who were abused in the boarding school became abusers themselves, creating a vicious cycle of abusers in the family and in the larger Indian community.

Those who work with Indian men and women in recovery estimate that up to 90 percent of them have been sexually abused. The resources to address sexual abuse in Indian communities have been lacking because, in the past, the tribal leadership was reluctant to support efforts to deal with sexual abuse. The unwillingness to deal with this insidious crime stems from a fear that the problem is much more prevalent than anyone cares to admit and has probably touched every family on reservations in some way.

When Native Americans talk of **"mending the circle"** they are usually referring to the need to acknowledge this trauma and to go through a process of healing the hurt within themselves, their families and their communities. The most successful Native American substance abuse recovery programs utilize traditional "tools" of healing, like **drumming, songs, dance, the sweat lodge, the Sundance, prayer,** and **other culture-specific recovery approaches** to get to the root of the problem. Native Elders say these tools are gifts from the Creator for Native people to heal themselves. Most all of these approaches utilize the **power of the circle** to heal the hurt within a person so that they can live their lives without having to numb the pain through drugging or drinking.

Mending The Circle

In the safety of a dark, heated, circular sweat lodge, for example, people are able to pray and to release pent up feelings of hurt, anger or guilt. Often the greatest healing comes in a place where a person can express the abuse inflicted on them, or that they've done to others, without fear of ridicule or condemnation. That safety in expression comes from the power of the circle and the recognition that the Native American experience is very common from one Native community to the next.

The Conversation Deepens

John's colleague was glad to explain her people's unique approach to their own recovery from addictions. As their conversation drew on, she grew comfortable enough to speak from her own heart. *"As Native people, we desire to bring back the values of our people that held us together and made us strong before our families were ripped apart by disease, forced relocation, boarding schools and alcohol,"* she said. *"This is the rebirth that was prophesied by our Native ancestors and handed down through the stories and legends of the people."*

"To talk of these things within a non-Indian AA or rehab group is uncomfortable to many Native Americans in recovery," she went on. *"How do you explain why you get angry when someone says,* 'Those things happened a long time ago, why don't you Indians get over it?' *The toughest part of the recovery process for Native Americans is usually the point where they are ready to forgive the unforgivable, whether it be forgiving the abuser, forgiving themselves, or forgiving an entire race of people for the way they treated Indian people when they came to America. When you are with a group of people who have no clue about what it feels like to carry the hurt of the past like a heavy piece of luggage, then it is hard to articulate why so many Native people are killing themselves with drugs or alcohol,"* she concluded.

In The Workplace

By talking to his HR colleague John learned that the most successful recovery programs recognize that the use of drugs or alcohol is only a symptom of the problem. The abuse of substances usually has an underlying issue that must be addressed before the individual is able to move forward without drugs or alcohol. Programs like AA and NA have done an exemplary job of characterizing the most common triggers of

substance abuse among middle-class white males and females, providing tools for them to get well. He learned that what is needed for Native Americans in recovery are specialized tools to address underlying causes of substance abuse that are specific to the Native American experience-- just as Dusty had been doing. Native people in recovery are finding that these tools are in the songs, stories, ceremonial expressions, and elderly people back home who are waiting for them to find their way back home and to ask for help.

Dusty and many other Native people in recovery are now leading the efforts in their communities to heal the people. Their help comes in many forms–be it working at the rehab center, hosting a weekly sweat at the local jail, serving on the Tribal council, or organizing a drumming group for kids. They are the new warriors.

When Can You Start?
John thought over what he had learned in his moving conversation with another HR professional. He remembered that Dusty had said, "I consider myself a servant of the people now." He also understood that the ability to stay connected with his people and local ceremonies is the reason why Dusty has been looking for a job in the local area rather than moving to the big city.

John still found it hard to imagine how or why Dusty feels an obligation to save his people. Recovery for John simply meant dealing with his own stuff and making amends to his family, friends and company. Just this glimpse at the complexity of the Native experience made him grateful that his own life growing up was relatively uneventful and stable—even though he always felt something was missing.

John and Dusty met for another interview. As Dusty talked, John tried to put himself in Dusty's shoes. There was a lot about their recovery experience that was the same and a lot that was different. Obviously, John had a hard time relating to the trauma that Dusty alluded to. John knew about the high unemployment rate among local Native Americans. He also knew that many local businessmen in town wouldn't hire them because they might have a drinking problem. It was a vicious cycle that needed to be broken *off* the reservation, unlike the circle that needed to heal *on* the reservation or in Native communities. John thought about all this and made his decision.

"So when could you start?" John asked Dusty.

Recovery Takes Different Forms
This story attempts to characterize the attitudes toward one another of both an employer, and a Native American with a history of alcoholism. Our stereotypes and attitudes tend to cloud our ability to treat one another as individuals first, rather than as members of a certain race. The less interaction we have with one another, the greater the likelihood that we will revert to a stereotype to form our opinion. As employers and human resource professionals, we can overcome these stereotypes within ourselves by getting out of our comfort zones (see Chapter 8) and interacting in the communities where our current and potential employees live. We can help ensure that Native Americans in recovery can succeed in the workplace by understanding that recovery takes different forms depending on the individual and their cultural context.

Chapter 12
A Vision For Us
The First Vision is For the People

We have a vision, a vision for us. We
can find our sobriety, recovery,
wellness and Wellbriety, and then go
on to achieve skills with which we
can give back. Our people are
doctors, nurses, lawyers, teachers,
artists, scientists, engineers,
astronauts, builders, government
workers, members of the military,
law enforcement officers, and much,
much more.

Chapter 12
A Vision For Us
The First Vision is For the People

A long time ago, farther back than our grandparents' grandparents can remember, the Medicine people of our Tribal Nations knew that a great wintertime was coming. In those ancient days, the prophecies of our First Nations said that a stranger would come from the direction of sunrise. The prophecies of our ancient Elders said that when a bearded man came from out of the morning sun the people would enter a long, hard wintertime. They said that during this **long wintertime** the Sacred Hoop of the people would be broken between youth and adult.

It was also said that this wintertime would last five hundred earth cycles, now called years, and that many of our Nations would perish. Those ancient prophecies said that in the coming wintertime our people would be forced from their ancestral homes. They said that the people would sicken with diseases for which the grandmothers had no cure. They said that our traditional foods--the white tailed deer, the great elk, the wild trout, the salmon, and the buffalo--would perish along with the people. They said that those of us who remained would be made to cut their hair short and be forced into stone and wooden lodges where our languages were forbidden. They said our own people would learn to drink an

unhealthy water which made us sicken and die. They said the **sickening water** would be our greatest enemy because we took it willingly into our Nations, communities, families and into ourselves. These prophecies frightened our ancient ancestors, and unfortunately, they came true.

But a few of the old Nations also knew of other prophecies that picked up where the dark ones left off. It is said that some of our wisest grandfathers and grandmothers had visions that also told of a **new springtime.** These prophecies said that at the end of the long wintertime, even as the strangers dwelt everywhere on Turtle Island, our people would still live. They said that although weakened, often beyond recognition, the principles, laws and traditional values of our Nations would survive. These springtime prophecies said that the visitor from the east would create such disorder in Turtle Island that he would begin to become receptive to some of our old values in hopes of his own survival. But even as some of our oldest prophecies told of a new springtime, they left us one dire warning. They said that unless we, as Native people, could throw off our craving for the sickening water, the Sacred Tree of our cultures would die. **We are now in that springtime.**

The Prophecies

In more recent times there are other prophecies. Early in the 20th century one of our modern peoples said that when the eagle circled the moon, it would be a sign that the new springtime was about to begin. In 1969 the Apollo 11 Lunar Lander carried an eagle feather when it landed on the moon. The name of the Lander itself was Eagle. Everyone knows that when the Lander touched down on the moon, astronaut Neil Armstrong said, **"the Eagle has landed,"** fulfilling the prophecy and ushering in a time of great healing for Native Americans. The eagle feather that traveled to the moon is now in the care of AISES, the American Indian Science and Engineering Society, one of our own Native organizations.

A Vision For Us

Another modern community told us that when the sun was blocked in the seventh moon it would be a sign that the healing time was going to deepen. You may remember that there was a solar eclipse in July of 1991. A week after that, an important Elder's gathering was held in Loveland, Colorado. The Elders told us many things. They said that we would begin to see **young people with old spirits,** really young kids who would sound just like Elders when they spoke. They said that the youth would **seek out the old songs** and begin to **bring back the language.** They said you would see young people sitting at the drums—young men and young women—and that's what we do see now.

The Elders also told us that at this time you would begin to see **women step forward and begin to lead.** They said our nations were so out of balance that our women would come forward and begin to put our families and communities back in balance in a good way. They told us that when you see our women become leaders, go there and support them, don't make fun of them, because they have been holding our communities together for a long, long, long time. They said if we cooperated with all that was coming to pass, harmony and balance would come back. And they started to tell us that this is the right time.

In August of 1994 a white buffalo calf was born in Janesville, Wisconsin. It was also prophesied that a total of four White Buffalo calves would be born over the next few years as a sign that the **mending of the sacred hoop** of our nations was about to begin. The buffalo calf born in Janesville changed color four times as it matured, going through white, red, yellow and black color phases to fulfill a prophecy that the healing time for Native Americans was also to be a **healing and coming-together time** for all the races of the world—the red-brown, the yellow, the black and the white.

The Elders say that what you see on the outside is called an **"earth suit."** We each have different colored earth suits—but we are just one race, the human race. They said that during this time all four colors would come together and we would sit down together because each of the four colors was given what was called **"original instructions."** In order for any of us to heal, we have to have the original teachings from the other directions. They told us the nature of these original teachings. They said that the white direction holds the gift of **fire,** the red direction holds the gift of **earth,** the yellow direction holds the gift of **wind or breath,** and the black direction holds the gift of **water.** The fulfillment of the prophecies means that the coming together time of unity among all the peoples of the earth is close at hand.

The Hoop of 100 Feathers

In 1994 an Indian man had a vision. In this vision there was a circle of white light surrounded by darkness. All of a sudden something began to break out of the ground in the center of this white light and begin to grow. It was a willow sapling that began to grow, and as it grew straight and tall it then shed its leaves like in the autumn of the year. Then it bent itself into a circle, into a willow hoop. Next, the man saw a small dot form itself up in the northern direction in the circle of light. The dot began to

move very slowly towards the willow hoop and it soon dipped to the earth. When it came up, it had become an eagle feather that attached itself to the hoop. The same thing next happened from the eastern, southern and western directions, bringing the first four eagle feathers to the hoop. All of a sudden, other dots began appearing from all the directions until 100 eagle feathers were attached to the hoop.

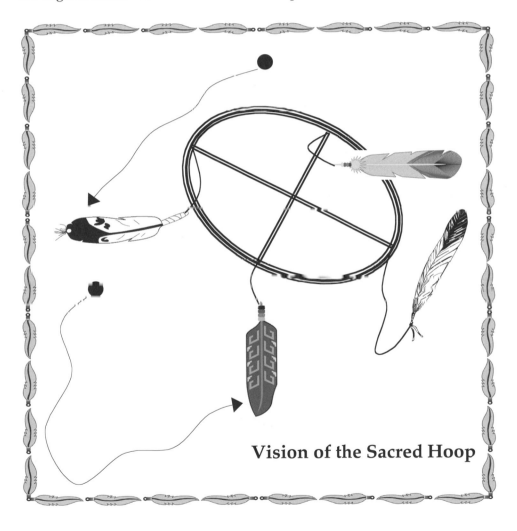

Vision of the Sacred Hoop

When the man woke up he knew he must visit the Elders in order to understand the meaning and intent of his vision. He traveled to South Dakota where seventeen Elders talked with him for many, many hours in order to understand his spirit and intent, in order to look into his heart. The Elders smudged him with sage and sweetgrass and revealed that they themselves had been having visions. They said they knew someone was coming. And they said, **"Build that Hoop. You are to build that Hoop of 100 eagle feathers just like in that dream, that vision."**

The man didn't know where to get one hundred eagle feathers, but as soon as he arrived back home they began to come. One by one they came, in the mail, handed to him on the street, and from relatives of famous people like Sac and Fox athlete Jim Thorpe's grandson, who gave his grandfather's feather. They also came from the Indigenous people of other lands. It took a year for them all to come. When they had one hundred feathers, just like the vision, a willow hoop was built inside a sweat lodge over a period of four days of fasting, singing, sweating and praying.

When the Hoop of 100 eagle feathers was complete, a **multicultural Elders gathering** was convened in Janesville Wisconsin. There were Elders from 27 tribes present, as well as Elders from the Asian culture, the Black culture, the White culture and the Hispanic culture in order to honor the coming together time which the prophecies spoke of. As the Elders, representing all cultural and racial directions of the earth prayed at the Hoop, they placed four special gifts into the new sacred element.

The Hoop stood on a bed of cedar and people approached it from the four directions in order to pray. The first gift the Elders placed into the hoop was the gift of **healing.** The next gift was the gift of **hope.** The third gift was the gift of **unity.** And the last gift was the power to **forgive the unforgivable.** It was a loving day that these four gifts were placed into the Hoop--a day of unforgettable love.

Spreading the Four Gifts

The Hoop was present at a **gathering of Native American women tribal leaders** in the fall of 1995. Many important issues concerning the healing and governing of Indian nations were discussed at that gathering, and all were able to pray at the Hoop and receive the four gifts into their hearts.

In late spring of the next year, a **Gathering of Native American Men** was held in the mountains of Colorado. Two thousand Native men, as well as their family and friends, came from far and wide to find healing at the men's encampment. Over five hundred veterans participated in a **wiping of the hands ceremony** in order to release their harms and hurts. Everyone prayed at the Sacred Hoop and received the gifts the Elders had placed there.

The Hoop was carried to many Indian and non-Indian communities in the US and Canada over the next few years. People from all four directions came forward to find **healing, hope, unity** and **forgiveness** for themselves, their families and their communities. Wherever people sought recovery from alcohol and drug abuse, there went the Hoop. Wherever people sought healing from family violence, the Hoop was there.

The first of the great organized Hoop Journeys began in 1999. **(Hoop Journey 1)** Starting from the Longhouse of the Onondaga Nation in upstate New York, the Hoop was carried from east to west to 31 of the Tribal colleges in the US and Canada. Each college hosted the first Hoop Journey in a Wellbriety Awareness Day. **Wellbriety?** What was that? As each local community sponsored Wellbriety Awareness Day, those who carried the 100 Eagle Feather Hoop told of the journey into sobriety and freedom from drugs and alcohol that each and every one of us must take. Those who carried the Hoop on that first Hoop Journey were helping to fulfill the prophecy that we, as Native people, must let go of our craving for the sickening water if the culture was to live. They spoke of the next step after sobriety and recovery--the step into wellness and a life balanced physically, emotionally, mentally, spiritually and culturally. A life of Wellbriety. **The Wellbriety movement had begun.**

The next great Hoop journey **(Hoop Journey 2)** traveled over 4000 miles from west to east, ushering in the new century in the year 2000. Starting from the Los Angeles area in the spring of 2000, the Sacred Hoop was run, walked and driven through hundreds of Native and non-Native communities across the southern route of the US. Over 10 conferences were held to carry the message of Wellbriety, including the ending of family violence, to many Indian nations along the way. The second Hoop Journey concluded in Washington DC, in July of 2000, where its gifts and intentions were honored in a ceremony attended by many leaders of the US national government in a day of presentations. This took place not far from the American White House.

The third Journey of the Sacred Hoop **(Hoop Journey 3)** took place in 2002 as the Hoop was carried to 16 urban Indian communities on a 7000 mile Journey west of the Mississippi River for the **Healing of Native women and children.** This Hoop Journey saw the birth of a Wellbriety for Youth focus and special support for Native Americans in Al-Anon, as we discussed in Chapter 9 of this book. As this is written, **Hoop Journey 4** is in planning. It will take place in urban Indian communities east of the Mississippi in 2003. It will concentrate on **healing Native men and children.**

Firestarters and the Healing Forest
The Journeys of the Sacred Hoop carried with them the birth and growth of the Wellbriety movement, as well as a new commitment: **The Firestarters.** Between Hoop Journeys One and Two, many people came forward because they had been touched by the gifts of the Hoop or had been on their own sobriety, recovery and wellness journeys for a long time. They came forward because they were on fire with the desire to see all people free of violence and the sickness of drugs and alcoholism. They came forward to help start little fires of Wellbriety on the grassroots level

in their own home Native communities. These wellness warriors are known as Firestarters.

NATION

COMMUNITY

INDIVIDUAL

Kindling a Flame

FAMILY

Firestarters work the Medicine Wheel and the 12 Steps Program just as you have read about in this book. They go through the Steps in a cultural way, just as the Elders said was possible. They hold **Circles of Recovery** in their own communities so that others can become sober and well. Perhaps you have come to know about Wellbriety through a Firestarter in your community. Firestarters may have a lot of recovery, or maybe just a little. Firestarters know that it takes a whole community to heal a community. They have stepped forward because they know that in order to keep it, they have to give it away. And Firestarters know **the story of the Healing Forest,** which we tell many times:

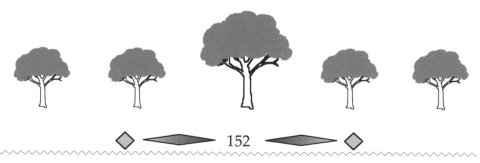

Story of the Healing Forest

Once, a long time ago, there was a forest of about 100 acres. You could tell that it was once a beautiful forest of many different kinds of trees, bushes, rocks, the four-leggeds, the winged, those that crawl on the earth, and those that burrow into the earth. But now it was a sick forest. The trees no longer sang their songs when the winds came to visit. The birds no longer chirped.

One day, a few of the trees got together and talked among themselves. "We know healing is possible," they said. "But we can't heal in this sick forest, we can't heal in our home." So these few trees left one night under the cover of darkness and went down the road to check themselves into a thirty-day program at a local nursery. While at the nursery they were given all kinds of good foods and good, pure water. They even got to work programs for healing trees like themselves. At the end of the thirty days they were feeling much better and decided to go back to their home forest.

It wasn't long after being back in the sick forest that the trees who had had some good healing began to become sick again. There was sickness all around them. When they tried to talk to some of the other sick trees, those trees even managed to convince them that they were the sick ones after all, because they had left to go to the nursery. And so the brave trees became sick once again.

As we begin to heal ourselves one by one, we must also help create a Healing Forest in our own families, communities and neighborhoods. We can't only work on ourselves in isolation because the principle of interconnectedness says, "We are all related." To truly heal the individual, we also have to heal the community and the family—otherwise even the individual won't stay healed. Firestarters who learn about the Medicine Wheel and the 12 Steps, or other sobriety and wellness ways, are helping to create Healing Forests where they live by facilitating Circles of Recovery right at home.

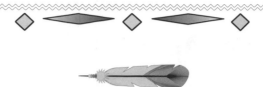

Many Visions

We have a vision—a vision for us. In our vision we see hundreds of **recovery groups** out in our communities and neighborhoods. We see our **schools and colleges involved in the prevention of unhealthy behavior**, utilizing culture to help us walk the Red Road. We see the **family system back in place.** We see the **clan systems** of our traditional cultures coming back to provide the wider support that it takes to have healthy families and Nations. We see some of our **traditional societies** coming back—warrior societies, men's societies, and women's societies, just like we had before the long wintertime came to our people. We see our **traditional religious ways** being revived--ways such as the Sun Dance, the sweat lodge, the longhouse ceremonies, and sober, non-competitive powwows. Our vision is that you can take traditional thought—not to go back and live in a teepee by turning back the clock--but to **take traditional thought, and function today in the modern society.**

Our sobriety movement began in the 1970's just after the eagle circled the moon. In those days, if you were sober 30 days and you could say "counselor," they would make you one. But now there are thousands of us sober. Some of our sobriety Elders who addressed the gatherings on the two Sacred Hoop Journeys have been sober since the time when the eagle landed. Now we have in our communities young people who have never tasted alcohol. The Bald eagle has been taken off the endangered species list. The buffalo is returning, thanks to one of our own Native organizations, the Intertribal Bison Cooperative **(ITBC).** We are fighting for our sovereignty as Tribal Nations and winning, thanks to **NARF** (Native American Rights Fund), another of our Native organizations. We have found voices to reach our own people and to speak for us nationally through the National Congress of American Indians **(NCAI)** and similar organizations. **You probably know of others.**

But there is no sovereignty without sobriety and we have to achieve that for ourselves. We can't blame the government or the "system," although we have to know how we were harmed, for example, by the boarding or residential schools, and by other historical trauma. We can learn about what happened so that we can better walk the Wellbriety road. We have to do it for ourselves, and the Wellbriety movement is a way of putting a safe road under all our hopes, dreams and visions as a people.

There is a spark of healing in our communities and we can become part of the movement by **setting up a Firestarters Circle.** We welcome other Indigenous sobriety ways into our circles. There are many people achieving sobriety now and going beyond sobriety into Wellbriety by participation in the **Native American Church.** Many people have fought hard for our rights to use peyote as a Medicine in our all-night meetings in the teepees of the Native American Church.

We can welcome **two-spirited people** into our Firestarters circles like the brothers and sisters that they are. The Two-spirited are usually taken to be gay, lesbian or transgendered people. They are also people in touch with both the male and female parts of life. Two-spirited people have always been a welcome part of the circle in traditional ways throughout our history. They took care of the young. They took care of the elderly. In traditional times they ran many of the ceremonies. In some Nations they were the ones who took care of the injured, the wounded, or the dead. Many two-spirited men and women leave the reservations now because they are not welcomed or comfortable there. But the Wellbriety vision is that everyone and everything is part of the circle. We may have adopted some attitudes that are not our traditional ways. The two-spirited belong in our Firestarters circles, working the cultural 12 Steps right alongside everyone else.

Our people have suffered greatly from the effects of alcohol on pregnant moms. Fetal Alcohol Syndrome (FAS), and Fetal Alcohol Effects (FAE) afflict some of our youth and adults in proportions higher than in the rest of society. But through education about what alcohol does to the unborn child, and through the Healing Forest model that is growing in our communities, we are bringing FAS and FAE numbers down. Our vision is that **we can beat FAS and FAE** and be compassionate to those among us who came into this world with the effects of alcohol or drugs already upon them.

A Vision For Us

We have a vision, a vision for us. We can find our sobriety, recovery, wellness and Wellbriety, and then go on to achieve skills with which we can give back. **Our people are doctors, nurses, lawyers, teachers, artists, scientists, engineers, astronauts, builders, government workers, members of the military, law enforcement officers, and much, much more.** For those of us in recovery, it all begins in the circle. The circle is not an Indian circle—it's the circle of the human being. When we connect with others in the circle, the energy starts to flow. The only rule for the talking circle is this: This circle is sacred, respect it. What you hear here... Who you see here... When you leave here... Leave it here.

The circle connects the individual and the community. The circle allows us to create a Healing Forest in our communities and neighborhoods. The circle allows us to participate in all the future Journeys of the Sacred Hoop that will come through your community and you can be a part of. The circle allows us to receive the four gifts of the Hoop:

To **Heal** from our historical trauma as Native people, and from the stress of today's world.

❖

To find the **Hope** that gives us the faith, courage and strength to become Wellbriety warriors.

❖

To experience **Unity** with others, regardless of the "earth suit" each may wear.

❖

And to have the courage to **Forgive**, so that we may not be burdened and weighed down by what was done to us or what we see being done today.

❖

How shall we begin this Wellbriety Journey? This is our vision:

**Build a better world said God
And I answered how?
The world is such a vast place, and so
complicated now.
And I am small and useless
There's nothing I can do.
But God in all his wisdom said,
Build a better you.**

❖

May our Creator bless our journey to wellness!!

Personal Recovery Stories

White Bison

A Misplaced Indian

He never fit anywhere. He was always different. But after a hard struggle, sobriety and self-acceptance came to him.

First, I want to tell you a story.

*O*nce there was a young man who was endowed with everything necessary for him to be successful in life by society's standards. He had the financial means and the intellect by which he gained an education. His education offered him the opportunity to join with a giant corporation. He climbed the executive ladder, which is membership in the country club as well as a fine, beautiful home and all the automobiles that go with it. The people in his community called him successful.

The young man looked at his life and realized something was missing. There was a void. To fill this void he felt he must have all there is of life's fill. In the beginning, because he had the financial means, he tried the psychologists, psychiatrists and group therapy sessions that were then popular. He expended a lot of funds in this endeavor but it gained him nothing.

Before long he found himself on the streets with groups of people like him, people who were seeking an answer even though they weren't sure what the question was. One morning after he came

to in an alley after a night of heavy drinking he began to look back over his life. He recalled that during his education he had acquired a great set of books introducing him to the philosophers of the past and the philosophers of our time. He decided to return to those books to find the answer that might lie at the cause of his drinking. Philosophically and intellectually he could understand the words that these people shared with him but he could not practice them in his life.

In this great set of books there was a study of the religions of the world, including one of our Far Eastern religions whose wisdom keepers were referred to as gurus. According to what he read, these gurus had all the answers, all knowledge, and all understanding of life. The young man said, "That's what I need. I need a guru in my life." So he boarded an airplane, landed in New Delhi, charted a boat and went up river. When the boat docked many days later the young man disembarked with his belongings. The people of the village approached him, and even though they couldn't understand each other the people in this place had seen many men like him come up this river. They knew why he was there. When he posed the question, "Where is the guru?" they pointed towards a mountain.

There was a vast wilderness between the river and the mountain. The young man began to have second thoughts about his journey, but since he had studied philosophy he thought, "Well, maybe I have to suffer some more before I find my answers." So he began his trek across that wilderness. After a hard journey of many weeks he came to the base of the mountain, broken in body, broken in spirit, and feeling his endeavors would once again gain him nothing. But at the base of the mountain he looked up and saw a small crow perched in a tree and smoke coming from a cave just behind a ledge. He said to himself, "That's where the guru lives." Rejuvenated in spirit he climbed the mountain,

arrived at the base of the ledge, and saw a ladder leading up to the cave "This is it," thought the young man. "At the top of this ladder lies the answer to all my questions." And so he climbed the ladder and stood upon the ledge. Just back inside the little cave he saw an elderly man sitting in the lotus position meditating upon the setting sun. The old man saw him and regarded him quietly. He knew why the young man had come. "What is your question?" he said."

"Guru," said the seeker, "What must I do to find peace, happiness, serenity, and an understanding of life?" The guru broke from his meditation upon the setting sun, turned and regarded our brother. Time seemed to stand still. After what seemed to be a lifetime the guru spoke. **"Don't drink, and go to meetings,"** *he said.*

The first time I heard that simple quotation was at my first meeting of Alcoholics Anonymous. I screamed within myself, "No, you don't understand. You don't realize where I've been. You don't understand what kind of a person I am. *Don't drink, and go to meetings* is not the answer to my problems," I screamed to myself. But now, as I follow that simple philosophy one day at a time, *Don't drink, and go to meetings* was more of an answer than anything I could have conceived on my own.

Following that philosophy, one day at a time I grew into a thing called sobriety. At moments in that sobriety there have been times when I've gone beyond, when I've stood in oneness, wholeness, and completeness with spirit. At times when it seems just too difficult to continue on, I'd look back on those moments of completeness and those are what kept me going, those are what keep me on this path that I'm on.

A Misplaced Indian

I had my first drink when I was twelve years of age on a small reservation in South Dakota where I was growing up. I went to town with some friends. We got a bottle. We went to a field and sat under a tree and proceeded to get drunk. It was our intention to get drunk—there was nothing about the social graces of consuming alcohol motivating us. When you drank under that particular tree, that's what your intentions were. I got drunk and blacked out. I came-to some twenty miles away from that spot on the following afternoon. Then we went back to town to get some more to drink.

During the early AA meetings that I went to, they used to say, "Keep coming back and listening because one night someone's going to tell your story. You're going to identify." So I went to meetings and waited for the guy to get up and tell me he left the reservation, went to town, sat under that tree and got drunk. I was looking for words and actual situations because I didn't understand anything about life.

One night at a meeting a guy talked about growing up on a small farm in Kansas. He talked about the parties they had at their house when the cousins, brothers, sisters, aunts, uncles and all the people of the family would come together to gather at his house. And he was always in the kitchen with his grandmother who did all the cooking. He'd look through the door to see that the family was celebrating and having a good time. And he said, "I never could go through that door and be part of that." And that's how I feel. I can see all those things going on out there but I can never be part of it. I'm always separated from it. It was then that I began to understand the concept of identity that we talk about in Alcoholics Anonymous.

I began to realize that it's not how much we drank, or where we drank, or what we drank. It's the question or feeling of "Who am I?" that we ask ourselves which is really important to our sobriety. I began to approach the philosophy of living through the Twelve Steps of Alcoholics Anonymous, combined with the things that I was taught by my

grandparents. I began to utilize them and to set off on the journey of knowing who I am.

When I left the reservation to go to the government boarding schools I wasn't comfortable at all. My older brother had set some sort of academic standards there and they expected me to do the same thing. I didn't know if I had the discipline or intellect to understand the words that are written in books or to be able to pronounce upon them and utilize them in life the way my brother did. I couldn't be an academic so I attempted to become an athlete. I joined the track team but they caught me smoking on the bus and kicked me off the team. I didn't have the discipline to be an athlete.

As I wandered around that school, I joined a group of guys who wore black leather jackets, Levis, white t-shirts and black motorcycle boots. I became a tough guy. I belonged to something with this group of guys and I fit in. We wandered around the campus creating problems and picking fights with people. There was usually one or two of them to seven or eight of us so it was always easy to be a tough guy.

Now I had two patterns in my life. I had a drinking pattern in which I always got drunk and passed out. The other pattern was that it was so necessary for me to belong to something. I would throw away my principles and feelings about what was right or wrong just to belong. I didn't have the courage to stand up and say, "No, I'll be who I am," because, in fact, I didn't know who I was. That pattern followed me through life. I will change to fit whatever the situation is. I will be whatever you want me to be. I was expelled from that school and sent back to live with my grandparents on the reservation.

A Misplaced Indian

When I was sixteen I left and joined the United States Navy. While I was in the Navy my drinking increased. Everybody around me was a drunk. I attempted my best to fulfill the Naval traditions of being a drunken sailor. They used to tease me about being an Indian. They called me Wahoo. They'd tell jokes about the Indian and his firewater. Nobody would go on liberty with me. I couldn't understand it. I felt they didn't like me because I was an Indian. I never did realize that when you went on liberty with Wahoo you always got in trouble—like fights with the MP's and the shore patrol. I didn't last long in the Navy.

So one day I found myself standing on a street corner in San Francisco. I was eighteen years old, had some change in my pocket and a train ticket to Los Angeles. I had less than what society deemed a proper education. I had less than an honorable discharge from the United States Navy. My grandfather had died and I couldn't go back to the reservation because there was no one to take care of me. But most important of all, I'm afflicted with a disease called alcoholism. I wasn't willing to accept any program or therapy that would help me recover. I was about to have many more years of misery. In my life it was necessary to experience all these horrible things so I could come to that point of surrender within my innermost self.

Standing on that street corner in San Francisco, I'm an Indian forced to live in a white man's world. That's why I am like I am and that's why these things happen to me. But then I began to realize nobody ever tied me down and forced a drink down me. I had to realize that my problems are of my own making. I had to accept that. I had to accept the fact that where I'm at is because of ME. It's a concept called honesty. A principle called honesty. Honesty is what I tell *myself*. Honesty is what I tell me about me.

My life is unmanageable. What does that mean? That I can't keep a job? That I can't balance a checkbook? That I can never pay my bills? No.

Manageability has to do with direction. I have no direction in my life. I'm not really sure what I'm going to do from one moment to the next. How do I seek direction? In the beginning it's *Don't drink, and go to meetings.* That's direction. Today I don't take a drink. It has to start simple like that. And surprisingly, almost twenty-four years later it's still that simple. Today I don't take a drink. There are a lot of other things I do in my life today, but that's the basis and beginning of it.

Then there is the lack of sanity in my life. I go out into a park and pick a fight with four cops. They bloody me pretty bad with their billy clubs. I come out of the hospital in a body cast and I am on crutches for six months. And on those crutches I walk two blocks to a beer joint and say, "I'm going to have a beer, and *this* time it's going to be different. I could never understand what always happened when I took that drink. "This time it's going to be different," but it's the same thing over and over again even though I'm looking for different results. The insanity of what I am was not just related to drinking—it was related to everything else I did. How many times in life today do I do the same things over and over, again looking for different results? Something has to change in order to get different results.

In order to get different results I had to learn about some principles and what they meant in my life. There is a principle called *humility* found in the Third Step. Humility talks to me about depending on someone else: surrender. Until you learn about surrender, hate, anger and self-pity require that you cannot depend upon someone else. You can always blame them for your problems but you cannot depend upon them. I had to learn about that. Today I understand that without *you* and without my God I am nothing. I had to practice that for it to become a living reality in my life.

I learned about other principles but they were only words until I utilized them. For example—integrity. Integrity is, *Am I the same person when somebody isn't watching? Do I act and feel the same way?* You can act OK with your family, or your work companions, or your friends, but you know they don't accept you as what you are. It always comes back to a point where I have to accept who I am. And what does that really mean?

Then they talk about freedom. What is freedom? The most difficult thing about freedom is that it requires that you stand alone. "I will stand alone. I will be who I am. I will not compromise on what I feel is right for me in my life." One of the old timers in the program said this to me. "When the whole world tells you you're wrong, but inside you know you're right, then its OK." But you know it's so much easier to just maneuver along and let people agree with you, and you agree with them, and you change what you are to gain acceptance—to be part of. As a result of the freedom I have in Alcoholics Anonymous, I have stood alone. It's been only God and me. At first it was scary, but now it feels good.

We talk about a number of principles: honesty, faith, integrity, humility, courage, perseverance, dedication, discipline, and especially *freedom*—but they mean nothing unless I practice them, unless I understand what they mean in my life. Alcoholics Anonymous gives me the freedom to stand alone. It also gives me the freedom to be an individual.

When I was drunk in the border town near my reservation, my grandfather used to pick me up on a sidewalk or in the back alleys of that town and take me home. I can still recall the hurt I saw in his eyes. Not long ago when I went back home to bury a sister of mine we went to that place where my grandfather now lies. And with eighteen inches of snow on the ground, and with the wind blowing, I stood there cold but sober telling my grandfather *I'm sober and I'm gonna stay that way.* I was able to make those amends that day and a warmth came over me. It was like my grandfather had said, "I understand, and it's good."

A Misplaced Indian

Years ago my grandfather shared a story with me that I never forgot. He said that in the Northwestern part of our country there is a tree they call the Douglas fir. If you ever stood before a forest of Douglas fir you would be awed by their majesty and perfection. They go a hundred or two hundred feet straight to the sky like an arrow. Every one of those trees is the same—tall and beautiful. But deep in the forest you come upon a small, deformed tree that does not grow straight and tall like the other trees. It is bent and crooked. It's ugly. But if you can look beyond that which you can see, you will realize that in the perfection of the creation there is a hole in the sky where that tree was supposed to grow. And through that hole in the sky the rain and the sunshine can come through. Throughout the rest of the forest floor there is nothing but pine needles except in the place where the ugly tree grows. But because the rain and the sunshine can come through, the wild plants, the green grass and the flowers grow there. Its imperfection creates beauty.

Let me look beyond that which I know and that which I see. Let me allow you to be what you are and nothing less. Hopefully, you will look at me and allow me to be what I am and nothing more.

It's Up To You

Our culture has a lot of lessons to teach, and the land does, too. When we get rid of alcohol and drugs, the culture really starts to teach.

Our culture has started coming back in recent years and this is how we're dealing with our alcoholism. Sweat lodges, drums, the Sundance, and other traditional ways—that's what it's going to take for us to become sober and really prosper.

Our culture was almost destroyed. For example, we enjoyed watching western movies, like when John Wayne passes around the peace pipe and goes through Indian country. Peace pipe my foot, there is no such thing. There is the sacred pipe, but never a peace pipe where I come from. We watched these movies and saw what they were doing to our kids. We brought in a cowboys and Indians movie to our remote community once and paid attention to our kids as they watched it. When it looked like the Indians were starting to win, the Cavalry came riding over the hill and saved the wagon train. All our little Indian kids started to cheer. We decided we had better to teach our kids which side they are on.

There are four directions and four colors. The white, the red, the yellow, and the black are living right here on mother earth. How come they can't live in harmony? We're saying we are Native people, so let's straighten out one another like we believe. When we go out in the bush we don't see the cottonwood tree kicking over the fir tree. You don't see the spruce pushing over the willow and telling it to get out of there. They live in

harmony with one another. We are supposed to be the smartest species on mother earth so how come we can't do that?

Our learning comes from our culture. Forgiveness is part of our traditions. One day when I was going out the door late for work, I stumbled over a dog that was lying right on the doormat. I kicked him out of the way. I went back into the house to get the keys to my truck and that dog was sitting there wagging his tail, looking up at me. He was telling me, "I forgive you for what you did to me." Some of us carry a grudge around for years and years. We forget that these little things that teach us are always right here. But we don't see what's behind everything. We don't see the teaching behind the little things.

Like water. That water is our life. It runs everyday. It's like time. That river. That river is you. If you go down there and try to make it go backwards, it's like stopping time. If you dam it up, is it going to go backwards the other way? Are you going to say, "I'm 23, and I'm going to stay here forever?" No way. You're going to get older. That river is the same way. If you put a dam there, that becomes a problem. Every one of us has a problem almost every day. But we find a way around them. That river does the same thing. It keeps going and it finds a way around the dam. It will keep going. That water is you. That water is your life. The trees, the willows, and everything else in your life have been like that.

We've been called savages for hundreds of years. But how about our kids who are starting to drink? When our kids pick up that bottle, <u>then</u> they become that savage. I think we ought to start telling them to look at their lives. They aren't savages. Let's not make that same mistake Columbus made when he landed on this island. He called us pagans. But he didn't study how we prayed. Now there are wars because of religion. Our drums and our past were burned because they believed we were pagans and savages. But they who drum came back and we enjoy listening to the songs. There's nothing wrong with it. It's a teaching. It's a learning experience.

It's Up To You

In their wars, one religion wants to be right. But if you ask them who they are praying to, they'll tell you, the Creator. Everybody is praying to the same one, maybe with a different name, but it's still the Creator. And yet there's wars going on because of that.

Throughout my alcoholic years I had hatred for where I went to school, which was a residential school in Canada. On my first day there I hated the priests, the brothers, and the nuns. I walked in there, a child proud of my culture. They grabbed me and put me on a high chair and clipped off my braids. They wrapped my braids in my buckskin vest, dragged me downstairs, threw it in the furnace and made me watch it burn. When I talk about that today I can still smell it burning. I hated those guys for a long time, and I drank because of it. Forgiveness came really hard. But today I can learn forgiveness from a dog—but it took thirty years to learn that. Our traditional cultures taught us that and that's where we can find learning.

Our marriages and our people who are now getting drunk need all the help they can get. Sometimes the people we fear the most are waiting for us to tell them that one word—"hey, why don't you stop? Talk to me." This happens in my community. Sometimes all a person needs is one word. "Help yourself and I'll help you." It's always been that way. Alcohol can be a powerful medicine for other cultures, but to us it isn't.

Sometimes we talk to couples. We know a couple which has been sober for a long time, but they are always fighting. They said to us, "Grant, you and Lori have been married for a long time. How the hell can you do it?" I said I guess its luck. They said, no it has got to be more than that. How do you do it? I didn't know what to tell them. So one day in April they were riding in my truck and along came a learning experience. I didn't

expect anything and had no idea what to tell this couple that was riding with me.

I stopped at a barn and near a log fence where two bluebirds were making a nest. I told the couple, just watch those two birds. Pretty soon everything started coming together. The female bird took a piece of grass to the nest and flew away. The male came and put his piece of grass in. We watched those bluebirds for a long time and my friends were quiet. We noticed if the female put her grass in the wrong way, the male didn't come and beat her up. They were working in harmony with one another. To me that is first-class marriage counseling right there.

We talked about what would happen next. The female would lay the eggs. And so I said, "When the eggs hatch, does the male go out and get drunk and beat the hell out of her?" No. They work in harmony, protect and feed the young, and they live together. When the young ones fly away, then they go their separate ways. My friends had children at home. I asked them what <u>they</u> were doing. They got real quiet and maybe something happened. They gave each other a hug and got in my truck and we went home.

We see symbols when we start looking, but we are usually looking in the wrong places. I think if we do our counseling in a willow grove or out in the high grasses you can probably learn a lot. We forget that all our teachings and all the things we talk about as Native people are out there in the land. We can also learn from our kids. If six-year-old kids can sit in their talking circles at school, pass around the talking rock and cry on each other's shoulders, and share all their hurts, then why can't adults do that same thing?

Our culture is something to be proud of. Our religion is something to be proud of. In our culture we didn't drink, we didn't abuse. Our language barrier is starting to break. In my age group we can talk our language and understand it. In the next age group down, from 45 to 25, that group can only pick up words here and there. The group after that can't understand anything. But the group that is still in high school is starting to learn our language again. They can read and write it. Our language expresses our culture and our understanding. The biggest mistake we made is not teaching our children our languages and our Native tongue. Because to us it's sacred and it always will be.

Alcohol and drugs are getting in our way and they have to come out first. The leadership has to understand that. We need sober Tribal Councils. Up in Canada where I live people are not getting elected if they are drinking. In my community, if somebody saw you in a bar, when election time comes around—forget it! Don't even campaign because you're not going to get in. That's how powerful it can get. If somebody is going to be negotiating for me somewhere, for something of importance, I want them to have that clear mind. All the chiefs in the past, from Sitting Bull all the way down, would tell you the same thing if they were sitting here today.

We'll change when we begin to understand that alcohol is the problem. That drugs are the problem. It's not us individually. It's the alcohol and the drugs that do it. It's time for us to learn where our problems come from. To begin to realize that we are Native people and we believe in the culture. We believe in something and we have a life of our own. And that life is yours. Begin to believe in our Native culture, and when you do believe, things will happen. If you are not positive about it you are never going to move. It's easy to be positive. Doing the Sundance is positive. The sweat is positive. Each of you has traditional ways from your Nations. Do it. It's up to you.

A Long Road

This Native woman knew she was different. Half Native American, she felt she didn't belong to any culture. But after a lifetime of alcohol, she finally found sobriety and a new understanding of God

A Prayer For Honesty

What a relief! I'm learning to be honest! No more ducking or dodging, no more tall tales, no more pretending to be what I am not. My cards are on the table for all the world to see. I am what I am. I have an unsavory past. I'm sorry, yes, it cannot be changed now. All that is yesterday is done. But now my life is an open book—come and look at it if you want to. I'm trying to do the best I can. I will fail often but I won't make excuses. I will face things as they are and not run away. I want to be honest. I try to be as honest as I can. That's why I always pray for honesty, especially before I speak, because sometimes I don't know that I'm being dishonest. This is my honesty prayer.

I want to be honest. I'm an alcoholic and an addict. I have to say that I'm an addict because I took a lot of pills. I liked anything that could change my feelings inside, anything that could kill the pain, or the hurt, or the anger, or any of those feelings that I didn't know how to have when I came into the AA program. It's still not easy sometimes to be

honest with people. I didn't know what self-honesty was—really being honest with myself first, before I could be honest with other people.

I'm also a child of an alcoholic. I married two alcoholics, and I believe today that probably five of my children are alcoholics. One is probably not, but she's with an alcoholic. I know it's a family disease because it's in my family and it has been for generations. This disease touches our children even if they don't drink. It's a disease we get as a dysfunctional family. I had a lot of guilt over that but now I don't. I try not to, but sometimes it comes back. Guilt doesn't stay too long now because I know that alcoholism is a disease. I forgive a lot of people in my life for the things that have happened, for the hurts that I had because of this disease. That was the beginning of forgiving myself. They tell us we can't forgive other people until we forgive ourselves. That's what I had to do.

After I was in the program for about a year-and-a-half I began taking tranquilizers. I started my sobriety date over because I was learning a little bit about honesty. That was hard to do because I didn't want to tell anybody I was taking tranquilizers. It was the beginning of my honesty—trying to find out what honesty was.

I was born on the Pine Ridge Reservation in South Dakota, the oldest child in my family. I was that child who was probably never a child because I took care of my brothers and sisters a lot. When mom and dad drank I was the one who took care of the kids. I was the one who cooked and make the children go to bed so they wouldn't see my mom and dad fight. I was always a protector—like being a mother when I was only a child. I resented this a lot. I left home at the early age of thirteen years old and chose to go to a boarding school. I could isolate myself there. I didn't have to deal with family problems. Whether in my family or out of my family, no matter where I went, no matter how many people were around me, I felt alone all the time. I felt I was different and didn't know why.

A Long Road

I remember being depressed a lot. I went to an off-reservation school for the first grade and I remember being chased home at night. I was the only Indian in my class. Fear, hate and anger began to build up in me for being who I was. I never wanted to be what I was. I was always wishing to be somebody else or to be some place else—then I would be OK. Those feelings began real early.

Another feeling really affected my life. One day my mother told me that when I was born my father came to the hospital to see me but I was a girl so he walked out and got drunk for two weeks. That really bothered me all through my childhood. I tried to be likable. I fought a lot to protect my brothers. I rode horses and I tried to do everything better than my brothers did because I wanted the acceptance of my father.

When we come into this program they tell us that many things will be given to us that we could never imagine. In just this past year I told my father's sister how I had disappointed my father because I wasn't a boy. I never wanted to be a girl. I told my aunt what my mother had told me and how I had thought about it all those years. But she said to me, "Charlotte, that's not true." She said, "I remember the night you were born. Your father came and woke everybody up in the middle of the night to tell us that he had a baby girl. He named you after his mother because he loved his mother so much." She told me he wasn't drunk for two weeks. She said he gave the family money to get you clothes and he was waiting for the day when you'd come home. I wasted all that time thinking that my father didn't want me because I was a girl. Each one of us has a perception of something that happens, and each one of us sees it differently. I guess my mother saw it differently too. I went all through my life feeling I wasn't what I should have been. It was painful at times trying to please people.

A Long Road

For many years my prayer every night was, "Please God, stop my dad from drinking." I always said I wouldn't be like my father and I wouldn't be like my relatives. I never planned on being an alcoholic—it was the last thing that I ever wanted to be. I wanted to be different, and I was. None of us wants this disease, but so many of us couldn't help ourselves—we became alcoholic.

I didn't drink through grade school or high school—I guess it was control or maybe it was God taking care of me. I was always at the head of my class and a leader at school. Being children of alcoholics and the oldest in the family we become the "hero" or the responsible person. I was over-responsible. I thought my parents would love me if I made A's. Everything had to be perfect and I had to be perfect.

I always wanted to leave the reservation because I knew that place wasn't for me—I didn't want to be like everyone else. I got married real young, right out of high school. I married a boy I knew all my life. I picked him because he was one who didn't drink. We went to church together all the time. He was a model boy of the community, a boy who went to church, a boy who studied. He was everything that I was then. We got married so young we were only children having children. I forgive myself, and him also, because we were children having children without any knowledge about life.

When my husband came back from the Army I knew he was a different person. Until I came into this program I never knew that we showed our alcoholism even when we weren't drinking. When he got off that plane I knew he wasn't the same man who went to Korea. We stayed together for a time and went back to the reservation, but it didn't work. His drinking got worse. We left the reservation for San Francisco and the first month there was the happiest in our marriage because he didn't drink. We had two children and I did all the things I said I was going to do as a mother

and as a family. But as soon as he met other Indians he was off drinking again. I stuck with that marriage for a long time and had five children.

I began to drink as a binge drinker, but when I drank I got beat up because it gave me the courage to say the things that I wanted to my husband. I knew that if I drank more regularly I probably wouldn't live too long.

We lost a daughter in San Francisco, born with a congenital heart defect. I remember going through that alone as she lived for a year and my husband's drinking got worse during that time. The night she died I was alone and I remember the hatred for that man. I vowed never to cry again. What's the use of crying? And what's the use of praying, because God just doesn't answer your prayers. I had given up on God. I thought, "I'm alone in this and I'm going to do it myself. I don't need anybody and I don't need God either because he's let me down so many times." That's how I went for a long time.

I think about the abuse I took. I thought I had to take it. After I got into this program I was able to forgive my former husband because it was my own fault that I was abused. It was my own fault that I was beat up even when I wasn't drinking because I really didn't have to be treated that way. It was more my fault than his for taking it. I came to Arizona after five children and I knew that his drinking and violent behavior was getting worse. I was getting crazier and crazier. We went without food too many times. A lot of the time I didn't want to live. I had hopeless feelings that nothing was going to get better. Every Friday night I stayed up praying until the bars closed, never knowing what condition he would come home in.

A Long Road

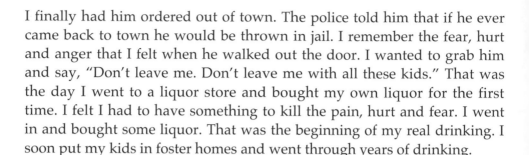

I finally had him ordered out of town. The police told him that if he ever came back to town he would be thrown in jail. I remember the fear, hurt and anger that I felt when he walked out the door. I wanted to grab him and say, "Don't leave me. Don't leave me with all these kids." That was the day I went to a liquor store and bought my own liquor for the first time. I felt I had to have something to kill the pain, hurt and fear. I went in and bought some liquor. That was the beginning of my real drinking. I soon put my kids in foster homes and went through years of drinking.

I always drank over people, places and things. Every time I drank it was somebody's fault. Every time I drank it was because you hurt me, you got me angry, I was afraid of you, or I was afraid of everything.

As time went on I wanted my kids back so much. I asked God to help me raise these children. I eventually found a good job as a secretary on a reservation in Arizona. I got my kids back, and at one time I had three different boyfriends. I told myself that no man is going to hurt me again. I always had a backup in case one didn't work out. I went around as a tough person. Everyone thought I was responsible and OK because I had a house, a good job, and got my kids back. But they didn't know how I felt inside.

Of my three boyfriends, I picked the one that I thought was the most responsible, the one who would take care of me. I wasn't going to make a mistake like I did the first time. He had status in the community as well as having five children, which he was raising because his wife had died. Together we had ten children as well as one we had together. But it was a real crazy household. Nobody could feel, and nobody could talk about their feelings. There was a lot of friction and a lot of fighting. My kids never felt that that was their home. I kept drinking, hoping that maybe things would be better. So that one was also a pretty stormy marriage. I was still a very critical and angry person inside even though as a Catholic I went to confession and to church all the time. It's only now that I am in

this program that I have truly found my God. It wasn't the God that it used to be—that punishing or hurtful God.

When my second husband and I had our child together I thought that maybe everyone would become close and the family would become a real family. But of course that wasn't true. When my new son was nine months old I got a chance to go back to college. That was one of the things that I always wanted to do. Even though my father was dead by then, everything I did in my life was to please him. But I went back to college so I wouldn't have to depend totally on a man any more.

After I got my degree I went back to my community and began to teach. But things didn't get better. The children started acting out the dysfunctional part of our family that was created by the disease of alcoholism. The children were drinking. They were not coming home and not going to school. My drinking got worse, too. I became very violent during the last three or four years of my drinking.

During the last couple of months of my drinking I almost killed my husband. They told me that it took four people to drag me off him. I had guilt about that and about my growing violence and unhappiness. I had guilt that I had also been drinking with my children. The household was going to pieces.

My last drunk was on a three-day weekend. I wanted to die. I bought a bottle of Vodka to make it easier to die. I went to Salt River Canyon and was sitting on the edge of the canyon in tears just as it was getting dark. I looked across the canyon and saw a sunset sky that was so beautiful. There was something about the beauty of the sky that I thought there

must be a God. Somewhere inside of me I felt there has got to be something. I can't kill myself. I've got a son to take care of. I knew that I had to live for him. I turned around and came back to Mesa, Arizona and called Alcoholics Anonymous. They directed me to a meeting at a church in Mesa. I was shaking so bad I don't know how I found that meeting. When I arrived at that meeting I looked at some people and thought, "these aren't alcoholics." Everyone looked so beautiful. I looked at one woman who reminded me of my sister and saw the beauty in her. She hugged me. She was the first person in AA who hugged me. I went away from that meeting really hurting, but for the first time there was some hope.

Right after that meeting some of my first thoughts were that I wasn't really an alcoholic but I would go to meetings because I had a son to raise. I'd go to meetings because maybe my husband would begin to come to AA since he was also drinking. I didn't admit to myself that I was an alcoholic. I was only going to meetings because I had to take care of these other people and fix them. I thought I would do that, and then maybe I'd go out and drink later. Or, when my son got to be eighteen years old maybe I'd start drinking again. Those were some of my first thoughts.

About a year and a half into the program I began taking tranquilizers. I was a dry person with a lot of hate. I thought I worked the steps, but up until then I really didn't. I remember attending a New Year's Step program. When I came back, I told my sponsor I had worked all the steps in two days!

But finally I went to a treatment program where I started to learn something about myself and this disease of alcoholism. I had a counselor who was trying to make me feel my feelings. He said, "What's with you Indian people? I've tried to work with Indian people but you can't make them cry, you can't make them angry—they just sit there." He said, "That

song about the wooden Indian—that's what you remind me of!" But at that time I certainly couldn't show any feelings.

I began to learn more about this disease of alcoholism. Acceptance of my disease finally hit me. The surrender of the first step finally meant something to me. I finally got it that no matter what happened, I had to do it for ME. It wasn't for my little boy. It wasn't for the rest of my family or for my kids. For once in my life I had to look at ME honestly. Without that time at the treatment center I don't think I would have been able to really work the AA program.

I always think about my first sponsor, an Indian man, and the many things that man told me. I'm half Indian. I went through a lot of anger over that, too, because I wasn't accepted in my own tribe. And I wasn't accepted off the reservation because I was Indian. But today I'm just Charlotte. That Indian culture, that Sioux culture gave a lot of things back to me. It gave me a new God, and that's beautiful.

Who Am I?

An Elder asks some questions and directs this Native man back to the heart

Many, many times as we travel this country, we wonder what lies over the next hill. And many of our Indian people always wondered what was over the hill or over the next hill for them. But the one thing they always beheld was guidance of the Great Spirit. They always went to this Great Spirit to find leadership and directions. I didn't know what that was as I was growing up. I grew up in an alcoholic environment. I grew up in a very dysfunctional environment. I grew up being the oldest in the family, and you know what that does.

There were certain expectations of me, and because my values were just a little bit different than my father's values there was conflict. But being the oldest in the family I had chores that needed to be done. And if I didn't get those chores done there were usually consequences to that as well.

I started using alcohol when I was three years old—not because I picked it up to drink, but because my grandfather was my baby sitter. He had an alcohol problem and he had a bunch of friends who came to the house and shared their home brew or whatever they had to share. To get me out of the way, my grandfather would put whiskey or the home brew in my Kool Aid or whatever I was drinking at the time. He would put it in there and I would pass out and they would go ahead and have their good time.

Grandfather didn't know the affect of the chemical, alcohol, that was taking place in my body when he did that. He only knew that for him it

made him drunk. He only knew that it made him feel a certain way for a period of time. He saw no harm in sharing that with a little infant or a little child. I don't blame my grandfather for that. There is still ignorance as to the affect of the different chemicals that a young child can ingest.

Sometimes adolescents say to themselves, "I'm OK because I'm not going to become addicted like my dad, my uncle, or my grandfather." But for adolescents it's a very dangerous period because your cells are still developing. According to what I understand, you don't fully develop until you're around twenty-one years of age. I started when I was three and I had a real disadvantage when I sobered up at age twenty-six. I really had a hard time understanding my role as a twenty-six year old in society. I still wanted to behave like a four, or five, or seven-year old child. My body grew but my mind stopped. When I sobered up I found it very difficult to accept any kind of change.

I've gone to many different institutions and many different kinds of structures to try to find change for my life, but it wasn't until I came to that place where someone asked me the question, "John, who are you?" that anything happened. I had trouble with that question, *Who am I?* Well, I'm John. Are you really, really John? I had to ponder that question because I really did not know who I was. I knew that I had a Cherokee name, an Indian name. My grandfather gave me an Indian name and commenced to tell me, many, many long years ago, how Creator had chosen from amongst the people men who would go up into these hills. They would hold vigils for many, many days and God would anoint them, and choose them, and give them the medicine that belongs to the Indian people, the Cherokees especially. When they got this medicine they carried it with sacred honor to all of those who were members.

The Cherokees have seven clans, but I didn't know any of my clans. I didn't know my clan. I was lost. I was lost in a world that had all the makings of the great blessing that anyone could probably dream of and have. They told me I was an Indian. I grew up amongst a lot of

Caucasians and a lot of Hispanics, so I just looked at myself as a person. But every time I would come home and they would get around that fire and sing in Cherokee I would say, "Wow! That sounds familiar. I want to be part of that." And every time I'd hear those shackles shaking, every time I'd hear those girls shaking those shackles and the drum beat going, I wanted get in step with those shackles and with the music in the air. I thought, "Wow! This is so neat." And somebody said those are Indians. And here I am, I'm a full-force Cherokee, I'm a full-force Keetoowah Cherokee. But I wondered, "What am I?" Then I heard the term "apple Indian" and I had to really, really do some searching. They said that's the man who is red on the outside and white on the inside.

Back in 1970 I found myself dying from the abuse of my body. I was lying on a hospital gurney in Fort Worth, Texas, dying from internal bleeding. They had given me up for dead because I was an alcoholic, number one. I was a drunk. I was useless. I was not worthy of anything. They just gave me up to die. But something happened on that gurney. They say the body moves one last time before death. And my body moved. I had needles and tubes in my body but my body jerked and I pulled out those needles and tubes and hit my chest hard because I was fighting for air. When I hit my chest and went ahhh! somebody said, "he's alive!" I didn't realize that they had given me up to die because it would be the best thing for me.

The Creator had something he had for me to learn. First, I had to learn who he was. Then I had to learn who I was. I began to visit with my Elders. I have a very special Elder who I go to and I began to visit with him. I said to him in Cherokee, "I'm lost, I don't know who I am." And he said to me in Cherokee, "John, where do you maintain your life and where do you live?" I could tell him that. And he said to me, "John, you're an Indian." I told him I knew that. But he said to me, "you don't

understand me. You're an Indian in the heart." He said when Creator created man he had a relationship with men in the heart. He said, "you are a creation of Creator and you are very special. You are very worthy but your life doesn't reflect that. Your life doesn't show that. It shows that you are not worthy because you're treating your spirit unworthy of being worthy." I didn't know how to treat it any other way because I had always been told how dumb I was, how stupid I was, how unwanted I was, how unloved I was. "I wished you had never been born," was what I got. I'd always been told those things. How am I to rise above that? And he said, "Creator has provided a way."

One day I was visiting with a man who knew the Bible inside and out. He said, "John, I'm probably the worst example that Creator could have put on this earth for being a good example to someone." He said, "Creator forgave me. He forgave me of all those things that I ever did in my life." I wanted to be forgiven because of the many things I did in my life that needed forgiving. So this minister led me through a process. He said this is how you must come to that point of forgiveness.

After all of this I was confused because everybody had these steps and philosophies to forgiveness. When I joined AA they had twelve more. And one of those 12 said you have to take care of a sick person. I didn't want to take care of a sick person because I was too sick to be taking care of somebody else.

So that's where I was, I was looking for a direction. When that Elder talked to me about the heart it made me stop and take a look at what he was talking about. What does the heart have in relation to the brain? Most of the time we are who we are by choice. We choose to become what we are today. Life is a matter of choices. That's all life is—a matter of choices. The choices you make set up the consequences you're going to live with in your life. The choices I made were to live exactly the way my folks were living, exactly the way my dad had lived his life. The pattern that was set before me was to be dependent, dysfunctional, and to be that old

drunk Indian that everybody points to: "Aw, he's just drunk, that's natural. He's an Indian."

My grandfather said, "Listen to your heart. Listen to the drumbeat because the drumbeat is likened to the heart. The drumbeat is a replica to the heartbeat of our Creator. Whenever you hear that drum beat you know there's life there. You know there's activity there. And you know that you can be a part of it. So I began to listen to my grandfather about the heart and about the brain. Because of the terrible, terrible conditions our ancestors had to live through, our ancestors' reliance was upon the guidance and the direction of the heart. They maintained the connection with Creator. But the moment that connection is severed, our direction becomes confused and it is lost. Many of you have probably heard what God means. God simply means good, orderly direction. God has a good, ordered direction for everything that is upon this earth.

If you watch the sun as it rises, it rises from the east and has a perfect path to set in the west. If you watch the movement of the sun from season to season, it moves from the north in the summertime to the south in the wintertime. It has perfect direction. The trees turn green at the regular time they are supposed to. God has good, orderly direction. He gives and shares that order with us, but it must be shared in the heart. Your heart is where you really are in your creative state of being akin and likened to God. We get lost and a lot of us get trapped in the head. We start to *smartenize*. We start to intellectualize. We start to be academically acclaimed because we get a thing called ego. If I look better than you, smell better than you, and walk taller than you, I probably am.

That's why, as an alcoholic and a recovering person, it was hard for me to humble myself and step down and let God be the director. I was directing

my life all the time. It wasn't until I came to the place where I could begin to look at the core and to see what was there that I began to see that the Creator gave me something to look at, and that was the core of the earth.

The core of the earth is very hot and therefore it is a purifier. You'll also notice that in the center of our stomp dances we have a fire. That fire has been there for centuries, for ages, for a long, long time. That fire is a representation of God's purifying power. When we come to the fire we approach the fire from the east and we give God that opening to the east so that God will always be in the presence of us. When we go around that fire, we notice there are four logs put in four directions and there are seven different types of wood burning on the fire. I came to that point and began to understand that John was very, very special and there was a purpose for him. I realized he was truly Indian. I began to relearn my language and today I have the language to share because I realized from the heart that I must stay within my heart to be humble, to be lowly and to be respectful.

My grandfather told me I was living in a worldly atmosphere. He said I was living ON the earth, not IN the earth. Even in the Lord's Prayer I say "IN earth." We are the earth. Whatever is happening in heaven, wherever that is, must happen in us also. When it starts to happen in us we start to feel that serenity, that peace, that reconciliation. It wasn't until I came to the point of seeing that my heart was not connected that things began to change for me.

I know I'm made with limitations. I need God's power to keep me in that good direction. I need to do something. Those who have trouble with religion and with the name "Jesus," I want you to listen to this. I got this thing, and you know, it's Jesus. Have you ever stopped and pondered what Jesus really means? If you ask the religious folks they will tell you He's my savior, He's my reconciler, or He's God. You want to know what Jesus really stands for? Jesus stands for Just Enjoy Self Until Serenity. He's not standing there saying your going to hell. Jesus is standing there

saying, "You're a very special individual, you're a very important individual but you're not behaving that way. Your life is not reflecting that because you don't know who you are. You're operating in the *Made Self.* You're operating in the self somebody made you by conditioning you the way they raised you. You made yourself from the information picked up from the head. You were *smartenizing* with life and not being humble with it. Being humble with it allows the created self that you really are to come forward. It allows who you really are, that person you fight against, to come forward."

We are a spirit being, and being a spirit being we align ourselves with a spiritual nature that we seek through the Alcoholics Anonymous program. Number one, it says I am powerless over alcohol, that my life is and has become unmanageable. Therefore I came to believe that a power greater than myself could restore me to sanity. I realize that I am insane and I need some help. So I became willing to turn my life over to the care of God, as I understood him. Notice, *as I understood him,* not as someone presents him to me, but as I understand him.

I had to come to grips with who I am as an Indian, as being a castaway, as being an unloved person. And when I finally came to grips with that word "love," it really hit home with me. One day I got this definition of love. The definition of love is simply **L**etting **O**ur **V**alues **E**merge.

Creator has that same love for each one of us but we need to find that foundation. Have you found that foundation for yourself, to really know who you are spiritually and how you are related to a Creator who created the whole universe? Remember that Creator has created you for a purpose. Creator has created you very special. He created you honorably, so learn to honor yourself. As you begin to know yourself, take the

Twelve Steps to those who are still suffering. And extend that arm of love, that arm of joy, that arm of forgiveness to all.

My Vision

The moment we enter treatment we begin to create a world free of alcohol and drugs, a world that our ancestors, our children and the Creator would be proud of.

Once we're sober, life takes on a different look. Feelings we haven't had for years spring out and come back to us. It can scare the heck out of us. In the treatment center that I'm connected with, we ask you to write your autobiography in the first thirty days that you're there.

Your autobiography is your life story. It's YOUR story. We say HIS-story for men and HER-story for women. We ask you to look back at your earliest memory and write it all down—the good, the bad, all the way to your recovery. The autobiography is a tool. If you can put your life's story on paper it's the first big step. It may be a struggle to get it down on paper, but if you can do that the next step is to share it with someone you trust. It can be with another resident of the treatment program, or a counselor, or if you want to call in your aunty or someone else you can confide in and who will listen to you. Just let that person listen to you. That's another step.

A third step is to take it and read it to a small group or just talk from your heart. If it's the right group and it doesn't say, "Oh my god, you're awful," that will be another major step. And another really big step is if you can get up in front of an AA convention and tell your story. Then you

are free. When you have the freedom to share your story to a large audience like that you'll know in your heart that your story is someone else's story. Each part of your story is someone else's story and you are helping so many people. When people ask, "How do we help each other?" or "How does AA work?" we have to realize that the autobiography is exactly AA.

Another big thing that we really stress and emphasize is to do this for yourself and no one else. Sometimes we say I came into treatment for my kids. Or I came into treatment for my husband or wife. You are still in denial if that's what you're doing. You have to come for yourself first. YOU have to be the first priority. Number one. Numero Uno. One.

When you get sobriety and are working on your recovery, without even lifting a finger things around you are going to get better. We often see one family member come in for treatment, and then a second member, and maybe we'll hear that a third is going to the outpatient center and a fourth is starting to attend meetings. Pretty soon you'll have a family of ten on their way to recovery, working their program, and attending AA meetings together. When you are clean and sober and you have your recovery in place your family members around you are going to grow. We see our children growing strong because their role model is clean and sober. They think twice about what they are going to do. Our kids have a lot of peer pressure to drink or to use, but even if that child goes out and uses there will be a mentor they can turn to who's significant in their lives.

If you are the only sober person in a family that is still using, that's a real tough place to be. It takes all your determination and conviction to hang on to it, but if you can hang on to it you are going to change someone's mind without having to do anything else but being clean and sober everyday and offering your family members an example. You might say things like, "Let's go to a movie," or "Let's go fishing," or "Let's go to the rodeo," or "Let's go to the powwow." That might be enough of an

example without giving them hell or reminding them about their sobriety. We have to really look at our approach and look at how things can be with our family members who are still using. And we can look at our communities that are still using.

We have our favorite jokes about the tribal council that drinks, where the chairman is the biggest drunk of all while they sit up there making critical decisions about our people. If they represent us to the government or the courts about our treaties, and someone's intoxicated or really hung over, that's really rough stuff. It's worse if you come before an Indian judge who was passed out in the bar last night. We really have hard times in our communities where people are still using.

We as a people can DEMAND clean and sober tribal councils. We can DEMAND clean and sober judges. We can DEMAND clean and sober community members who represent us. It's really hard to do something about that. You can't go out and change this world right away, but you can work on things.

Drinking behavior no longer disrupts our powwows. We don't see that in powwows anymore. We may see some in the background, but you have a thousand Indians out there who are enjoying themselves clean and sober. Those are the kinds of things we must expect from our communities—to demand the kind of behavior you want for yourself, your family members and your sobriety.

I want to speak just a bit about substance abuse counselors. Many of us new in recovery have a strong desire inside ourselves to give back what we have and that's a really good tradition. You want to be a substance abuse counselor. You want to turn around and help people the way you

were helped. We honor that with the greatest of honor. If there's anything in the field I honor more, it's a recovering person who is a good counselor. It warms my heart and spirit to see them because they really relate to that person who's still suffering because they've been there. Those are really sacred people among us.

We have a really big task in front of us. I've been wearing a button that says One Day at a Time now for seven years. I keep it with my jewelry and wear it at least once a week. But where are we going to go? It's One Day at a Time but what are we moving toward?

My vision is that we as Indian people take the strength, the heritage, the culture and all the beauty that was given to us by the Creator and by our ancestors to go forward and make a world that is free of alcohol and drugs. My vision is that we join together arm in arm, walking together, supporting and caring for one another, as well as with the non-Indians who are our allies.

This Has Got To Stop

*Turning alcohol and drug problems around takes
personal work and a new look at traditional heritage
and values*

I have been affected by alcohol for my whole life but I never became alcoholic. In my teenage years growing up on the Blackfeet reservation in Montana, the real cool thing to do was to drink with all your friends, and I did that.

My memories are of skipping school with my friends and going to my friend's aunt's house. We thought no one was home but her uncle was there and they had been drinking. There was liquor all over the house, bottles of wine with a little bit left. We gathered them all up and poured them all together so we could have a full bottle of wine and that's how we spent the afternoon. We got so drunk we couldn't walk. We couldn't even get outside the house. That is the kind of pattern I saw as a young Indian woman and a teenager.

Our only way of having a good time was to see how much money we could get together so somebody could buy for us. When I was a teenager the reservation wasn't open. You had to get someone to buy alcohol off the reservation. Our big deal was to see how many times we could drink together and where we could drink. We used to tell each other how many times we'd been drunk, who we'd been drunk with, and how much we had to drink. If there was a prom in the high school it was who you were going to drink with after the prom, not who you were going to dance

with at the prom which was important. So I grew up in a drinking world, a reservation that was ridden with alcohol.

As I think of AA traditions, the twelve steps and twelve traditions, I really look at them as a way of life, a way to live, and a way for us as Indian people. In the early days when AA was introduced to American Indians, about ninety per-cent of Indians turned away. They said, "That's not our way. The AA, that's not our way." But then many Indian people took the twelve steps and the twelve traditions to some of our elders and asked the elders to hear what these twelve steps and twelve traditions were about. The feedback was just unanimous even from different tribes that never talked to one another. The elders and the spiritual leaders said that those are the teachings of our own people. Those are the words and ways that have been among our people for thousands of years. I always say to Indian people that AA is our way. AA has our values. AA has our traditions. They're interwoven and they're one.

In AA it's always said that what we have we want to give away. That's also an Indian tradition. You know, if you visit any tribe in this land they will give you what they have. If it's their food, their house, or a place to sleep, they honor you. I was thinking in that context about some of the connections between AA and our cultures.

When I was a teenager growing up, alcohol was just everywhere you went. Our Blackfeet reservation in Montana was dry prior to 1953. "Dry" meant that you couldn't sell liquor on the reservation, and you especially could not sell it to an Indian. So in order to get our alcohol we had runners. The runners were usually the non-Indians who lived around us. Or it was really a treasure to have an Indian that looked, or who could pass for a Mexican because they could go and buy liquor for us. They were real popular. Everyone took them to their party so they could buy alcohol off the reservation.

This Has Got To Stop

When our reservation was opened to liquor in 1953 I witnessed the devastation of our Indian people because they had unlimited access to liquor. My grandmother never drank, but when the bars opened on the reservation she began to drink. Grandmother was the caretaker of her grandchildren because her grown children were drinking. I remember one time walking by the bar and two little kids of about four and five were sitting outside the bar and looking in through some slats at the bottom of the door. They were saying, "Grandma, come out. Grandma, can you hear us, come out!" they were asking their Grandma to come out and take them home.

I also remember a beautiful Indian woman friend of mine who had six children and who really took care of her kids well. I knew that her husband drank and that he was cheating on her. One day, he and another woman were both walking down a street really drunk. And my friend and her children were also coming down the street. And this woman who was with my friend's husband challenged her to a fight. She attacked her right on the street and tore her blouse wide open. It was such a shock to see this woman being treated like this. She got angry and fought back but no one stopped them. It was nothing for two Indian women to be beating each other up, to be bloodied with their clothes torn from them and for their bodies to be exposed to the public.

As a young teenaged woman I saw all these things and all the devastation that was happening to our reservation. Today there are many reservations that are dry. I can't say that that's the answer, but somehow this has to stop. This kind of abuse, degradation of our lives, and sacrifice of our children, of our families, our mothers, our fathers, our grandchildren, our great grandchildren, grandparents and community members—somehow this has got to stop.

American Indians have only been doing something about alcoholism from about 1965 or 1970. We have over five hundred years since the first non-Indian came to these shores to destroy what we have. It's just been a short time that we've been working to change our lives, to take this alcoholism by the horns and turn it around, to realize that it is not our way of life. And now we are beginning to say "No more. We've had enough. We're going to change our community. We're going to be the proud, wonderful people that we are. We're going to bring back all those values and traditions."

When we look back at our history we see the genocide of our people, the forced removal of our culture, the forced abandonment of our traditions, our ceremonies, our heritage, and our languages. We always ask "why?" But it's starting to get better because we are making it better, not because somebody else is making it better. It's because Indian people are making it better. We were ashamed to be Indian. Some of us tried to pass ourselves off as white people or of a different nationality. For a race to be ashamed of who they are, is really a crime for society at large.

I have a real tough time with missions. My mother was forced into a mission. Like many of our relatives and grandparents who spoke only their own language, she was forced to learn English and to give up all the Indian ways. She was told that those were heathen ways or the ways of the savage. We were all supposed to live this new way that is so good.

We have a lot of work to do on our own Indian self-image to turn our alcohol and drug problems around. We have a tribal history and it's a beautiful history. We have to turn around and look at the values our tribes had and our family had. We have to identify those values and keep them strong and good. Someone in the early stages of recovery might want to charge home and change their whole family and their community over night. That's how we think and its OK to think like that because we do change a lot in recovery. But we first have to change ourselves, and by the miracle of the creator everything around us will change.

I want to talk about treatment programs because I'm the director of an American Indian Family Healing Center in a large city. The treatment program is one of the many ways we can sober up. We have talking circles from our own Indian traditions, which blend ceremonies and heritage with a sober life. For many of us the sweat lodge has really been instrumental in our lives. We greet each other by saying, "Ho, my sweat brother or my sweat sister." It reminds us of the good way.

In our treatment program we use a social model. You probably know that there is a medical model, a behavioral model and other kinds of approaches in treatment centers. We also use some therapy along with our meetings or whatever else is happening because there is usually more to us that needs to be explored than just alcohol or drug problems.

Coming into the treatment program, we look at the return of self. We don't try to mold you into anything you are not. We like you to look at who you are. You already come to us with great beauty, great strength and lots and lots of experience. We look at that to see what makes you feel positive about yourself and help you to look at that. We blend the twelve steps and twelve traditions, the meetings, workshops, and smudging all into the talking circle. Smudging has really worked for us and we will continue to have it in our program.

When I say that we have the return of self, I always say the return of your Indian heritage too. Ours is a culturally based social model. It's very important to look at "Indian" first and then see how we are going to recover in terms of what are you going to do, and where are you going to live.

We are looking toward our future as American Indians and our future with clean and sober communities. We see men and women now who have their sobriety, who have been in recovery, who have decided to be companions, and who have decided to be parents. We have a whole new generation of children being born who are not touched by alcohol or drugs at birth. They've been born to a clean and sober mom and a clean and sober dad. If our ancestors, our teachers, our grandparents and our elders ever hoped and prayed for us, this is the generation that their prayers are being answered. We who are sober are the educators, the role models, and the recovering people who are the main characters in the lives of our children.

A Double Winner

AA and Al-Anon work together for a peaceful life

I'm a Northern Cheyenne from Montana who's both in AA and in Al-Anon so I guess you could call me a double winner. I didn't take my first drink until I was twenty-one years old. I was raised in a very nice Christian home and the good book tell us that we must go back to the way it used to be. I went to treatment and not long after I was in treatment I started drinking again. Some time after that I had a spiritual experience and sobered up, but to make a long story short, I wasted fifteen years of my life. Even though I wasted so many years of my life, I'm thankful today that I'm sober and that I can live a happy, peaceful life like I did when I was a teenager.

When I was nine years old I got into a fight with one of my Anglo friends and she told me, "Oh, you're just a drunken Indian. You're going to be drunk in that ditch just like all the other Indians here on the reservation in Montana." Twenty-three years later that happened, but today I can say that I'm sober, and I live one day at a time.

I went into Al-Anon because a friend of mine told me that I should go into Al-Anon to learn about drinking. Before that, I went into treatment, came out of treatment, had a spiritual experience and sobered up, but I couldn't understand why my husband wasn't able to quit drinking. Because I didn't have Al-Anon, I just covered up for him, lied for him, and did everything I could to fake it because I was ashamed that he was

drinking and that we had a problem in our family. Al-Anon taught me that I have as many character defects as my husband did, and Al-Anon also taught me that I had to look at myself, keep an eye on myself, and to work on my own character defects. I started the steps all over again in Al-Anon and I'm so thankful today that I did. I'm an adult child of an alcoholic and I work and believe in the twelve steps.

Step One tells me that I can't stay sober and serene myself. Step Two tells me that God heals. And Step Three tells me that I must let him do that one day at a time.

I'm so thankful that we can get together today like this, as Indian people celebrating sobriety. It's good to be with people who know about the twelve step program, about AA, and about Al-Anon. I also thank God that I'm not just sober, I'm not just a dry drunk, but I live my program one day at a time. When things like resentments and jealousy come into my life I can work on them, I know I can turn them over and give them to God, and he'll help me.

In Al-Anon, I learned about letting go and letting God. That was real hard for me to do, but one time a person told me in a meeting that if I didn't let go and let God, it was like putting God in a little box on the shelf and saying, "I can do a better job than God can." I appreciate all the sayings in the program and I believe in the program one hundred percent.

A Re-Emerging Man

He got sober and connected with the culture

My first drink was at the age of fourteen in a little community in Colorado called Ignacio when I was in the ninth grade. I liked what alcohol did to me, the freedom it gave me. The experience of drinking alcohol did lots of things to me the first time. It set the foundation for the things that were going to happen in my alcoholism. I got in a couple of fights that night with fellow students, got the hell knocked out of me. I met with my dad later on that night and got punished by him. And the principal of the junior high school kicked me off the junior high varsity team. The feelings I had after that night of drinking were about to become very familiar to me. I was depressed, and I had the feeling that I had violated my life in letting down my parents because of my being drunk that night.

From the age of fourteen to the age of thirty-nine I always had those feelings every time I drank. Depressed feelings. I lost lots of jobs, which was just like my getting into fights, and my being kicked off the junior high varsity team. These were the things that I had to put up with in my life. I drank from the ninth grade to the time I graduated from high school. I managed to stay out of trouble. I drank when I went to college. My college career started out at Bacone College out near Muskogee. I spent almost two years out there before they decided to kick me out of school because I smoked too much, and I drank too much, and I liked to chase the women. I forgot that I was there to study and to learn some things in school.

A Re-Emerging Man

From the time I got kicked out of college at the age of twenty, to the age of thirty-nine, my life was an alcoholic career. I drank to get drunk and I drank to have that feeling of being high because it created this false thing that I wanted in my life. I didn't want to deal with reality.

Being Native American I had lots of excuses to drink. I drank because I was an Indian, I drank because I didn't want to be an Indian, I drank because I couldn't compete, I drank for a lot of reasons, defeatist reasons in my life. I don't understand why it is I became an alcoholic. I never will and I don't care, but I drank to cover up a lot of things in my life. My first marriage at the age of 23, I had to drink for that. My wedding night, I had to drink for that. When my son was born, I had to drink for that. If I got a new job, I had to drink for that. I had to drink for Christmas, I had to drink for New Years, and I had to drink for every celebration that existed on the calendar. They were just an excuse for me to drink.

My life and my career took me out to the West coast to study electronics in 1965 on the BIA (Bureau of Indian Affairs) Relocation Program. I was in a thirteen-month training program. I didn't learn anything about electronics but while I was out there I did connect with the National Indian Youth Council when I was 25 years old. Working for that organization, I began having lots of cocktails seven days a week, 24 hours a day, crisscrossing the country, being involved with National Indian Civil Rights cases, being involved with the American Indian Movement (AIM) and the people who were involved in those activities. When I was twenty-eight and one-half I lost every thing. I lost the job, I lost the family, and I lost all the contacts I had made in my life. There was nothing left. It all fell apart because of my alcoholism. I had three children by that age and I destroyed their lives. I had destroyed the life of my wife. I let people down in my life who gave me a chance to survive.

I was given the opportunity to work with federal agencies after that but I didn't last long because I was an alcoholic and preferred to practice my alcoholism. I had good jobs. I began to work for the Indian Health Service

in 1972. They gave me access to the country. I could fly any place I wanted and rent cars to travel around. I could fly all over this country and drink. I didn't have to be accountable to anybody. I abused the travel status I had with the federal government. I flew lots of AIM people around, we drank a lot, we went to lots of demonstrations, and I went on behalf of Indian Health Service, making that public a lot of times. It didn't take them long to catch up with me and let me go.

A friend of mine then gave me a job at the University of Utah to head up an urban Indian health Program. I lost it about five months into that job. I was treated two or three times for alcoholism when I was in that job. It just didn't last long.

My life was a comedy of alcoholism, but the tragedy was what was happening to me. The tragedy was what was happening to my family, what was happening to my parents, and the other things that went on in my life. I never realized that these things were happening. I didn't give a shit any more whether I lived or died.

My parents were the only people who would let me stay with them. There were many times that I would go out into the back yard at my parents house at three in the morning, crying, with a bottle in one hand and asking to die. I didn't care to live any more because I didn't understand what was happening to me. Things were always OK when I began drinking but they were horrible when I quit. I was not a continuous drinker—I was a binge drinker. I became a liar, a cheat and a thief. I could be your best friend and be stealing your money. I could be your best friend and try to steal your wife or your car. I'm the guy who would go through your medicine cabinet and steal your pills, your

tranquilizers. I would drink up your almond abstract from the kitchen. I drank anything that had alcohol in it.

I went to treatment eighteen times from 1973 to 1981. The FBI classified me as an Indian militant or radical back in those days. But all I ever was was a drunk. I don't have a great history of being in jail. I went to jail a few times for domestic violence. I embezzled money. I rolled cars two or three times and got up and walked away. I should have gone to jail but I'm one of those guys who just didn't get caught.

I got sober about ten and a half years ago in Albuquerque, New Mexico, where there were almost no sober Indians at the time. I think you could probably count five or six in those days who were sober, who were actively participating in the fellowship of Alcoholics Anonymous. I walked into a meeting one night and there was a gentleman called big book John who was a big book thumper and he insulted me. There were two or three Indians in that meeting of 35 people, and in the course of the meeting big book John insulted me. It got through to me. I made my mind up that night that I would not give this white guy the opportunity to ever see this Indian drink again.

So I got sober on a resentment and lived on resentment for about ten months before I found a sponsor. After going without a drink for ten months I decided I needed to actively look at sobriety and what other people were talking about. They were talking about reading the Big Book of Alcoholics Anonymous. They were talking about practicing 12 steps recovery. They were talking about having a sponsor. They were talking about going to AA meetings. I never understood any of that.

I picked a guy for a sponsor who was half white and half Sioux. I saw this guy go to meetings around Albuquerque all the time and I didn't like him, to tell you the truth, because he was always dressed up nice and he always seemed to have a nice looking lady on his arm. I used to say, "this

guy isn't an Indian, Indians don't act like this." All the Indians I knew were on skid row.

I was still sober and full of resentment. My resentment grew and grew until one day I called up this guy who we knew as Indian Bob. We met and I asked him to be my sponsor. He looked at me and smiled and said, "Stan, we're going to get sober one day at a time." I said, "OK, I'm ready." He took me through the Big Book of AA and taught me how to work the steps. He always said to me, "Stan, you are a beautiful person." I never understood that.

He was my first sponsor for about the first four years of my sobriety. At the age of 46 he passed away from a massive heart attack. For the first time in my life, I began to understand what it was to love somebody. He was the first person who I ever loved in my whole life. He was somebody who understood me. When he passed away I knew that my life and my sobriety had to go on, so I had to go out and find another sponsor. I'll never forget him.

Today I work with lots of people. I work with lots of Native Americans, I work with lots of white people, and I work with lots of Hispanics and black people in Albuquerque. I have lots of people who call me from around the country. I can be having the worst day in Albuquerque and I'll get a call from somebody in Massachusetts who will say, "hey Stan, I had a feeling you were having a bad day. I just wanted to call you up and tell you I loved you."

In all those years of practicing my alcoholism nobody ever called me up and told me they loved me. I had several women who took care of me when I was a practicing alcoholic. They bought my clothes and they

bought my booze. I never had to work for a long time. We were co dependent with each other.

On December 10, 1981 I had my last drink.

After I stopped drinking I made fourteen to eighteen meetings a week. I went at noon, at six in the evening, and at eight-thirty. When Christmas came around that first year, I had to go to the Alcathon because I was afraid to stay by myself. We met continuously for twenty-four hours. I needed to be around people who understood me because I never understood myself.

I'm a Chippewa Indian. My dad is from Minnesota, my mother's from North Dakota. I was born and raised in the Southwest. I grew up in New Mexico, Arizona and Colorado. I don't know my language, I don't know my tradition, and I don't know my culture. But growing up around Native American people, I understand and I respect. And that's given me more than I ever asked for. I'm a product of the BIA. My dad worked for the BIA. My mother was a nurse for Public Health Service.

Now I'm involved with a whole process, a healing process. The spirituality that's involved in my recovery includes being around Native American people and watching people grow. It includes the reemergence of our ways, being involved with the Sundance, with sweat lodges, being able to talk with friends about spirituality and the things that go on in my life and your life. This is what's happening in my life today.

My wife remarried and had two more children. My three kids grew up and each one of them has given me a grandson. My oldest son has five-and-a-half years of sobriety. He got sober at twenty-one. My youngest

daughter got married. I had to pay for that wedding. When you get sober you have lots of responsibilities. I was sober when my folks celebrated their 50th wedding anniversary. I got to pay for that too. We had over three hundred people come from twenty-seven different states. I met relatives I had only heard of. Seven years ago I met a young lady and I married her three years ago. I have a daughter who is two years old. I'm a reemerging father with tremendous responsibility.

I want to be happy, joyous and free. I want to trudge the road to happy destiny. I do know that if don't take a drink it's going to be OK. I have to be responsible and accountable today, and that's something I couldn't be ten-and-a-half years ago.

Ten-and-a-half years ago I changed my life. I became what I always wanted to be. I began to paint and draw, and I'm beginning to have some success in that business. We contribute a lot of imagery back to Native American healing programs, scholarship programs, and educational programs.

The community I grew up in Ignacio, Colorado is the Southern Ute community and that is where I spent my growing-up years. For the last six years I've been going back to that community during their Sundance time. I don't Sundance, but I go and I share my spirituality at that Sundance. I share my support at the rehab center and I share my support at the AA meetings they have in that community.

I can't find words to tell you what this fellowship has done for me. It has given me the ability to be responsible, the ability to grow up a little bit. I'm fifty years old but emotionally I'm somewhere between twenty or thirty I suppose. But what a life it's been! I can never begin to compare what I've gotten in sobriety, to all the years prior to that. The hardest thing I ever had to say when I got sober was a term called "love."

When it comes to we Native American people, we have a lot of problems with the term called love—in particular, us Indian guys. We still don't know how to hug each other. We don't know how to hug our spouses. We don't know how to love our children. But we're getting there! Ten-and-a-half years ago I could not have said that to my parents, and I certainly could never have said it to another Indian guy. But today I can, and I give freely. I'd much rather tell somebody that I love and care about them as human beings than let them go out and drink themselves to death.

As Indian people we have the highest statistics in the country for alcohol and drug abuse. And the highest statistics for FAS and FAE (Fetal Alcohol Syndrome and Fetal Alcohol Effect). We also have the highest statistics for AIDS. Nobody's going to stop that stuff but we Indian people. We, as individuals, are going to stop it.

Creator gave me a chance to get sober ten-and a half years ago. Nothing else could have changed my life. I tried doctors, I tried psychiatrists, I tried counselors, I tried priests, and I tried religion. I tried a lot of things.

This is what it's all about: It's about sobriety, it's about getting sober, and it's about sharing your life with another human being. It's about recovery. I don't have happy days all the time. But I don't have as many bad days either. If I really need to share with somebody, I know where to go. I go to a meeting.

It wasn't many years ago that you'd have thought this could not happen. That Indian people could get together and share sobriety. But this movement is going on all over the country in the Indian community. Wisconsin, Minnesota, Montana, Alaska, the Northwest—it's going on all

over. I never thought this could happen to Native American people. I was ready to drink myself to death. I thought it was over. I thought that Indian people were going to vanish. And we haven't. We're getting sober, were getting educated, we're challenging those treaties. We're going to get the country back—all we've got to do is get sober.

Our Whole Family

Indian shame and an alcoholic home began early for Katie.
She learned that she couldn't fix other people. She learned to
take care of herself.

When I came into Al-Anon I was real oblivious to everything. I didn't want to come to Al-Anon. My husband had been in recovery and I didn't want to go to any program because <u>he</u> had the problem, I didn't. I blamed him for everything that happened. I came into Al-Anon because my son had just gone into a treatment program. At the treatment center they said, "Katie, you have to go to Al-Anon." Being a people pleaser all my life, and a person who likes to follow directions, I went. But I wasn't too happy being there.

I remember my first meeting. I walked into a room and a group of people was sitting there. They were all talking about their problems and I really wanted to give them advice. I just wanted to say, "well, if you do it this way, this is how I did it, and this is how it worked for me." I never listened at all. From October when I came into the program, until December, this is how hard-core I was. I would go to these meetings and I was really resentful for being there. Every time I left the meeting it was like a steel band around my head got tighter and tighter. It was like I was ready to go off. I knew that.

Later on I debated for a long time. Which should be my birthday, October or December? Because in December I finally realized what Al-Anon was about and how sick I really was. Before then I was very stubborn. I was just there to people-please as usual. But in December I finally realized

that alcoholism is a disease, a family disease that affects every family member. Before then I thought it was just a moral issue. I thought only a weak person would do that kind of stuff. I was just very arrogant when I came into Al-Anon.

All my life I thought I was very strong and tough but actually I was in oblivion. I was a dark shadow of pain, guilt and shame. Deep shame. I think I was infected with shame from a very young age. I was more or less an observer in life. I never participated. I was always on the outside looking in, trying to do what people wanted me to do, or what I <u>thought</u> they wanted me to do. I would watch people and that was the way I responded. I didn't want to give my opinion because I figured I would be wrong, or I waited until somebody made a statement and I would agree. That's the way I lived. This is what I was all about until I came into this program of Al-Anon. It was a joy coming into recovery and learning about *me* for the first time, discovering who Katie really was. I think I lost myself back when I was three years old.

Alcohol came into our home when I was in about the third grade. Before then my father had tuberculosis. He was in a hospital so I never really knew my dad until he got out of the hospital. And then he started drinking. I don't remember if my mother drank at that time but I knew that we were very poor. Things happened to me that made me figure, "I'm different, I'm not like everybody else."

The first thing that happened to me is that I had rheumatic fever as a small child. My parents had my aunt take me to the hospital. She said, "don't cry," and she left. I thought I was abandoned. And I didn't understand a word of English. The nurses came in and talked to me but I had no idea what they were saying. They put me in a room with a girl who understood English and she said to me in Indian, "Katie, when they talk to you say 'yes' or say 'no.' But I had no idea what they were saying so I couldn't say yes or no. So I didn't say a word.

When her parents came, I said to them in Indian, "tell my mother and father to come because I need help." After that my parents came. I had parents but they were never really there for me because they had there own set of problems. My mother was too focused on my father, and my father was too focused on his drinking. As a result I didn't get the nurturing and the love that a small child needed. They were not there to read to me or to tell me I was important.

The next thing that happened was that I went into school. I was taken to school and was left there with no instructions or explanation from my parents. The abandonment feeling of alone, scared, fearful was very strong. I remember I cried. I went into that school, once again not knowing a word of English except yes or no.

That's how it all started. I knew then that there was always something wrong. I never knew what it was. I couldn't put my finger on it. I am trying to go back to when all this toxic shame for me came about. In school I knew it was not OK for me to speak Indian. I remember sitting in a corner because I couldn't read. They all acted like I was supposed to know this English language. As a result I had to sit in a corner, I was humiliated, I was shamed, embarrassed, and I knew then *there is something wrong with me*, I'm not OK and I better forget about this language, I better not speak Indian again because for some reason it's gotten me into a lot of trouble. So from then on I was determined to forget that language. I didn't want to be an Indian, I was ashamed to be an Indian, I was ashamed of my culture, I was ashamed of my language.

There were two people in my life who said, "no Katie, that's not the way it is." That was my grandfather and my grandmother. My grandfather said, "when you talk to me, you will talk to me in Indian. You are an

Indian and that English language is your borrowed language. You speak that out there. With me you will talk Indian."

The other one was my grandmother. She did a lot of beading and she encouraged me to dance, she encouraged me in all the things that were important in my culture. They were the only two people. I never understood why my mother and my father said, "you're not to speak Indian." And today I understand that, because they were ashamed when they were sent into the boarding schools. My mother talked about the spankings and the beatings they got when they spoke their language. They wanted to spare me and my sisters and my brothers so we were told to forget that. I think that's where the cultural shame came from.

I remember how the alcoholism started. My father was put in jail while I was in a hospital. My father went to jail for drinking and driving. He had my little brother with him who was three years old. It must have been a traumatic experience for my little brother to be taken to jail with my dad. There was a lot of pain in my family that was denied. We were told not to talk about it. "You don't talk about this family or what is going on in this family. What we do in here is our business You don't tell anybody else." There was a lot of anger in my home. It was OK for my mother and my father to yell and scream. But it was not OK for me to get angry. If I got angry I was told it was not the thing to do. I got those messages: don't talk, don't cry, don't get angry. Early on I knew it was not OK to be Katie. From that time on, I did everything to forget who I was. I was going to be somebody else.

I remember telling my parents before I left home: I said, "If I leave here, I will never come back." I must have really hurt them with that remark. But I meant it. I also said I was going to marry a man who is not going to drink. I'm not going to ever take a drink, and I'm going to have a lot of smart children and I'm going to have a lot of money. And that's what I set out to do.

I went to the Bureau of Indian Affairs employment assistance and I graduated and I went to school in California. I finished the business school and then I met my husband.

I met my husband and said I wasn't going to marry an alcoholic, but I didn't even know the word "alcoholic" at the time. I was never going to marry a drinker. I met him at a party. He was the life of the party. He carried the party. He talked, he laughed, and I thought, "I'd like to know that man." He was going to college and had just come back from Vietnam. I thought he was so much fun. Before then I had boyfriends who didn't drink. I would drop them. They were not exciting enough. He was everything that I ever wanted. He was exciting, handsome. He would take me in his car and we would go over one-hundred miles an hour. I needed excitement. I didn't realize how I was setting myself up.

We got married, stayed in California for two years and had our oldest son. Then we moved back to Alaska. Back up to Juneau. And as soon as we hit that town of Juneau things started to change. I was often left alone with my son, surrounded by people I didn't know. Before then I was very sick, but I got sicker there. I went into a lot of deep depression. My husband would stay out to drink and wander home at two or three in the morning. I would be so angry. I had a lot of rage, so much rage. Once I beat him with a broom. But he was too drunk to help himself. I tried to control that sick situation we were in.

My husband got sober when our oldest son was in a car accident because he was drinking. The police called us, and that was the first time I saw my son drunk. We went to the emergency room and I was shocked. I chose not to see the signs that he was a drinker.

My husband took him to a treatment center in Seattle. He said he thought, "I'm the one who should be here, not him." Our son's drinking affected him deeply. He said he went back to the hotel room and had his last drink. The next day he knew he was not going to take another drink again.

My husband never took a drink again. He went to AA. He's been sober. He's doing really good. I have to keep hands-off because now he's totally focused on our son. And again, that's none of my business. I would like my husband to come into Al-Anon but I have to let that go. Now there's tension between him and my sons because he would like them to be sober just like he is, working a program. That's not happening, so I have to turn that over to my Higher Power. I have to take care of *me*.

Since I've been in Al-Anon a lot of healing has begun for me. I understood why I am a people pleaser. Why I have so much guilt. Why I have so much shame. So much rage. I think it's the children who are the most affected in an alcoholic home. When my husband was drinking, I was so angry I took it out on my children. Everything I said I was not going to do when I was a child, I repeated in my home. I wasn't there to nurture my children. I was not there telling them they were important to me. I picked at them. I criticized them. I took all my frustration and rage out on them.

When I try to do things my way, I screw it up, I hurt myself, and that's what I've done all my life. This program has taught me that I need to take care of *me*. This program has taught me that I am really this important person, I am a good person. The best example I can be to my family is to work this program the best that I can with the help of my sponsor and my groups. I work the steps and try to attend a meeting every day. Now I know I am a human being on this earth just like every body else, with the same needs. I've come to know myself and continually take care of myself.

I'm trying to have more fun today. I'm trying to be more spontaneous and not sit there and plan something for weeks and obsess over it. I'm trying to do things that would be fun for me. This summer I went out and bought myself a kite. I went and flew my kite on a Saturday afternoon and I had so much fun! It was something unplanned. I just wanted to be that spontaneous, happy child I left so long ago. That's what this recovery program has taught me, that I am really this important person. I am a good person.

I just had my fourth birthday in Al-Anon. I see the little lessons today that I missed before I came into Al-Anon. If this was six years ago before I came into Al-Anon, I would not have even looked at the scenery, I would have been bored while traveling to this meeting. Things are clearer today. I recognized the mountains, the flowers, the birds and the clouds. They were there and they were so clear. I felt a lot of gratitude for recognizing all those miracles. These are tears of gratitude.

I say a prayer that always helps me when I get real, real scared or when I start slipping again, when I start having the slips. Like on a Friday night. Friday nights are not good nights for me. Growing up, that was the night my parents wouldn't come home. In my marriage, that was the night my husband didn't come home. When my kids became teens, that was the night they didn't come home. So I started saying this prayer, but now its become a prayer for me all the time. *"God help me. God, God, please help me. I can't help myself—and I don't know where to turn."* And every time I have said that, that peace that has never been there, that peace always comes back.

My Past is My Mirror

This Native man is clean and sober. He knows there is still more work to do.

I could tell you many thoughts that swirl through my mind. Many of them would frighten you. They frighten me at times. I think of the future and the struggles that my children and grandchildren might face because of the decisions we are making today.

I grew up somewhat disoriented and confused as to my purpose on this planet. Neglected and abused in certain amounts, I found a way to hide my true dreams, strength, and pride. Using alcohol, drugs and sexual acting out became my behaviors early in life. It was a shame-based existence coupled with low self-esteem that guided my adolescence.

At thirteen years old I was selling marijuana on the streets of Lakota Homes in Rapid City, South Dakota. One of the hardest things I remember about being a teenager was watching my father disintegrate into his beer and wine. At fifteen dad died and I ran away from my mother and attempted to kill myself with alcohol and drugs. I ended up in juvenile detention and was sent to a drug treatment center. It worked for a while but eventually I was back with my old friends, partying, raising hell.

At seventeen years I was incarcerated in Youth Forestry Camp. At eighteen I was on a non-stop road to self-destruction. I drank and did

drugs all the time and was incapable of having respectful relationships with women. I was all about sex, using and being used.

I straightened up for a while early in my twenties. Got married. Had a couple of boys. Soon my diseases had taken them away. I was angry , hurting and confused. Several trips through alcohol treatment did nothing to help me. I wanted a better life. Deep down inside I wanted a better way to live. But each day I would rise, looking for my clothes, wondering who she was, did I get in a fight, am I in jail? I would drink some more. I was a streetwalker looking for a hustle or trying to bum a cigarette.

I was tired of getting beat up by, and beating up my girlfriend. We would always drink, fight and go out on each other. Then we would come back and apologize, saying it would never happen again. We always had our little honeymoon, but eventually the cycle repeated itself. I was unhappy.

At twenty-seven years of age I skipped out of Bismarck, North Dakota on a warrant that was hanging over my head and checked into Hope Lodge in Rapid City, South Dakota. I learned of the Sacred Seventh Direction inside of me, the spark of the Creator. That's been more than eight years ago now. No alcohol or drugs. I feel proud, yet realize there exist many behaviors that are detrimental to myself.

I realize there is still a lot of anger, pain and shame going on inside of me. In a sober state of mind I am still guilty of abusing myself, my family, my people. I feel insecure sometimes. I have honest and good intentions of helping, yet I question myself as to whether I should have permission to counsel others. After all, my life is still screwed up.

But I ask myself: should I hang my head in toxic shame? Should I make no attempt to help others? Should I ignore my people who stand at the place I once did? Should I offer nothing? Should I allow myself to be

knocked down and not get back up? Should I ignore the issues facing my children and my grandchildren yet to come? Should I say I am beaten?

No, I shall not! I will offer my best until my dying breath. I will challenge myself to be more than that confused little boy ever thought he could be. I will be generous and good-hearted to children and elders. I will confront my peers when they get off-track, and I will allow them to confront my behaviors in a good way. I will work to unite my people in health, healing, and wellness in whatever way that means. In a humble way I will hold my head high!

My God is a She, and She is an Indian

Adopted out at six years old, this Native woman took a long journey to God

My name is Brenda, I am Assiniboin Sioux and Navajo.

When I first came into the rooms of Alcoholics Anonymous, I was fourteen and court ordered. After having consumed large quantities of Wild Turkey throughout an afternoon and evening at a friend's house, I was rushed to the hospital. I had literally almost poisoned myself to death. The next morning I didn't even remember what had happened. My punishment was being grounded and to go to Alcoholic Anonymous. As I walked into "the room," I looked around and saw a table surrounded by wrinkled, old, gray haired, white men, drinking coffee and smoking cigarettes. I was the only Native American in the room. I left and didn't return to these rooms for another fifteen years.

Never would I have imagined what those fifteen years had in store for me. At fifteen I hopped on the back of a motorcycle that my boyfriend found in a friend's garage. I woke up a few days later in intensive care. He had jumped the curb and hit a fire hydrant. In the hospital I was tied down because I kept ripping my catheter and IV's out. I couldn't move my left arm. My injuries consisted of a concussion, the entire left side of my face scrapped up, and my upper left lip ripped open. My neck was fractured, and my left kidney and spleen were removed. Stitches down the center of my belly told the story. My left arm was paralyzed due to

the spinal cord injury. It was two weeks before my sixteenth birthday. I left the hospital thirteen days later and joined the ranks of the disabled.

At the age of thirty, it was as if I was balancing on a tightrope. If I fell to one side I would dive into a pool of alcohol and become one of the unknown drunks in the gutter, or die. If I fell to the other side, it meant facing my drinking and me. My daughter turned six and I realized I didn't want her to go through the life that I had. I actively sought an out-patient program that would educate me about alcohol. I called various Native American agencies and found one. They said there was a waiting list, but that I could go to AA until an opening was available. I asked to be put on that list too. The woman laughed. She said the doors of AA were always open and there was no waiting list. As I left that agency, I spotted a flyer on the bulletin board. It said "2nd Annual Red Road Convention." In my alcoholic mind, my motives and intentions weren't in check. I thought I would find a sober Native American guy. When I arrived at the convention, I saw all these sober Native Americans and felt intimidated. I didn't stay for the dance they had that night, but returned the next morning. I sat alone and listened to the speakers. One man told my story.

Alcohol had been a constant foe in my life even before I was even born. Both my parents were alcoholics. I later learned that both my maternal and paternal grandmothers had died from alcohol related causes—one from cirrhosis of the liver, and the other a car wreck. My biological mother told me that my father had gone out drinking the night I was born. She said I was a breach baby and that she had to deliver me by herself. My brother was two, and my sister one. Around the age of three or four, my brother, sister and I were taken away and placed into a mission on the Navajo reservation. There we were given immunization shots and our hair was butchered. I remember my sister crying. I tried to quiet her. I didn't cry when I given a shot. When we were placed into foster care, the foster sister would later tell me how I kept saying my hair used to be longer and how traumatized I was by that loss.

On my sixth birthday we were adopted into an Anglo family that had three children of their own—two sons and a daughter. That day my sister was spanked for something and she came crying to me. I told her that that lady couldn't spank her. My sister said "Yes, she can, she is our mother now." I remember glaring at that woman and saying, "She's not my mother." Abuses by their middle son began on the three of us, including his own sister. They moved us all to Kansas where we worked on their farm, and later moved back to New Mexico.

There was a time that my sister showed my brother and I the bruises on her bottom, inflicted by our adoptive mother. My brother stated it was child abuse. I didn't know what that meant. I didn't have a name for my abuse. That family was well to do financially. We went on vacations, had swimming and skiing membership, and lived in the upper middle class. But it didn't shield us from our past. We were not taught our heritage, and were told Pow Wows were a reason for Indians to get together and get drunk. We three were always reminded that our parents were alcoholic and the statistics were against us. I always claimed I wouldn't become an alcoholic.

When I turned eighteen, I began my search for my biological mother. I found my grandfather and mother within two weeks. They came to see me the next day after finding them. I remember calling my brother who had left home at eighteen and moved to California. I told him of my find. His response was that "You owe mom and dad." I replied that you can't go through life owing people. He stated that I had been the black sheep of the family, and had always been looking for something. I told him I found what I had been looking for, I found my mom.

My God is a She, and She is an Indian

Several months later I visited my newfound family in Shiprock, New Mexico at the Shiprock Fair. My grandfather was at the stove stirring mutton stew. He turned and asked me how it felt to be home. I said in amazement, "I have never seen so many Indians in my life!" Growing up, my brother, sister and I were always the only little Indians in the classroom or at the swimming pool, Sunday school, and in the grocery store. A year later I made contact with my father. We kept in touch by letter.

During my teenage years I had a permanent in my short hair, and long fingernails painted the color of burgundy. Today I can joke that I was a "Mary Kay Indian." My best friend and I had gone to a Mary Kay cosmetics store and had a makeover. The lady said it would make me pretty. I remember a time when I sat on a boyfriend's tailgate drinking beer in a canyon at the age of seventeen. He asked why I didn't grow my hair out. I looked at him as serious as I could be and said "But then I will look like an Indian." Shocked, he said, "You are an Indian, and you are beautiful!" That was the first time that I was acknowledged for who I was and what I was—a Native American. I say today that the rest is history. My hair is past my bottom, and I am aiming to grow it to my knees.

Several life-alternating incidents happened that seemed to solidify how I had always viewed myself. When my adoptive father let me drive through the Navajo Reservation one day, he yelled at me to get into the other lane. He looked in disgust and said there was a drunk Indian in the road. I thought to myself, if it were a white man in the road, would he have yelled there is a man in the road? The man was walking along side the road. I thought to myself, he must look at me in disgust, because I am an Indian, and no different from that Indian man walking alongside the road.

When I took an interest in continuing my education after high school, I was told I could go to the Southwestern Indian Polytechnic Institute and become an Accounting Clerk because I was Indian and could get a free

education. They paid for two of their own children's college education. I put myself through school with the aid of the Navajo Scholarship, state and city grants, and work-study employment.

At the age of twenty-three I broke the silence of the years of abuse I endured at the hands of my adoptive brother. I called my sister and told her I was going to report him to the authorities. The next morning I received the call that she had died instantly in a head on car crash. She was drunk. Even after her death, my adoptive family, would not acknowledge the abuse. I walked away.

A year after my sister's death I gave birth to a baby girl. I stayed sober during my pregnancy, and for the following year that I breast-feed her. I named my baby after my sister, in her honor. I left my abusive marriage when she was 6 months old, but I started to drink after I weaned her. Alcohol became my relationship.

I came into these rooms of AA thinking I was unique and special—that no one could possibly understand why I drank. I wallowed and bathed in my self-pity. At a meeting I heard someone laugh as I spoke. In my mind I thought he was laughing at me. I didn't bother to stay long enough to understand he was laughing with me. I left the rooms and found myself picking up that drink once again. When I came back to AA a few months later, I came with a vengeance. In true form, I looked at the Twelve Steps and Twelve Traditions as rules and regulations, fighting everyone who dared to cross my path. I thought I had to fight all my life to survive and that I would have to fight for my sobriety. It wasn't until I was a year sober that I heard someone say, "This isn't a death march." I stopped my battle.

When I started to hear the message about God, I closed my ears, my mind, and my heart. I believed that the God they were talking about was a White God. As I continued to come to these rooms my perception changed. I began to believe that there was a White Big Book and an Indian Big Book. When it came to the part of a God, as we understood him, I found my God. My God was a She and She was an Indian. This gave me the honesty, open-mindedness and willingness to open my ears, my eyes and my heart to this program. This program introduced me to a God that was not punishing God or one who threatened me to damnation. My God is an understanding God: loving, patient, and teaching me to forgive myself and others the wreckage of my past with unconditional love. I had always been Spiritual, but confused it with being religious. I was a "closet Spiritual person," but now I am out.

In my thirteenth month of sobriety I started dating a man in the rooms of AA. I remember that when he chaired the meeting he would say, "We'll love you until you learn to love yourself." Because he said this while he was looking at me, I heard him say "I'll love you, until you learn to love yourself." I was pregnant by my fourteenth month of sobriety. Out of the hard times of that relationship and its ending, I have a miracle. And that is a baby who has never seen her mother drunk. She is an AA baby.

I completed my fourth and fifth step in my second year of sobriety. For the first time in my life, I entered the sweat lodge and completed my sixth step. In time, I became willing to make amends to those I harmed. My first amends was to a boy I used to viciously harass when I was thirteen. From my experience of tracking down my birthparents, I used the same tactics in tracking him down.

I also knew I had held a thirty-five year old resentment towards my father. He had come back into my life acting like I was his daughter. I didn't feel like he had that right. In fact, all my life I didn't let anyone close to me, or touch me, unless I was drunk. Nine years prior I had a falling out with him, but now knew it was time for me to face this resentment and to forgive him. A few years ago I took a journey of healing to see him at his home. This was the first time in over thirty years that I slept under my father's roof. It was overwhelming and I didn't know how to "feel, deal, or heal." It was also the eleventh year anniversary of my sister's death. I left my daughters with him and sought out meetings in the surrounding towns. After that weekend, and several meetings to help me through, I felt like the weight was lifted off my shoulders. I thank Alcoholic Anonymous and the people in those rooms for being there.

Today, I am aware when my self-centeredness and self-will are taking over and my solutions are not working, or feel the insanity return when I stand on my laurels, stop going to meetings and I think I am well. I am reminded that this program requires action and that you get out of it what you put into it. I remember a time when I didn't like who and what I saw in the mirror. I didn't love myself but I knew the one thing I could do for myself was to go to a meeting everyday whether I wanted to or not.

When I first entered an out patient program, I logged a timeframe for getting well. I thought if I worked real hard in the three-month program, and read a step a week, that I would pass this "course." Today I know that it is a life long process, and even after six years of sobriety, I still have a lot of growth ahead of me. When I first came into the rooms of Alcoholic Anonymous, it was my Native brothers and sisters who showed me I belonged.

Today, I don't sit and wait for my prayers to be answered, nor put conditions or time frames on my prayers. I still continue to grow up in the rooms of Alcoholics Anonymous, and have gained a sense of family

through the many people I have met along the way. Today I can reach out and ask for help, and even give or receive a hug and mean it. I look at the gifts that have been given to me and am grateful that *today* I don't have to, or want to drink. Today I realize that the miracle did happen.

A Woman of Two Cultures

She found Spirituality in the Ways of the North

I had blackouts from my first drink at age 14 but didn't know it was a sign of alcoholism until I got to AA when I was 30 yrs old. I thought *everyone* didn't remember what they did when they drank. I was scared into sobriety in May of 1973 after my second or third suicide attempt—a night when I had wandered in a blackout beside the C & O Canal in Washington, DC. I realized even then that I was fortunate I hadn't been attacked because there have been many rapes and several murders along that stretch of the canal over the years.

The next day I sought help at my family doctor's office. He didn't know much about alcoholism, but he had pumped my stomach at the hospital two or three times in the previous months. He recognized I had a problem. I am grateful that he took the time to get on the phone with a colleague and find out where local AA meetings were. I began to attend AA. At first I thought it would be like a college course I took. I thought I would go twice a week and take notes and come home and practice what they taught me. Only the last part was right. The women I met made sure I went to meetings every night.

Getting sober was one of the most exciting periods of my life and I often wish I'd kept a journal because the insights and changes were coming fast in those first years. I was still a teenager emotionally. I felt like something old and rotten left too long in the garbage can. Sober, I began looking at

the world and my past in a new light. Slowly, I was transformed into a new person.

I often I grew resentful when I'd hear AA speakers say that when they got sober, they had their wife back, their job back, and had two cars in the garage. My sobriety story was the opposite. I lost things. Friends moved away or died. My grandparents, parents, and a favorite aunt all died. They went so fast I felt as if someone had put my family up against a brick wall and shot them.

My marriage broke up in the second year of my sobriety and I had trouble collecting child support for years until my ex-husband died. Some of the saddest days of my life were during this period. I loved my husband with all my heart since we'd met in 1958 when I was 15. When he first touched me, my bones liquefied.

We had two children, a boy and a girl. I have never gotten over the feeling of betrayal that invaded me when he left in 1975. My husband was handsome and couldn't say "no" to the ladies. He looked a lot like the musician Rick Nelson, and, as a matter of fact, he knew and admired Rick Nelson. They died two weeks apart in December of 1985.

I've often told the story of my drinking life and it appears in a book published in 1980. I'm in the housewives' chapter. By the time my story was published in that book, I had completed college and was working as a professional in the substance abuse field; I was astonished to find my story in the housewives chapter, but a housewife is what I was in the last years of my drinking, although I worked earlier as a secretary at the Bureau of Indian Affairs in Washington. Since my drinking story has been told, I am going to tell my sobriety story here. I find it amazing that I've now been sober longer than I drank.

I got sober in the northern Virginia suburbs near Washington, DC, but my continued sobriety and personal growth would not have been

possible without the help of many American Indian people, including a Cree medicine woman in northern Alberta, Canada.

I met Carla at a psychologists' conference in Montreal in 1980. She was short and round and wore beaded moccasins up to her knees. When we met, she told me that she'd had a dream about me the night before and that we were going to be good friends. I was awe struck by this. We had dinner together that night and promised to write each other—which we did for two years before I ventured out west to visit her.

Before I left home I had a lawyer draw up my will. I left my children with my parents and sensed I was saying goodbye to them for the last time. I felt as if I were going to the ends of the earth. Carla lived 700 miles north of the Montana border in a community of less than 500 people on the shores of Lesser Slave Lake. I was scared of going so far alone but felt compelled to make the trip.

My fears disappeared when I arrived at her home. It was the first of many trips to Alberta, but the first one is special. I had been seeking a spiritual path in the seven years I'd been sober. In 1978, I took a business trip to Seattle and met Peter, a Squamish Elder who led an AA meeting and invited me to meet his family and take part in a Talking Circle. We passed an eagle feather and each person spoke from their heart. I felt more comfortable in this meeting than I'd felt since I had gotten sober.

Peter said to me, "You know, Jennie, white people won't understand what you are doing, and Indian people won't like what you are doing, but it's the right path for you to learn Our Ways. If you really want to learn Indian ways, go to Canada. They still have their language up there, and that's the place you will learn the most."

So when I met Carla and first went to Alberta in October 1982, it felt like it was more than a coincidence. It was an unfolding of my life's journey. I experienced my first sweat lodge ceremony during my visit that October. I remember looking out through the oval of the door when it was open to bring in more hot rocks. It had begun to snow on the tall stately evergreen trees that stood like sentinels all around the meadow on which the sweat lodge stood. I thought to myself, "If I were an artist, I would paint the world as I see it right now, looking out through the door of a Cree sweat lodge in northern Alberta."

At another time as I was sweating, I prayed to be relieved of the terrible anger I felt toward my ex-husband. As Carla and the others prayed and the steam rose, I felt weaker and weaker. My body became a rag doll. Scared, I asked, "But what will <u>hold me together</u> now??!!" I realized I'd used the energy of anger to work three jobs, take college courses, and care for my children; but the anger was damaging me and my relationships, especially with men. The answer came in the sweat lodge, "Depend on the Creator now."

During my visit, Carla asked me if I wanted an Indian name. I replied that I thought I'd have to come up to visit lots of times before something that important could happen. But I said, "Yes, I would like very much to have a spiritual name." She told me how to make the proper offerings and took me into the nearest town to buy loose tobacco and four meters of cotton cloth—red, yellow, black, and white, representing the Four Directions and also the four races of humankind.

My naming ceremony was held in a totally dark room in an old log cabin. We sat on a buffalo robe. The blackness of the night inside that room was beyond doubt the darkest room I've ever been in. There were about nine American Indian people present. One man, Sky Wind from Saskatchewan, played a handheld drum and sang. When Carla received the name from the Spirit World after praying hard, she told it to me: "Your name is Two Moons Owl Woman. That means that you are a

woman of two cultures, and the White Owl of the North is your Helping Spirit." She told me that, unlike some Indian spiritual names, mine is not secret and can be told.

Over time I learned that the Creator knows us by these sacred names. When our lives end, the Creator will call us by our spiritual name to come join the Heavenly Spirit. But my name is more than what I will be called at the end of my life. It is what I am called <u>to do.</u> My name defines who I am as a human being. It is a prized possession.

Sometimes I think of the Jewish religion as being about the Father, and the Christian religion being about the Son. But Indian Ways, now that's about the Holy Spirit.

Many people stopped by Carla's house for tea or dinner, sometimes staying for days, weeks, or even months. Even though their people had been enemies of the Cree in the past, the people who came were Blackfoot, Blood, Chippewa, and Stoney, as well as many Cree. Carla was always cooking, but when someone called for help, such as to go doctor a child in Saskatchewan, she'd pack up and leave within the hour. When I was there, she'd often throw me the keys and say, "You drive so I can rest." I felt important. I now had a name and work to do. Sometimes Carla would hold sweat lodge ceremonies while she was visiting in another place. I was her helper on these trips. I didn't know until later that she taught apprentices that way—by <u>doing</u> the things she was doing, not teaching by just saying words like teachers do in school.

We visited some of the poorest homes I've ever been in. They would always give their bed to Carla and sleep on the couch or floor. They'd share what little food they had. Sometimes we would take some food

with us, and Carla was always collecting clothes and other items to give away. I remember telling one old couple that their view out over a beautiful northern lake—just that view—would be worth half a million dollars around the DC area where I lived. I don't think they believed me, but they smiled and humored me.

Carla holds special ceremonies at the changing of the seasons, spring and fall, and I often made a trip at those times in order to take part. I never had much money, but I had a VISA card and would charge my plane fare, spend months paying it off, and then go to Canada again. Sometimes I would sob when it was time to leave that wide western sky and my friends there.

At the seasonal ceremonial occasions the pipes of the Elders and Carla's apprentices would be put up on the hill to be cleansed. The pipe carriers were the main participants in the ceremonies. However, many people would attend, lend support, and fast for four days and four nights. When they fast in that part of the world, Cree people do not eat or drink water. I found that the hardest part—not having anything to drink for days.

The first time I fasted, it was for only one night. Carla said she'd left the cabin door open because no one thought I'd make it through the night out there in the bush alone. But they prepared me with a sweat ceremony and prayers. Someone started a fire for me.

"Just keep the fire going," someone told me. "That will keep the wolves and bears away."

I kept the fire going!

In fact, it was wonderful not to have any other job than to keep the fire going. No phones to answer, no children's demands to respond to; just quietness and the sound of the wind blowing through the tops of the spruce. What a sound that makes. It was as if I could ride off on it.

Time slid forward, and the next morning when I put out the fire and left the woods, I saw everything differently. I was seeing clearly. I could see each leaf on a bush even two feet away. I could see each needle on a pine tree. Colors seemed to sing in my eyes. The world had changed. This altered perception slipped away as each hour passed, but it is a very special memory.

Later that day, Carla's son Eddie went back to where I'd fasted to make sure the fire was out. He said there were fresh bear claw marks all down the tree I'd leaned up against. Perhaps a bear had been watching me all night.

One time I fasted with seven Indian women on top of a mountain in the foothills of the Rockies. The men had put up a large tepee for us, and we slept there at night, making a fire. During the daytime hours, we would spread out all over the nearby woods, out of sight and sound of each other. Then at night we would come back together. Some of the women told stories. The stars were many, and so low I could almost touch them.

Every day, those of Carla's helpers who were not fasting would come and check on the people who were fasting. I never knew what they were checking on. Were they checking just to see that we were still alive? Sometimes they would cut firewood, but mostly that was something we had to do for ourselves.

I became involved with an older Cree man who attended the ceremonies. Carla was critical of our relationship. She said it would never work out—the 5'2" educated, book-reading white woman from the eastern city, and the 6'8" Cree hunter/trapper from Sucker Creek were too different. However, we got married in December 1990. It was forty degrees below

and we left the pickup running when we went to see the Justice of the Peace. If we hadn't left it running, we might not have been able to get the truck started again. We stayed a lot of the time with Joan, a woman friend who lives in Edmonton and reads cards and tea leaves for a living. Joan has always been kind to us, but my relationship with Carla has never been the same.

After about two years of marriage, I told Paul I had decided not to move to Canada. Soon after that, I heard he'd gotten drunk and thrown in jail. The police had to shoot him with the darts they use to tranquilize large animals because they couldn't calm him down when he was in a drunken rage. I've never seen Paul drunk and I don't want to. He had been sober for 14 years, and now in an instant he had become someone I didn't know.

We were legally separated for two or three years. Eventually I heard that he'd been forced to go to alcoholism treatment in Grande Prairie for several months. After that, we got in contact with each other and resumed seeing each other. Each visit is different, but we fight or bicker every time. We get along better in our conversations on the phone every Sunday. Perhaps we should have remained good friends and not gotten married. Perhaps Carla was right.

It's been ten years now and I rarely see her anymore. But perhaps, like other apprentices and students she has had, I would have eventually moved on and not been so dependent on her emotionally. Like an AA sponsor, she helped me when I needed it the most.

My job has worked out better than my marriage. I work for a Government agency that awards grants to States and communities for running substance abuse prevention programs. I often have the opportunity to work with American Indian and Alaska Native people. The experience and knowledge I learned from Carla is invaluable. I see life differently, although not ever as clearly as that day coming out of the

woods after my first fast. I attend AA meetings and am friends with a group of Indian women who work in Washington.

I continue to pray with the sage I picked in southern Alberta and with the special Cree smudge from northern Alberta, a tree fungus, which Paul gives me from time to time. I pray in the mornings facing the rising sun. I try only to ask for continued sobriety and to be allowed to be of service to the Creator and to the people around me.

The purpose of my life becomes clearer to me now. It is in my Cree name. I am Two Moons Owl Woman, a woman of two cultures. I advocate and work for programs that promote sobriety and wellness among Indian people. No one can speak for Indian people but themselves, but often what I do is simply sit in a business meeting and at the appropriate time, ask, "What about Indians?"

The rest of the group usually looks surprised: they had totally forgotten about them in considering programs and initiatives. But more and more often, there are Indian people in the meetings now; fortunately, that makes it harder for Washington to overlook the needs of Indian people. Less and less often now do I have to ask, "What about Indians?" My Helping Spirit, the White Owl of the North, has helped me become a friend and ally of Native people, and that's my work in the world. That, and praying, and staying sober myself.

I Forgot Who I Am

Many take a journey of <u>cultural</u> recovery even if they didn't need to take the journey of alcohol or drug recovery themselves. Culture is prevention and culture is healing. Here's a story to gladden the heart.

I know this may sound funny to some people, but I forgot who I am. At least momentarily. This happens from time to time, and most times I don't even realize that it happened until I remember who I am.

I don't look like the majority of Americans today. As a matter of fact, my race makes up maybe 1 percent of the population of this land we call home. When I say "home" I really mean home. My people were the first ones to occupy this territory. For thousands of years my people thrived on this land. My ancestors are buried all over this continent. I guess you can say my roots are buried real deep, so deep at times that others forget they are there.

Pow-wow season has started for us in my little family of six. For several months now we had gone back to the grind of daily living. We put our roots behind us and blended into the rest of society. It was time to put away our feathers and hang up our regalia. The season started a little later for us this year, but no bother, because we don't realize what we are missing until we attend our first pow-wow of the year. That is when the reality of who my children and I are really sets in.

I Forgot Who I Am

I am full blood Native American, my husband is white—Scottish to be exact. Our children of course are mixed. Growing up on the reservation enabled me to always remember who I am. But I didn't always like what I saw going on in our own little Indian world. Things were not perky and rosy. We didn't live in teepees or ride horses. We spoke English as well as anybody else and attended the same schools as children of other races—only we were treated differently from the start.

Born and raised in Washington State on an Indian reservation, I attended kindergarten in public school. I don't remember much about it. First thru fourth grades were spent in parochial school. My mother was fed up with how little credit we were given as Indian children in the public schools. Those years in parochial were fun because my family was a kind of token Indian for the school but without the stereotypical myth that we were academically challenged because we were Native. It is in this school that I learned to love every race. Yet at the same time my race was still being viewed in the history books as the inferior race.

My best years were in the Indian-run school, Chief Leschi Elementry School. It actually started out as a summer program entitled "Back to Mother Earth," which was geared to bring the Native youth back to our roots. It went so well they decided to make it a full time school. That was in the nineteen seventies, a real tough time for the Indian people of Washington state. While being taught about who we were and why we were there, the rest of society was trying to take away every ounce of respect we had left. It was at this time I learned about the true tragedy of the American Indian people. It was here I learned about racial hatred and how hard it can be, while at the same time receiving the teaching I would need to survive later in life. My roots were planted real deep and later I would have to dig them up just to be happy. I think our Elders and parents knew that, that is why they put us in this school.

Seventh through twelfth grades saw me through public school again. Only this time it was harder, because now I knew what society really thought about Indian children. My mother was up at the school on a daily basis to straighten out differences between my brothers and their teachers. Because the tribes on the coast of Puget Sound were fishing tribes, a teacher told my brother that he should drop out of school like the rest of the Indians and go fish on the river. My mother came to school and got in the face of a teacher over this. While fishing is not a bad thing, what upset my mom was the fact that this teacher wasn't giving my brother credit for having the ability to do anything else but fish. My Indian brother now runs the Indian Casino on our home reservation. Does he fish? No. Does he have an education? Yes. He is a graduate of the University of Washington along with his Native wife whom he met in college. Stereotypes can't hinder us if we don't let them.

By the time I got to high school I didn't want to be Indian anymore. There was too much bad medicine going on as far as I was concerned: too much drinking, too much drugging, and too much death. By the time I hit high school there was so much death under the Native bridge I didn't want to be a part of it any more. There seemed to be no way out of this cycle of death on the reservation unless you immersed yourself into white society completely, which I pretty much did. All my friends were white by the time I graduated.

I remember going out with my white friends one night to cruise for guys. We were hanging out at a popular spot when a car of good looking boys pulled up to talk to my friend. When I walked over to see what was going on they looked at me and asked if I was Indian. When I said yes, they pulled away without one more word. How embarrassing that moment was! Not even my group of friends could disguise the color of my skin and the color of my hair.

I knew the hate people had for my people, and it was easier to pretend I was someone else than it would have been to try and change society's view of my people. I guess what hurt the most was the fact that my people were proving to be what society had claimed they were—a bunch of drunken Indians with nowhere to go but the river. By now those real Native roots were way down under ground and I didn't want to pull them up. I guess it's because it wasn't time for them to sprout yet.

Not long after high school I fell in love and married a white man. I didn't marry him because he was white, but I did by this time forget I was Indian. We stayed in the inner city for about 4 years, struggling to survive the day-to-day grind. I held a couple of jobs in food service and then my favorite at a large department store. I was so proud that I had made it to the big time in women's clothing sales!

I was there for 21 days when they let me go. I was so upset that I couldn't even talk to my husband when I called him to come and pick me up at the store. When he got there he asked me why I had been fired. I told him I didn't know why—they just said I wasn't working out, even though a day before several of the woman who worked there had told me I was the best hire they had seen in a long time. My husband was so outraged he drove me back to the store, walked me into the office and made me ask for the personnel manager, the man who fired me. When we got into his office I asked him who had made the decision that I was no good. He stammered for a second or two then pointed to a chart on the wall listing about 20 floor supervisors. I looked at the chart and did not recognize a name on the wall except for one, someone who hadn't been on the floor with me to see me work. I asked if he had talked with the people I had worked with in the past 21 days. He again pointed at the chart. I said, "I know none but one of those people. I want to know that you have talked to someone who has worked with me."

I told him I was a good worker and knew it—that he was making a big mistake. He said he would go and personally check with these people

but felt he was in the right and would get back with me in a day or two. In the mean time, he told me that if I was as good as I said I was then I should have no problem getting a job at another department store—and that would prove him wrong! I said I didn't want to work at another store, that I liked this store and that if things didn't go that way I would be seeing an attorney real soon.

The next day I received a call from the store telling me I had got my job back and could return to work on my regular schedule. I never received an apology but did receive hoorays from other employees for having the guts to stand up to the big guys. My husband was convinced this was racially motivated and actually is the one who wanted to bring a law suit against the store for the hurt they had inflicted on me. But I wasn't about to go crying about injustice because that would only rip out the roots before I was ready to deal with them. I went back to work.

After working at this job for seven months, I received the "customer service award" for the whole district for the month of February. I honestly believe had I not been with a man that was so proud of his own Scottish heritage, as well as his wife's Native heritage, I would not have had the guts to do what I did.

In August of 1990 we had our first child, a beautiful baby girl. Things were still difficult for us financially, so in May of 1992 we uprooted and moved to Georgia. In August of that year we had our first son.

I remained home with the kids in our single-wide two bedroom trailer while my husband went to work at a local RV dealership. The money still was not good, but at least he had a job and we had a place to live. It

was real easy to not be Indian at this time because there were so few around to remind me of who I was.

I became very active in a local Christian fellowship, serving as part of the worship team and helping in the children's ministry. I had the opportunity to attend some college-level seminary courses and even held two jobs at local daycare centers during this time. Believing my ministry was to children, later I would realize that wanting to do good for others was hurting my own children. The church broke up after six years and everyone went their own way. I was hurt because I was left without a church family again.

Around this time I noticed some roots starting to pop up in my life, and these roots held pain both for me and for the Native American. I had always been one that didn't believe in crying over spilt milk, figuring it was in the past. Why cry over something you can't change? So when I started to get choked up watching Geronimo on TV, as well as the way Native Americans were depicted by the network, I was shocked. What was going on here?

I had also run into what I felt was a road block in my relationship with God. I was at a dead end and couldn't seem to get anywhere. One day while I was praying, I heard this little voice in my heart say, *"You threw away your heritage and your culture—I never asked you to do that. Ask for it back!"* I knew at that moment that God wanted me to be Indian. That is what He had made me and this is what I had to be.

That one brief moment in time changed everything I thought was important and what I thought was expendable. I was Indian, and it was time to pull up the roots and replant them in a spot where they would flourish and reflect the beauty God had intended.

Over the next few years things took off for me in my personal and emotional life. I went through some counseling to help me deal with life

issues that I think we all face no matter the color of skin. And then I had to deal with issues that only Native people have to deal with. God put in me a heart to love my people and enabled me to experience the pain and sorrow that still lives within Native people today. My attitude of "get over it and get on" has changed to, "I know it hurts—I can feel the pain. What can we do together to make this better? Let's heal the pain!" I was given the chance to feel the hearts of a wounded people—*my people!* But it took a lot of running before I could face up to it.

I began dancing at powwows. I'll never forget my first grand-entry—the opening ceremony of a powwow. I had tears in my eyes as I watched everyone line up. I knew deep within my heart that the only reason we were about to do this was because the extermination process had failed. I knew deep within my heart that we had a Creator who loves us. We now have four children and each one is going to know the heritage that they carry—Scottish as well as Native American. In Georgia there are few Natives because of the Cherokee removal in the 1830's. Yet at the same time, just about every person you meet claims to have Cherokee blood somewhere in their ancestral tree, usually back with their great, great, great grandmother.

I know what it means to be Indian and I tried to run from it. I know many others that have done the same thing. I once went to see a production called "Spirit" by Peter Buffet and other Native performers and traditional dancers. I was so moved by the production because I felt it was so much of what I was about: being Indian, forgetting who I was, and struggling to find a way home to happiness. We were given wonderful balcony seats so we could see the show from above. I was so excited until we got to our seats. I got in and sat down with my husband, his mother and our children. As the show began I noticed that the people

seated all around us seemed to know each other. They were all as white as can be, but had feathers in their hair. I found myself becoming annoyed at these people and at their presumption that dressing Indian made them Indian. By the time we left the show, I was so disgusted at the whole thing I just wanted to go home.

Later I understood my disgust. I realized that my anger was not at these people but at myself for being Indian. All my life I tried to be someone else, not wanting to be a Native American or associated with Native Americans. And here was a bunch of people doing all they could to be what I was. I remember thinking, "...if they really understood the things that Native people had to endure just to exist, they wouldn't be putting those feathers in their hair." I realized that the problem was not with these white people wanting to be Indian, it was about *me* not wanting to be Indian once again.

How could self-hate well up inside of me after all this time? Why did I once again have to face the issue of color, *my color?* Or was I experiencing the shame of generations past, something that had burrowed into my hereditary memory? All the pain of my people came back to my own heart. I felt the cry of the peace chiefs as they were betrayed into horrid concentration camps along with their dying people, helpless to relieve them of their pain and hunger. I felt the agony of the alcoholic brother and sister as they struggled to hide their unimagined pain in a bottle. I felt the whimpering of a sexually abused child in the government funded boarding schools that housed only Indian children, the cry of the mothers as they watched all hopes for their little babies crushed at Wounded Knee and Sand Creek. I felt the hidden pain, sorrow, shame and regret at being an Indian woman surface in my soul once again.

Sometimes it's just easier to put all these things aside and pretend they never happened. It's easy to say, "That was a long time ago and has nothing to do with me." It's so much easier to forget who you are when faced with these memories. I know they may not be my direct memories,

but somewhere in my soul a distant ancestor cries. Pain was so real for this person. That person could have been me. Because I am my father's child, I am the child of an Indian man and woman. I look like the mother that lost her child at Sand Creek. My father looks like the Chief who was betrayed at the treaty table. My mother was the alcoholic woman in agony. I am all of these things because this is the blood I carry in my veins. I am a reproduction of generations past.

My mother says, "We are not responsible for what happened to us, but we are responsible for making ourselves well." I carry this saying with me now. I am responsible for making myself well, just as my mother before me was responsible for moving through, and clearing herself of the alcoholic pain and agony that she lived. Through her triumph and recovery over her addiction, she can now lead many more people down the road to recovery. So when I find myself in times of shame over my identity, I remember that the things that happened to my people were not their fault. Yet now I must do what I can to heal the pain.

Someday, my children will not feel the pain that I feel. That pain will be replaced with dignity—dignity restored to my people by Creator Himself. Dignity as we walk in the fullness of who God made us to be.

Yesterday I forgot who I was. Today I grasp onto who I am: *I am Indian, I am whole.*

Strengthening Fatherhood

Sobriety, fatherhood, and a men's circle are part of this Native man's commitment to single parenting. Native men can support each other as dads by taking the Wellbriety journey.

I grew up in a school district that bordered the reservation, and probably 90% of the teachers were non Native. There was no Native American curriculum in our school. We Indians were constantly expelled. We were constantly being told that we were no good, that we lived in poverty, that we ate *commods* or couldn't afford to go to the grocery store, or the ones who went to the grocery store were all on food stamps. When I turned 18 years old I believed everything all these people were telling me. They told me I was going to be nothing but a drunken Indian. My white counterparts were all going to college, but there were no Indians going to college because the guidance counselors wouldn't encourage that. They said, "Why spend time on you Indians because you're not going to school anyway, that's not part of who you are, that's not important to you." When I turned 18, I felt that--I was ashamed of who I was.

When I went into the Navy I started drinking really hard. I was your typical sailor. Sailors were expected to be drunken in every port. As an Indian, I had every right to be the drink-till-you-can't-even-walk-back-to-the-ship kind of person. People said, "Aren't you ashamed of yourself?" I was playing a role that was already foreseen for me. I said, "I am who I am. I'm a drunken Indian sailor, that's my life. Who am I to change my life? It's already been presented to me. All I got to do is stay alive and live out that life." A lot of men grow up that way, being ashamed of being

Indian men because there are no positive role models out there to tell us who we are.

Our community prepared to do a memorial feast on a national prayer day recently. Someone gave me tobacco to go talk to a medicine man and ask him to come so we could do a prayer. When I talked to the Elder he said, "I'll take this tobacco from you, but I want you to take some more tobacco and go to the other Eagle Staff carriers in the community, to those veterans." I learned something there. In Indian country we honor our veterans all the time. As a veteran, I love carrying the flag during powwow. It makes me feel good. But the Elder told me that the veterans have a daily role in our communities. Veterans--men and women--all have a daily role, but no one is telling them that, and no one is asking for their roles to be achieved.

The Elder told me that when something traumatic happens in our communities it's not the domestic abuse personnel, or the AODA (Alcohol or Drug Addiction) program people, or the Tribal Chairman who should run there and fight the crisis. The medicine man told me that those aren't the people who we should be going to. It's the people with those Eagle Staffs, it's those people we honor at the powwows. Those are their rightful roles. Those men in the community who are fathers--that is their role.

I think its time we get back into some of those traditional roles and allow our veterans to have a more functional role in our communities. We honor them every time we do a powwow, we honor our flags and we honor our Eagle Staffs, but the only time these men and women ever come out in the community is when we honor them. They serve a bigger purpose than just being honored all the time. They are there for the healing of our communities. But these community programs have to let that happen.

Strengthening Fatherhood

Family violence programs are pretty powerful on our reservation. What they say is usually what the Tribal Council follows. If they proclaim that women are the victim and men are the perpetrators, and that's the way it's going to be forever and ever and ever, then that's the way it's going to be. As a counselor, and as an Indian man, and as a Tribal member in our community, I see many Indian men come into my office who are victims themselves. When they and their mates start drinking they become emotional and mental victims when they get into an altercation. We've given women who are alcohol and drug users power, and they can use it in a dysfunctional way. The woman will say, because she has power, "...get out of the house." They kick their men out of the house because the man can't kick them out of the house in our society. In our society the house belongs to the woman--and I agree to that. But some women who are still using, use that tool, and soon we have wandering men in our community, not welcome back in their own home--because if they approach their own home they are going to be thrown in jail.

When I got kicked out of the house I didn't feel very good--I was ashamed. Looking back on it from my sobriety now, I was abused. She abused both of us because both of us kept that house. When we got in a disagreement, I was the one who got kicked out. I had to wander around. My wife and I didn't have the tools to resolve that conflict. I see a lot of our men like that. We need to give men back their roles.

When I got sober, I went to a Medicine Man and he told me that all Anishinabe had pipes. Not the big community pipes, but the family pipe. He brought me to Pipestone Creek and I quarried out a piece of pipestone and made a pipe. He told me it was for me and my family, and not to bring it out into community functions. He said, "If you want a well family, use some of those tools." We smudge down in our house, and

other things like that. We use some of these teachings in our men's group back home to create our philosophy.

I was introduced to the *Seven Philosophies For a Native American Man* in 1996 out at Badger Flats when White Bison held the Gathering of Native American Men. I had met someone from White Bison about six months prior to that who said, "I hope that you can come out for the Gathering." I went back home after meeting with him and told my rez group that there was a great Native American Men's Gathering coming up near Colorado Springs at the end of May. I said, "Would you guys like to go?"

They said, "Yeah, we'd like to go, but how are we going to get there?"

I said, "We have no budget money to go, but if we want to go, I think we could make it there." We all made a compact at that time to do what we had to do to get there. We had to fund-raise money to get there. But as we know, confidentiality is a big, big thing. My boss in the community program where I work, who is a non-Native, asked me how we can do fund raising but keep the guy's confidentiality intact? That was a good question that I had to deal with.

At our men's group, we talked about getting to the Men's Gathering by fund raising, and the issue of our confidentiality that it brought up. We always held our circles in rooms with the blinds drawn to keep our confidentially because our youth were coming in on the same nights to use the gym. I said, "Everybody knows when we drink, but how come we have to hide behind blinds and confidentiality when we are trying to get sober?" So we talked about it and agreed not to close the blinds, but to go out in the community to fund raise and tell the community who we are.

We went into the community and said we were the Bad River Men's Support Group and that we were fund raising to go to the Men's Gathering. We had great support from the Elders, we had great support from all the local stores, and we made it to Colorado for the Men's Gathering. We had a great time and we learned a lot of stuff. All the guys in our group who went to the Gathering were fathers. As a counselor, I didn't have any training about how to talk to fathers about fatherhood, let alone talking about our culture. I had to learn from them what ceremonies were important to men. I know now from working in two different reservations that men have a pretty good idea of what they want and what they need. We need to ask them what their needs are.

We have a lot of programs that are centered around women, especially the family violence programs. They are centered around the woman as a victim and they center around the man as a perpetrator. I was a perpetrator.

I sobered up about three weeks before the white buffalo calf was born in Janesville, Wisconsin in August, 1994. I feel so connected to that because I needed to be sober to understand the significance of the white buffalo calf. Before I sobered up, my wife and I kept saying that alcohol was the problem in our relationship. It was always alcohol that she and I could both blame. When I went into treatment for the sixth time in my life, my wife told me that if I couldn't stop drinking it would be best for me to get out of my kid's life because I was a danger to them when I was drinking. For the first time in my life, I believed that I was a danger to somebody else.

I've done many things to myself, even attempted suicide, but since the day my wife said that to me I haven't had a drink.

Today, I have good friends and I'm a single parent. After getting sober we found out that our problems were not just centered around alcohol. The alcohol was gone but we still got into fights. We learned how to fight better, we learned about time outs and other things like that, but that didn't solve our problems. I went from a married life to being a single person living all by myself. But now I have my children who live with me. I single parent my children, along with other men around me who are doing that also. It's a good feeling.

I was scared in the beginning. Could I do this? Could I get up in the morning, get them on the bus to school, help them with their homework-- but I'm doing it and it feels good. I know that it's my role as a father. It surprised me that their mom would give up the children to me now that we are separated. The children helped make the choice. They said, "I want to go live with you, dad."

These are some of the things I feel about sobriety, being an Indian man, and fatherhood.

Two Spirited

"You, my gifted child, will learn to see both sides of the spirit," his great grandmother said. Her words proved to be true, but he still had to find his own sobriety and freedom from drugs before life became good.

My story is a simple one. I was born in Kentucky in 1948. My family were farmers who relocated into the city life. It wasn't until forty-five years later that I learned just how difficult a move that was for my parents.

My great-grandfather was Appalachian Cherokee. He won my great-grandmother in a poker game while fur trapping in Canada. That's right. He won her in a card game. She was French Canadian Blackfoot. He brought her back to Kentucky and built a cabin for her where she lived until she died. I remember when I was as young as five years old that I was the ONLY child that she permitted in her cabin. I had many cousins, sisters, and kin, but I was the only one she took under her care. For many years I never understood this. During the summer, I was permitted to stay with her and help her with the farm chores. Many, many nights she would tell me stories of her life. Many I didn't understand, but they always made me feel good. I was her "Special Child!" "A Special Gift from the Creator!" "You, my gifted child, will learn to see both sides of the spirit," she said. "You are Two Spirited and gifted!"

Grandmother taught me how to predict the weather. "Child, if the animals build their nest close to the water line it will be a long, hot, dry summer. If you see them building high on the hill, or in the tops of the trees, it will be a wet and flooded spring. Watch and mimic how everything lives around you and you will be able to live comfortably!" she said.

Being educated in a Roman Catholic School and raised as Irish Catholic caused me many problems early in my life. The conflict of my great-grandmother's spirituality with the upbringing of a Catholic marked me as a heathen. Instead of going to study hall, I preferred reading the Bible while sitting in a tree. I felt closer to the Creator being held in the arms of a tree than in the man-made cathedral. All of the gold, stained glass, ritual, and statues scared me. They were man's creation. Not creations of the Creator.

By the time I reached the age of seven I was no longer permitted to visit great-grandma. The last time I saw her she cried as she held me and said, "So it begins my child, life for you will not be an easy road. Many will hate you because of the gifts the Creator has given you. Never lose your trust in what you know your heart is feeling." I never saw her again. I was never even told, or permitted to attend her funeral. I felt she had abandoned me and I never knew why. It wasn't until twenty or so years later that I found the truth. I'm getting ahead of the story here so let me back up.

My father was a loving man but a nasty alcoholic. All of my youth I can remember my mother hiding my older sister and me in closets, behind furniture, or in a neighbor's house because whenever dad was late for dinner, he was drinking. When he drank he became violent. My sister

and I would try to sing loud enough to cover his yelling, but not loud enough for him to find us.

In our neighborhood, all of the men worked for a brewery and came home drunk almost everyday. As children, we would make bets after school to see whose mother would be the first being chased down the street by her husband. Seeing women being chased with guns, or a knife, 2 x 4's, pipes, was nothing shocking. It was an everyday event in our lives.

This is why I could not understand "religion." To pray Sunday and ask for forgiveness, promising the Creator to change, and then repeat the same behavior within hours of returning from church was totally unacceptable. Why could the church not see the violence, fear, and damage to the family all of this was producing? Why couldn't the church God stop this? Was the church only interested in the 10% of my family's income? Were they afraid that if they said, or did something, they would lose this income? Why did grownups preach one thing but yet practice another?????

When I was ten, my mother gave birth to a baby girl. At the age of twelve my mother gave birth to another baby girl. These two girls became the daughters that I would never have. I was their older brother. I was their protector. Or at least I tried. When dad would come home drunk I did everything I could to keep them from hearing dad accuse mom that "those two little bitches were not his children!" I tried to hide them from his anger and violence. My mother, older sister, and I would take turns getting dad to aim his anger and violence at one of us so he would forget the little ones. Most of the time it worked, but not always.

As soon as my older sister graduated high school she married and left home. That left me to care for the little ones. I had to grow up fast. When I was fourteen, I came home from school to find that my mother and little sisters were gone. Vanished. It was as if they never existed.

Did they leave on purpose or were they murdered? It could happen that way. I spent many nights as a young boy trying to think of ways that I could kill my father so he would leave the family alone. I can't remember how many times he told me I was a mistake, so lazy I stank, that I had no right to breathe the air, that I was nothing and would always be nothing, so what did I have to lose?

The night my mother and sisters disappeared I lived in great fear. I knew that when dad got home, and if he didn't know what happened, I was in for the beating of my life. He would beat their location out of me. It didn't matter that I had no idea where they had gone. I just wish they had taken me with them. When dad got home that night it was late. I climbed out of my bedroom window and crawled onto the roof where I spent the night. Naked and cold, I hid in the darkness on a rooftop. I could hear him screaming our names. Sometimes I could hear him crying and asking for forgiveness. But I knew not to trust him. I knew that if I went inside I may not make it out alive.

My mother and sisters were well and in hiding. My mother's family was hiding them. She could not take on the responsibility of taking me with her. The two little ones were all she could handle. I was fourteen, a young man that she hoped would understand. I did understand when I became an adult, but at the age of fourteen I felt abandoned by her and all of the family. I was left to live with the biggest fear of my life, my poor alcoholic father. Alcohol had cost him his marriage, his daughters, and his only son. I promised myself that I would NEVER become the man my father was. Little did I know what was in store for me...

The next three years are a blur. I really don't remember much. I did manage to complete high school. After I graduated, I joined the U.S. Navy. By this time I knew I was Gay.

I didn't seek out men for sexual pleasure. I sought men for revenge. After sex I would threaten to scream and blackmail them for cash. I had found a way to see fear in the eyes of these men, the same fear I had felt growing up. I began this behavior at the ripe old age of nine and continued until after high school. Once in the military I met a new friend, a young man three years older than me but with the same type of childhood. We both agreed that to be friends we would never permit each other to drink--and we never did. He introduced me to the world of drugs instead. By the time I left the military I was a major drug user. I could hold my head up high with false pride that I still did not drink. I did steal from my family and friends to pay for my drug addiction, but I WAS NOT AN ALCOHOLIC! Funny how we can twist truth to fit our needs.

By the time I got home from the military my father was sober. He did everything he could to get me to understand he was not the same man as I remembered growing up. God bless him--he was trying! But by this time my only desire was drugs. I didn't care what he had to say or what his excuses were. In my mind I was clean and sober and that made me better than him, so why should I listen? There was nothing he could do to get me to forgive him. Everything wrong with my life was HIS fault. I had found the perfect blame for my behavior. My dear old dad!

My mom tried to get me to listen to dad. She felt that it was important for me to have a role model and he had gotten sober--hadn't he? I was still angry with her for abandoning me. I was self-absorbed in my own world of addiction and WOULD NOT LISTEN to anybody.

Within a year, I left my home state and moved to California. I was looking for a world that would accept me, and my lifestyle as a gay man.

What a mistake. I didn't look for anything except more drugs. I did meet a fine woman and we lived together for seven years. During this time I started drinking along with my drugs. Nobody out there knew my promise or family, so what difference did it make? In the seventh year of our relationship, under the influence of drugs and alcohol, I struck her. Even in my stupor I could not believe that I had hit someone I said I loved.

All the nightmares came rushing back--the fears, lies, abandonment and mistrust. I had done the one thing I swore that I would never do. I had hit someone I said I loved. She left me. It hurt, but I cannot blame her. Why would she want to go through what my mother, as well as her mother and sisters had endured for so many years? I now turned my attention away from women for good. I was stupid enough to believe that living in the gay world none of this would matter. My life would be one big party full of happiness, living with those of my own kind. How close that delusion became a reality.

Shortly after losing the woman in my life I met a man. A man that began making me stand up to my realities. A man that insisted that if we were going to start a friendship/relationship there would be no room for alcohol or drugs. A man who loved me enough to support me every step of the way. A man who had been where I was heading. And for the first time in my life, someone who saw talents and abilities in me that no one ever had. He was a man who told me that I was good. I had a right to be here. I had the right to have goals and ambitions. He was a man willing to help me discover in myself everything he saw. This was a man whose friendship I would always cherish. This was NOT a sexual relationship but a relationship of one man that had been there, trying to help another man not to go where he had gone. A sponsor!

I spent two sober and clean years with this man. One night it all came crashing down. He was killed while riding in a taxi on his way to the airport to fly home. I crashed, blamed the Creator, my father, my family, and convinced myself that I didn't deserve any type of a successful life. I dove head first into the bottle and drugs. I managed to lose everything including my self-esteem and self worth.

I moved to San Francisco and learned the so-called pleasures of putting a needle in my vein. I cared for no one and nothing. I was dangerous to be around. I had an awful lot of anger, and no one, including me, ever knew when it would explode. When it did, I would be in a full, violent, anger blackout. I had no control over what I would do, or to whom I would do it, and could not remember a thing. Life was NOT worth living! Death would be a great welcome at that time but I didn't even have the courage to face death.

Somehow I managed to survive two years in San Francisco and then moved on up to the northwest part of California. The salmon rivers, redwood forest, and a coastline with crashing waves and cliffs was a primitive-feeling place that brought out a primitive-feeling state of mind for me. It called to my heart. I couldn't understand how or why, but I knew it was calling to something very deep inside of me.

A friend invited me to his new home in Grass Valley, Nevada City, California. I had never been in that part of northern California near the Sierra Nevada mountains and decided to go. It was very dark and late when we arrived and I felt very uncomfortable. My friend noticed it and asked me what was wrong. I could not explain it. I tossed and turned all night, couldn't sleep, and was terrified to walk out the door. It was a hellish night with no reason for the fear. The next morning when I awoke, he told me it had snowed and wanted to take me outside to see the view.

Two Spirited

I couldn't tell you what the view was. As soon as we walked out of the building, and within ten feet of being outside, all I saw was my own blood. I fell to my knees, screaming, having been shot in the chest. Not by gunfire but by an arrow. I felt my life draining out of me, saw my own blood coloring the snow crimson red, and passed out. Of course when I came to I was back in my friend's house and there was nothing at all wrong with me. My friend thought I had gone totally crazy, screaming and carrying on like that. I scared him half to death, the first of many past-life visions I would experience in the coming future.

I explained the whole experience to my friend. I was waiting for him to either start laughing or throw me out of his house. Instead, he smiled a very old smile and said it was time for me to return to my home state and discover my history. Yes, I do believe I had died in the same spot in his yard, but during a war fought many generations ago. Needless to say, I returned home to Kentucky, not knowing why and afraid to find the answer.

Life was standard. Dad was sober, Mom was remarried, all my sisters were married and raising families of their own. I was still drinking and weekend drugging, but this was a major cut down from what I had been doing. I was actually holding down a job, paying rent, and making my own car payments. I met my current partner and life was OK.

As the years went by, both of us gave up alcohol altogether. He supported me in giving up drugs as well. For the first time in years, I felt as if I really did have a future and many years went by smoothly. During that time my father died, but we had talked and all was explained, examined, and understood to the best of my ability. It still took several years after his death for this to happen, but all was finally forgiven.

By this time I was working in the field of HIV/AIDS. Many, many deaths had crossed my path and many more were to come. The number of people that came to me because they were told I could assist and understand any and all of their problems, confused me. I had compassion that felt old and comfortable to them. They all seemed to be more at ease when they left after spending time with me. Where was this coming from?? What should I do with it? Why me?

In 1995, a good friend of mine convinced me to participate in his support group called "The Spirit and The Flesh!" It was a ten-week support group for gay and bi-sexual men. It was during this time that I really started studying Native American history, ritual, and spirituality.

At the same time, my mother had a really bad year. She flat-lined three times and each time they were able to bring her back. During that year, she and I had many talks and I keep her informed about the excitement of studying the Native American ways. She finally told me of my true Native American heritage during one of these conversations. It was at this same time that I discovered all the missing information about my great-grandmother.

The family was afraid of the things she said about the Native ways and me. They were trying very hard to fit into the new lifestyle in northern Kentucky. In the mid to late forties in northern Kentucky, you were white Irish, Negro, or a Red Skin. The least accepted by society was being a Red Skin. That was the main reason that the family did not tell me of my heritage. They were afraid of what would happen to us in the community we were now living.

By working with my doctor friend in his support group, I realized the importance of maintaining my sobriety from both alcohol and drugs. During this time I studied many different religions, but the Native American Spirituality was the only one that filled me with the true feeling of being connected to the Great Spirit. Learning to re-connect with Mother Nature and the Creator put me on the path to health and healing for the community. Not just the gay community, but also all of the communities that were dealing with HIV/AIDS, death and dying, or simply having someone sit and listen. I have been shunned by many "true" Natives because I was not raised on a "Rez" or I look too white to be a true Native. It used to trouble me greatly inside. I was trying my best to live by the ways I was learning. I simply tried to remember all of the things that were told to me by my great-grandmother. She comes to me in many dreams now and was the very first to visit me in a vision.

I can only offer my experience, stories, and trust to those who ask for my help. I no longer worry about whether or not I am accepted by anyone. As long as the Creator is happy with what I am doing then I can be doing no wrong.

Being clean and sober is the greatest gift I can give back to the Creator. It has been a long journey and there is a longer path to follow, but I have learned not to question the reasons of what I do. I thank the Creator that I am still alive and have been given the gift of helping others. If my story can save just one individual from the life I have led, then I feel that I have repaid my debt to society.

The Medicine Gave Him Back His Life

This man found the Native American Church when he most needed it. He found the culture and sobriety in a tipi in Montana. Now he participates on a regular basis to stay in harmony and live a good life.

I was three days old when my grandpa gave me my Indian name *O-Kee-Ja-Tay*, which translates back into English as Westfork, the name of the creek where my family and two or three other families were camped. This was up by Four Buttes, Montana, which is very close to the Canadian line. This act then established my identity from then on.

My story is typical of many Indians who were raised without their culture and language. Instead, I was brought up to be ashamed of myself as an Indian person. I did not participate in any Indian ceremonies until I was thirty-four years old. This happened in 1980 when I attended my first Native American Church ceremony. When I look back I realize the Native American Church saved my life and I will always be thankful to the Native American Church and the holy Medicine, peyote.

I grew up in a one-room log house and this is where I started witnessing violence and domestic abuse. I grew up watching my dad beat my mother on a regular basis. Every so often us children got the beats. After a while you accept this as normal and you can't wait to get married and have kids and do the same. This behavior resulted in several divorces for me. I also have four children from these marriages and I feel sad sometimes that I never took part in their raising up. That opportunity was

taken away because of my dysfunctional behavior, caused by my use of alcohol and loss of our culture.

When I start to feel self-pity I do a personal inventory. And then I begin to accept the things I cannot change and ask the Great Spirit to give me the courage to change the things I can. I realize then what I must do to be happy. One of them is to stay sober. So I think this is why I continue to say that part of my recovery process was to be re-introduced to our traditional ceremonies and our history--and I mean to our *true* history of who we are as aboriginals or Indians.

Many times we make the mistake of identifying ourselves as how the Wasicus (whites) portray us to be. I am happy with myself as an Indian and I thank the Great Spirit for making me an Indian person. I was introduced to the beauty of our people through the Native American Church and the wonderful sacrament we use in our ceremony, which is called peyote. We like to call it "Medicine."

As Indian people, we all have our stories about suffering from racial prejudice and discrimination just because the Creator made us Indians. I even became a "red apple" in order to be accepted. But it did not matter because I was still Indian and brown. I wasn't happy being a red apple anyway because I was out of harmony with myself, and everything around me. I realize now I was very weak without my spirituality and our cultural values. This allowed me to be pushed around and taken advantage of. Now I am not afraid to stand up for my rights as a Native American and a human being. There are discrimination laws that we can use to protect ourselves. Before, I didn't care how I was treated as long as I had my bottle. But now it is different and I care about myself.

I was raised up to the idea that cowboys don't cry. I was in a reformatory when I was young. When you cry in those places, it's a sign of weakness. So I learned not to cry. I learned to become a cold-hearted man. Without my spirituality and our cultural values I was very weak, doing things I

really didn't want to do. Even though my spirit was telling me certain things were wrong, I did them anyway. The Native American Church helped me to find spirituality and helped me to find harmony within myself. The Native American Church performed a miracle on me when the Medicine turned my life around. I was one of those persons that society had given up on. The Native American Church did for me what state and federal reformatories failed to do. Those institutions made me worse because my major crime was only truancy and running away. If I got anything out of those places it was criminal thinking. No one ever asked me about my truancy and running away from home. I guess they took it for granted that the system was always right because it is run by adults and children are always wrong.

My spirituality was knocked out of harmony by so-called do-gooders. They made it too strict for me. I said the heck with it and turned away from my Christian up-bringing. My home life went from one extreme to the other. One day it was a strict God-fearing home, and the next it was drunkenness. The balance of good and bad was never there--it was like riding on a teeter-totter. When I hit the streets at 21 yeas old I didn't care about anybody. I couldn't. If I felt any caring it seemed I became weak. My whole value system was all distorted. It was very easy for me to hurt people, both intentionally and unintentionally.

I started to sober up in 1980 through the Native American Church--something the treatment centers couldn't do for me. The treatment centers kicked me out until I felt I had nowhere to turn but suicide. I didn't really want to go that way because I wanted to live. There I was in April of 1980 wondering how to get out of that life. I really didn't want to be myself, an Indian, because I was brought up to be ashamed of being an Indian. Back in those days it wasn't cool being an Indian. Everybody was

trying to be a red apple, and the powwows were the only Indian things going on.

By that time I tried just about everything I could get my hands on to be happy, but nothing worked. The only thing I never tried was to be me. I decided that's what I wanted to do. I know the Creator knew what I was thinking because he guided me into a tipi where a Native American Church ceremony was to take place. That's where I found myself and what I was looking for.

Twenty-one years ago I was contemplating suicide because I wanted out of the dysfunctional and alcoholic way of life that I was living. I was guided to a Native American Church ceremony at Wolf Point. I was invited and I participated. When I ate the Medicine, the first thing I realized was that I had come home. I regained my identity that night. I learned that the Great Spirit is real so I became a believer in the Great Spirit. I discovered love and compassion in that meeting. I saw real tears and that people loved and cared for one another in a good way. They didn't have to be drunk to be hugging each other. It was a beautiful experience and it helped me to sober up. The medicine helped me to break down my denial barriers.

I ate a lot of Medicine that night, and through the Medicine realized that God was real. I became a believer that night. I found the peace and happiness that I was searching for. I breathed a sigh of relief because I had found my way home. Now I know the way home, so when I make mistakes I know where to find forgiveness. I now understand what they mean when they say God is my sanctuary.

When I went into the Native American church 21 years ago I started caring for people again. I was able to cry and express my emotions, to be able to talk to God about all the things that were going on inside me. I asked him to forgive me for all the things I had done wrong. Man, it was a beautiful experience!

The Medicine Gave Him Back His Life

When I get out of balance I go to a Native American Church ceremony, or I sponsor one on my own to get back into harmony. The Native American Church is where I find refuge when I am seeking peace, happiness, safety and a place where you have the feeling that everything is going to be alright.

The Medicine has been with me every step of the way since 1980 while I was getting my life back in order. I went through a couple of divorces in the process of getting my life straight. I made some bad choices because I wasn't quite ready to give up the old value system I used when it comes to women. I had to get raked over the coals before I was willing to pay attention to the Medicine.

I lost my dad, my baby brother, my sister, and my beautiful wife and baby daughter, who died of childbirth complications, somewhere along the way. I was left behind with our 2 1/2 year old daughter when my wife passed away. In 1988 I married a beautiful Northern Cheyenne lady and we now have three boys and two girls in our family.

Some might say Native American culture is dead, but it's not dead. It's not dead because everything is still there. Mother Nature is still there. Mother nature and the natural laws have never changed. The animals that we learn from for the most part are still there. The ways in which our people have learned are still there. The sun still rises in the east and sets in the west. The moon, our grandmother, still comes up at a certain time. The four directions are still there. Everything is still there. It's just been that we are looking in the wrong place when it comes to our culture. It is still there yet...

The Medicine has been everything to me. I sponsor thank you ceremonies of the Native American Church whenever I can because I am so thankful for what the Medicine has done for me and my family. The Medicine has given me a real life and the balance and harmony I need to be happy. As long as I am in balance and harmony within myself that's all that matters, because I have to live with myself. If I can't help myself, how can I expect to help others? Every morning I do a personal inventory of myself and lay my weaknesses before God, asking for help and guidance.

My brothers and sisters, please remember this: the Wasicus may have taken the fat of the land and everything else that we hold to be dear to us, but above all things is your spirituality. If you are spiritually grounded you will make it anywhere. Once you become spiritually connected no one can ever take that away from you except yourself. You then realize the greatest enemy you have is you yourself and your spirituality will help you to conquer yourself. When you have conquered yourself you have conquered it all. Understand this my brothers and sisters and you will be happy.

Thank you my brothers and sisters for inspiring me to write this story. A-ho!

The Great Mystery Waited For Me

Sometimes it takes a really long time. Drinking and drugging, marriages, careers, and long dry drunks come and go. But if we do our part, and if we let it, the Great Mystery finds a way.

On my father's side, our family ancestry includes both Shawnee and Cherokee blood. In addition to my family's Native heritage I have inherited bloodlines of escaped African slaves and delinquent Scot Irish indentured servants who found their way deep into the Appalachian Mountains sometime before seventeen hundred. My dad was raised by his mixed-blood grandparents on a little mountain farm after his father left him and moved on to work in the city during the Great Depression of the 1930's.

I was not raised Indian. I was raised as a kid who didn't know what it meant to be poor even though we were often "broke." I grew up in a small mountain village in the midst of the Adirondack Mountains in northern New York. My father taught my brothers and me how to hunt and to fish and to see the Creator in the bark of trees and in the moss beds on granite boulders long before we learned to drive. We always had a freezer stocked with venison, rabbit, partridge, trout, and pike. Life was good. On my mother's side, I have inherited the blood of her Blackfoot ancestors who found their way north and east into Canada in the eighteen hundreds.

Of a family of five boys, two of my brothers and I were practicing alcoholics way before we were twenty years old and every one of us expected to live hard and die young. That didn't happen to any of us. The first time I drank I was thirteen years old. I drank my way through high school. Drinking was exactly what all of us expected to do, and we drank with the absolute intention of getting drunk. We drank as often as we could. We deserved to get drunk.

I won a scholarship to college my senior year. I had never expected to go to college but intended to enlist in the Navy as my father had. I won this scholarship, so I went to college. I was seventeen, and I was probably a bright kid. I might have done well in college, but I didn't. I chose to drink my way through instead. My grades were horrible.

At Easter time during one of my college years, another guy and I looked at our chances of pulling up our grades by studying through the holiday break. We decided it wasn't worth the effort. We took his Austin Healey Sprite to Daytona, Florida, and we rented a room on the beach. We drank every night and raced his Sprite up and down the beach at night. After a while, faced with the choice of paying for the room or buying beer, we opted for buying beer. We slept on the beach or in the car until it was time to go home. We both failed out of college that spring. Al, my guitar-playing buddy, joined the Air Force. I joined the Navy to stay away from Vietnam.

I was sent to Vietnam as a quartermaster on a River Patrol Boat (PBR) and served two terms in-country. I was there for the next twenty-seven months. I drank more there, and learned to do drugs, too, when I got off the squadron base. Getting drunk, and staying high and stoned to forget the terror of being there, let me get away from the jungle and gave me

heart and courage. It felt like victory, somehow. I think I left a lot of my spirit in the jungle. I didn't notice it at the time, but I've been looking for it ever since.

I finished my tour and I returned to college after my enlistment was up. I kept on drinking, but I had learned to drink in a way so that I could do what I had to do. I majored in secondary education and graduated on the President's list three years later.

In my senior year I got married to a white girl who was a harder drinker than I was. We fought and drank our way through that last year of college. That spring both of us were certified as teachers, and we decided to go to Alaska. The Bureau of Indian Affairs hired us straight out of college and we ended up in the Arctic that September. I was working with Inuit kids not much younger than I was. We spent two years teaching those kids. During those two years there were sixteen violent deaths in the village we lived and taught in. It was a town of less than two thousand people, both Inuit and white. Most of the deaths were as a byproduct of drinking, depression, and the violence that accompanied it.

After two years in the bush, two years of drinking and dancing, hunting, and taking long walks on frozen beaches, we returned to the lower forty-eight. I was offered a grant to go to divinity school from my father's church. He was an Elder there. I decided not to go back to Alaska.

I went to graduate school for the next three years without a basis in any spiritual system. This might have been more an attempt at finding a geographical cure than any quest for meaning. I didn't find meaning in divinity school. I drank my way through. Somehow I did incredibly well, academically. I graduated summa cum laude and was ordained as a clergyman in the mainline Christian church that had paid my way through school. I didn't have any feelings toward religion or any inclination toward a spiritual life. My courage and meaning still came from a bottle, and from building up an exterior that looked good from the

outside but had nothing to do with me on the inside. I worked in the gospel ministry for the next few years. My drinking progressed steadily, and I ran from church to church never finding any spiritual center. I left my congregations behind me when things got tough, and was a failure in the ministry. I didn't understand that. I'd been such a success at graduate school. Now my skills for getting by were falling apart, and I just never got the point.

In desperation I re-enlisted in the Navy. At a point where most people were raising kids, paying for two cars and a garage to park them in, and thinking about a retirement plan, I was looking for the easy way out. The Navy was the place I found it. I drank my way through five more years of Navy life. I trained for several months as a Medical Corpsman and was assigned to the Second Marine Division. I had married again and was the father of a son. My second wife was a Navy nurse and a party girl. We brawled and partied our way across several Navy bases.

My wife resigned her commission, and we moved home again to the mountains. We kept on drinking and partying, and we had another baby, a daughter. My daughter and my son were the center of my life, or as close as I could get to a center. I picked up a job as a teacher in the state prison system, and my wife worked as a nurse for the state. I worked all day and we drank ourselves into bed every night. Soon a second daughter was born.

One day, while my wife was still on maternity leave, I came home from pulling a late shift at the prison I was teaching in. When I got in, my wife was sleeping off a drunk and one of her girl friends was cleaning up after her. This wasn't anything I hadn't seen before, except for one thing. A

neighbor had called the local police to report our three year old daughter had been found wandering several streets away. She was in diapers, and it was April. April is cold in the mountains, and snow isn't unusual then. The state troopers had been called, and along with county social workers the police had taken the kids away. I didn't find where for the next three days.

Those three days were the bottom I had been searching for since I picked up that soda can laced with my father's "Sneaky Pete" when I was thirteen. I was thirty-seven. I hated my life. I wandered from room to room looking for the kids and seeing their shadows. I glared at their mother, and she glared at me. I never drank again.

I spent the next ten years doing a long, hard "dry drunk." I went to Alcoholics Anonymous meetings because I was ordered to. I didn't have a drinking problem. I wasn't one of these drunks. I had stopped drinking. Wasn't that obvious to these guys ? I didn't belong there. It took me three years to identify myself as an alcoholic during a meeting, I was filled with anger. That anger was all I knew about. It burned inside of me. No. That's wrong. I *was* the anger. All of me was anger. It was like being a boiling, black lake of anger--black, viscous anger. My skin was the only thing that kept the anger in, though the anger erupted just as soon as I let down the guard.

Those were a hard ten years and I didn't understand why. I wasn't drinking. I was going to meetings. I was making a living. I had two jobs, sometimes three. I was busy as a leader in my kids' Four H group. I was on the PTA. I was one of the good guys. Where was the pay-off? Where was the serenity people talked about at the meetings? I was happier

when I was drunk. I had never felt this miserable in my life, and I still didn't get the point. I did counseling. Family counseling. Alcohol counseling. Job counseling. Psychotherapy. None of it worked. When it was all over, life was too heavy to carry.

Then one night I was at an AA meeting. I didn't believe in anything AA had to offer. I never had a sponsor, didn't do the Steps, and believed people who said they did the Steps were lying. But I kept on going to meetings every now and then, kind of like a good luck thing. I stared ahead during the prayers that opened and closed the meetings. I listened, and laughed, and drank coffee. I never ventured information about myself, and when I was asked to speak I trotted out the same old war stories, but I didn't have a clue about being sober. I thought I was sober. I was simply a poor, miserable drunk who had stopped drinking, and that was all there was to it.

But that one night, something grabbed onto me and didn't let go. My marriage had died years before but my children's mother and I were still living together. Now, I realize, it was because I didn't have enough courage to do anything else. That night, and I'll never forget it, I walked up to a guy I had known for a long time. I knew him when both he and I were still using. He had started coming to meetings a couple of years after I had. I don't know why I asked this guy to be my sponsor, but I did. He was one of the guys I privately believed were lying when they talked about "doing the Steps." I asked him to be my sponsor anyway, and he took me on. That was the most humbling thing I had ever done, as well as the first free thing I had ever asked for from anyone.

I took on doing the Twelve Steps like a dog with a new bone. I chewed on them and didn't let go. Getting sober ate me up. I worked through the Steps. Looking back eight years up the road I chose that night, I know I was attacking the Steps intellectually. It took me a lot longer to ask the Steps into my heart. A couple of months later I did my Fourth Step. I did it rigorously. I did it honestly, and when it came time to do my Fifth Step, I was finally, for the first time, open to spiritual growth. The spiritual side of the program became real to me and I confessed my arrogance, my anger, my resentment, and my fears. My sponsor sat there and he listened. He didn't say a word.

Soon, my sponsor and I progressed through the rest of the Twelve Steps. I don't suppose I did any of them as completely as I might have. But for a guy who was used to never being honest with either himself or with anyone else, those Steps changed my life. I had not taken the easy way. I met my Higher Power in those Steps.

I have reworked most of the Steps almost every day, one way or another, since then. I have done ninety meetings in ninety days more than once. I've gone to so many meetings I've lost count. I've cried at anniversaries, my own and others'. I've laughed, too, and my laughing has been real. I've made amends. I've embarrassed myself at meetings, and I've come back to those same meetings and made coffee.

When my kids were little, one of their elementary teachers had asked me to come into school to talk about the "Three Sisters"--corn, squash, and beans--and their place in the Indian culture. Since I was the only Indian parent she had, and since I operated my own landscaping service, she must have figured I knew about those Three Sisters. I didn't know who they were, but I found out enough about them to make it through the

class by the time the day arrived to tell their story. I was called back to the school many times after that first story, and I became a sort of a storyteller without planning on being one.

At first I had self-consciously repeated the old stories, telling the kids as much as I knew about how and why those stories came to be. I guess part of me wanted my kids to be proud of being Indian. I had been raised to be embarrassed of being Red, and most of my family had always tried to "pass" for being as white as they could be, except my grandfather. But all the stories were way back in the old days.

After I began on this search for sobriety, I realized the stories were much more than a dead reminder of a dead Indian past. As I told the stories they started to come to life in my telling, and after a time they started to live in my heart. Then, I found myself seeking out the Elders and asking questions I could have asked long before but hadn't.

I found a mentor, a Mohawk artist. He guided me through writing a textbook about the old ways. The book was written at a beginner readers' level. That should have been easy for me to do, but it wasn't. My Mohawk teacher edited and commented on the text and sent me to other Elders who took time to teach me something of those ways I was trying to write about. Finally, when the book was written, it was cleared and used as an ancillary text in the prison system I was teaching in. By then, I knew the point had never been about writing a book. The point was about learning to be humble enough to allow others to teach me what they had learned about the Red Road and about being Indian today.

I had met the Great Mystery in the process. That was the same spiritual force I had discovered was my Higher Power while I was attacking the AA Twelve Steps with such passion. I began feeling the Circle's place in my life, and almost as if I had been shocked with live electricity, I realized I was part of that Circle. I wasn't telling school kids about old history that had passed a hundred or even a couple of hundred years ago. I wasn't

telling funny stories any more. I wasn't even telling stories so my kids could be proud of being Indian.

The stories began to live in my heart and gave me choices about the way I was living. Those choices were way different than the choices I had made most of the rest of my life. I learned to make choices based on reasons, which every day brought me closer to the Circle and the Great Mystery, and farther away from slipping through life the easiest way I could. The contradiction in all of this is that living within a spiritual framework is so much easier than trying to make sense out of the world the way I had for most of my life. Every day I continue to be shocked that life is so good. I had always thought life was so hard.

Now, having said all that, it would seem best to fade away and say, "he lived happily ever after", but that's true only in fairy tales. My story doesn't go that way. My story is a contemporary Indian story.

My second marriage fell apart. The separation was long and messy, and it isn't legally over yet. The kids were taken to court and both their mother and I played them off against each other. I can say that at this point two of them are in recovery, and two are in school. Their grades are up, and they are on paths that are their own paths, paths they have chosen for themselves.

I became involved in a series of heart-breaking love affairs with several women. I know at this end of that process that both the women I tried to love, and myself, were looking for someone to love, and to hold against the night, and to feel safe with. It didn't happen that way. I had to do this the hard way. I had to learn to love myself before I could say, "I love you" to any other human being. Without caring about myself, that phrase is

nothing more than a prelude to looking for fast sex and another broken heart. I am learning to care about myself, and when I tell someone I love her, it's because I love her. I love her not for what she can do for me, or even for what maybe she'll do with me. I love her because she is my partner on this part of our path toward being healed. We are part of the Circle.

I left teaching in the prison system. I couldn't do it any more. I was a year short of retirement, but I was free. Since then my physical health has spiraled downhill, mainly as a souvenir of an old Marine training injury and the subsequent surgeries I passed through to correct it. I can no longer walk without a cane, and I use a wheelchair for greater distances than a block or two.

Now I'm living on my Federal disability checks, but mostly, I have a place to live because a woman I love, a Mohawk woman, loves me enough to believe in me, sometimes a lot more than I believe in myself. We rent a house on the west coast of Florida, and I write. We both write. I write the old stories I used to tell, but I have begun to write new stories too, stories that the Mystery gives to me in waking dreams. Some people call these waking dreams "inspiration." It comes out to the same thing. The stories are part of the Circle.

The new stories are going out on their own and doing the Circle's work. Other storytellers are asking me if they can share my stories with audiences I will never meet. An illustrator is painting pictures to grace one of my stories, and it will be published in time. These new stories tell about becoming human, and being a part of the Living Circle of Creation. Being a small part of sharing the Creator's truths through these stories is a wonderful gift to be part of.

The Great Mystery Waited For Me

This gift is a direct result of meeting my Higher Power in the Twelve Steps of AA eight years ago, after living ten years as a dry drunk, and another twenty-four years as an active alcoholic. Life is good, because the Mystery waited for me.

I have learned I don't need artificial courage any more. I don't need the artificial courage of being fortified with my dad's flask of "Sneaky Pete." I don't need the artificial courage of being on the dean's list, or president's list, or graduating summa cum laude. I don't need the artificial courage of being the Reverend Mister ... or the Right Reverend Doctor ... I don't need those titles to give me status or a name. I don't need the artificial courage of making enough bucks to buy all the toys the other big boys want. I don't need the artificial courage of being in love in order to love myself.

I am loved. My Creator loves me, and so, I can love others and not be afraid of what I'm not, or what I am, or about what's coming around the next corner. I can feel the Creator's breath on my cheek, and I can feel the heartbeat of the Creation beneath my heart.

Is life perfect? Not yet, but life is good. It's about progress. I didn't have enough courage to go to a Christmas party last Saturday night. The party was going to be crowded with some very successful people, liquor was on the menu, and I was too scared to go. I'm not too scared to say so, and that's progress.

And progress comes a step at a time as I follow this path I have been given to walk on this living Circle.

Wa'do

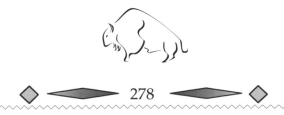

Appendices

SEVEN PHILOSOPHIES FOR NATIVE AMERICANS

6
To The
Creator

4
To The
Community

3
To The
Family

7
To Myself

1
To Women

2
To Children

5
To The Earth

A-1

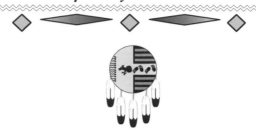

Appendix 1
Seven Philosophies For Native Americans

Our traditional Elders told us that there is a natural focus for our lives. It is not jobs, careers, cars, consumer goods, money, travel, success and the other things that are so strong today. But if we focus on our natural priorities, then any of these comforts might come. For us to be successful and get Wellbriety we have to be in harmony with seven aspects. Here are seven great aspects or philosophies that govern us as Native people.

1-WOMEN
The first of our natural values concerns our **women.**

One of our great Nations, the Cheyenne People say it this way. *"A nation is not defeated until the hearts of its women are on the ground."* But if this should happen, they say, *"Then it is done, no matter how brave its warriors or how strong its weapons."*

Violence against our women is not traditional. Sovereign women strengthen our sovereign nations. The woman has been given by natural laws the ability to reproduce life. The most sacred of all things is life. Therefore we should treat women with dignity and respect. Never was it our way to harm women mentally, emotionally, physically, or spiritually. Indian men were never abusers. We always treated our women with

respect and understanding. A woman's cycle of life is the baby, girl, woman and grandmother. Both men and women must respect this natural cycle because it is the basis for all life. We must also recognize and respect the female principle wherever we find it.

The Creator gave women the responsibility for bringing new life into the world. Life is sacred and new life is the basis for the survival of our nations and our people. In our traditional ways, the woman is the foundation of the family. As a man, I will work with her to create a home atmosphere of respect, security and harmony. If I have any feelings that might lead to abuse of women I will talk to the Creator and to counselors for guidance. Each woman is my own female relative. In a time of great diversity, the brilliance of a woman's mind and her many capabilities must be honored and encouraged to contribute to our communities in a good way.

2-CHILDREN

The second principle that governs us as Native people is our **children.**

As an eagle prepares the young to leave the nest with all the skills and knowledge it needs to participate in life, in the same manner so will I guide those younger than myself. I will use the culture to prepare them for life. The most important thing I can give to children is my time. I will spend time with them in order to listen to them and to learn from them. I will teach the children to pray as well as teaching them the importance of respect. We are the caretakers of the children for the Creator. They are His children, not ours.

In today's world it is easy for the children to go astray. I will work to provide positive alternatives for them. I will teach them the culture. I am

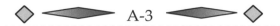

proud of our own Native language. I will learn it if I can and I will help the children to learn it. I will encourage education and I will encourage sports. I will encourage the children to talk with the Elders for guidance. I will heal and develop myself so that I may be a role model for children. I will not harm children through acts of domestic violence. I will make a commitment to children so they will have courage and find guidance through traditional ways.

3-FAMILY

The next principle that governs us as Native people is the **family.**

The Creator gave to us the family, which is the place where all teachings are handed down from the grandparent, to the parent, and to the child. The children's behavior is a mirror of the parent's behavior. Knowing this, I realize the importance of each Native man and woman to be responsible to the family in order to fulfill the need to build a strong and balanced family. By doing this I will break the cycle of hurt that affects our families today, and ensure the positive mental health of the children, even the children yet to be born.

I will dedicate my priorities to rebuilding my family.

I must never give up and be the cause of a single-parent family.

I am accountable to help restore the strength of my family. To do this I will nurture our family's spiritual, cultural and social health. I will demonstrate trust, respect, honor and discipline, and strive to be consistent in how I apply these values.

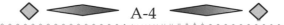

I will see that the grandparents and community Elders play a significant role in the education of our children.

I realize that the male and female together are fundamental to our family life. I will listen to my mate's council for our family's benefit, as well as for the benefit of my community and our Indian nation.

4-COMMUNITY

The fourth principle that guides us as Native people is the **community.**

The Indian community provides many things for us. The most important is the sense of belonging—that is, belonging "to the people" and having a place to go. Our Indian communities need to be restored to health so the future generation will be guaranteed a place to go for culture, language and Indian socializing. In the community, *the honor of one is the honor of all, and the pain of one is the pain of all.*

I will give back to my community by donating my time and talents when I am able. I will cultivate friendships with other Indian people for mutual support and strength.

I will consider the effects of our decisions on behalf of the next seven generations. In this way, our children and grandchildren will inherit healthy communities.

I will care about those in my community so that the mind changers, alcohol and drugs, will vanish, and our communities will forever be free of violence.

5-EARTH

The **Earth** and the natural environment is the fifth principle of great importance to Indian People.

Our Mother Earth is the source of all life, whether it be the plants, the two-legged, four-legged, winged ones or human beings. The Mother Earth is the greatest Teacher, if we listen, observe, and respect her. When we live in harmony with the Mother Earth, she will recycle the things we consume and make them available to our children and to their children.

As Indian men and women, we must teach our children how to care for the Earth so it is there for future generations.

I realize the Earth is our Mother. I will treat her with honor and respect.

I will honor the interconnectedness of all things and all forms of life.

I will realize the Earth does not belong to us, but we belong to the Earth.

The Natural Law is the ultimate authority upon the lands and water. I will learn the knowledge and wisdom of the natural laws. I will pass this knowledge on to my children.

The Mother Earth is a living entity that maintains life. I will speak out in a good way whenever I see someone abusing the Earth. Just as I would protect my own mother, so will I protect the Earth. I will ensure that the land, water, and air will be intact for my children and for my children's children—the unborn.

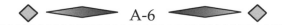

6-CREATOR

Relationship with the **Creator** is the sixth principle that is a focus of Indian life.

As Indian people, our tribes or Nations have hundreds of different words in our own languages signifying what we mean when we say Creator. I realize we make no gains without the Great Spirit being in our lives. Neither I, nor anything we do, will work without our Creator. Being Indian and being spiritual has the same meaning. Spirituality is our gift from the Great One. This day, I vow to walk the Red Road.

As an Indian man, woman, or youth I will return to the traditional and spiritual values that have guided my ancestors for the past generations.

I will look with new eyes on the powers of our ceremonies and religious ways, for they are important to the very survival of our people.

We have survived and are going to grow and flourish spiritually. We will fulfill our teachings and the purpose that the Creator has given us with dignity.

Each day, I will pray and ask for guidance. I will commit to walk the Red Road, or whatever the spiritual way is called in my own culture.

If I am Christian, I will be a good one. If I am traditional, I will walk this road with dedication.

If each of us can do these things then others will follow. From this day forward, I will reserve time and energy for spirituality, seeking to know the Creator's will.

7-MYSELF

The relationship with **myself** is the seventh principle that is important to us as Indian people. It is one that makes possible all that is good in life.

First of all, we must have a loving and good relationship with ourselves if we are to walk the Red Road in a good way. We must care for our bodies by having good eating habits and having physical exercise in our daily lives. We must be careful not to live in a stressful manner on a long-time basis or we will fall into poor health—physically, emotionally, mentally or spiritually. We must welcome relaxation into our lives day-by-day.

I will think about what kind of person I want to be when I am an Elder. I will start developing myself now to be this person.

I will walk with the Great Spirit and the grandfathers and grandmothers at my side. I will develop myself to remain positive. I will learn what it means to develop a Good Mind.

Each day, I will listen for the Creator's voice in the wind. I will watch nature and ask to be shown a lesson, which will occur on my path.

I will seek the guiding principles that guided my ancestors. I will walk in dignity, honor, and humility, conducting myself as a male or female warrior.

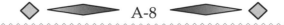

I will seek the guidance of the Elders so that I maintain the knowledge of culture, ceremonies, and songs, and so that I may pass these on to the future generations.

I choose to do all these things myself because no one else can do them for me.

I know I CANNOT GIVE AWAY WHAT I DON'T HAVE, so I will need to learn to walk the talk.

I will live up to my responsibilities and I will treat myself in a good, good way.

Wellbriety means to be sober and well. In our traditional ways, wellness was connected with these seven aspects or principles of living. When we study and discuss these seven ways in our talking circles they also become our vision for sobriety. You can use these seven topics to talk about in your recovery, sobriety and Wellbriety circles. The facilitator can read off one of the Philosophies after the check-in portion of a particular circle. Then people can share their experience, strength and hope about what they have heard.

Appendix 2
Native American Code of Ethics

Here are some good words to reflect on individually, and to discuss in our Wellbriety Circles.

-1-
Rise with the sun to pray. Pray alone. Pray often. The Great Spirit will listen, if only you speak.

-2-
Be tolerant of those who are lost on their path. Ignorance, conceit, anger, jealousy and greed stem from a lost soul. Pray that they find guidance.

-3-
Search for yourself, by yourself. Do not allow others to make your path for you. It is your road and yours alone. Others may walk with you, but no one can walk it for you.

-4-
Treat the guests in your home with much consideration. Serve them the best food, give them the best bed and treat them with honor and respect.

-5-
Do not take what is not yours whether from a person, a community, the wilderness or from a culture. It was not earned or given. It is not yours.

Native American Code of Ethics

-6-

Respect all things that are placed upon this earth--whether it be people or plant.

-7-

Honor other people's thoughts, wishes and words. Never interrupt another or mock or rudely mimic them. Allow each person the right to personal expression.

-8-

Never speak of others in a bad way. The negative energy you put out into the universe will multiply when it returns to you.

-9-

All persons make mistakes. And all mistakes can be forgiven.

-10-

Bad thoughts cause illness of the mind, body and spirit. Practice optimism.

-11-

Nature is not FOR us; it is PART of us. The land is part of your worldly family.

-12-

Children are the seeds of our future. Plant love in their hearts and water them with wisdom and life's lessons. When they are grown, give them space to grow.

-13-

Avoid hurting the hearts of others. The poison of your pain will return to you.

-14-

Be truthful at all times. Honesty is the test of one's will within this universe.

-15-

Keep yourself balanced. Your Mental Self, Spiritual Self, Emotional Self, and Physical Self all need to be strong, pure and healthy. Work out the body to strengthen the mind. Grow rich in spirit to cure emotional ills.

-16-

Make conscious decisions as to which you will be and you will react. Be responsible for your own actions.

-17-

Respect the privacy and personal space of others. Do not touch the personal property of others--especially sacred and religious objects. This is forbidden.

-18-

Be true to yourself first. You cannot nurture and help others if you cannot nurture and help yourself first.

-19-

Respect others' religious beliefs. Do not force your belief on others.

-20-

Share your good fortunes with others. Participate in charity.

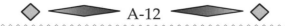

References

Chapter 2
The Solution is in the Culture

1- See the following website: www.runningdeerslonghouse.com
Either click on The Creator, or go directly to
www.runningdeerslonghouse.com/webdoc100.htm

Chapter 3
Alcoholism

1- Frazier, Patrick, *The Mohicans of Stockbridge,* University of
Nebraska Press, 1992, p7

2- In Armstrong, Virginia, *I Have Spoken: American History Through
the Voices of the Indians,* Swallow Press, 1971, p21

3- Lombardi, *Circle Without End* , Naturegraph, 1982, p34

4- Armstrong, Virginia, *I Have Spoken: American History Through the
Voices of the Indians,* Swallow Press, 1971, p43

5- Armstrong, Virginia, *I Have Spoken: American History Through the
Voices of the Indians,* Swallow Press, 1971, p40

6- Adapted from *Traditional Teachings,* North American Travelling
College, RR # 3, Cornwall Island, Ontario, K6H 5R7, (613) 932-
9452 voice, (613) 932-0092 fax

7- Vanderwerth, W.C., *Indian Oratory,* University of Oklahoma Press,
1971, p234

8- Vestal, Stanley, *Sitting Bull,* (1932), 1989, University of Oklahoma
Press, p284

Chapter 4
Many Paths to the Creator

1- Lombardi, *Circle Without End* , Naturegraph, 1982, p12

2- Lombardi, *Circle Without End* , Naturegraph, 1982, p22

References

Chapter 6
Interconnectedness of the 12 Steps

1- White Bison, Inc., *Medicine Wheel and the 12 Steps For Men. Medicine Wheel and the 12 Steps For Women.* Video sets, workbooks, facilitator's manuals.

Chapter 7
Steps 1-6 in the Native Way

1- White Bison, Inc., *Medicine Wheel and the 12 Steps For Men. Medicine Wheel and the 12 Steps For Women.* Video sets, workbooks, facilitator's manuals.

2- *The Twelve Steps of Alcoholics Anonymous Interpreted by the Hazelden Foundation,* Hazelden, Center City, Minnesota, 1993

Covington, Stephanie S., *A Woman's Way Through the Twelve Steps,* PhD, Hazelden, Center City Minnesota, 2000

3- White Bison, Inc., *Medicine Wheel and the 12 Steps For Men. Medicine Wheel and the 12 Steps For Women.* Video sets, workbooks, facilitator's manuals.

Chapter 8
Steps 7-12 in the Native Way

1- White Bison, Inc., *Medicine Wheel and the 12 Steps For Men. Medicine Wheel and the 12 Steps For Women.* Video sets, workbooks, facilitator's manuals.

2- Carlson, Richard, PhD, *The Don't Sweat Affirmations,* Hyperion, N.Y., 2001

Maisel, Eric, *Affirmations for Artists,* Tarcher/Putnam, NY, 1996

3, 4- *Alcoholics Anonymous,* Alcoholics Anonymous World Services, Inc., NY, 1939-2002, p76

References

Chapter 9
To Those Who Walk By Our Sides

1-   Beattie, Melody, *Codependent's Guide to the Twelve Steps*, Fireside, NY, 1990

Mellody, Pia, *Facing Codependence*, Harper SanFrancisco, 1989

Beattie, Melody, *Beyond Codependency*, Hazelden, 1989

Schaef, Anne Wilson, *Co-Dependence--Misunderstood, Mistreated* , Harper and Row, NY, 1986

2, 3   Al-Anon Family Group Headquarters, Inc. Toll free number for group meeting information: 1-888-4AL-ANON.
Web: www.al-anon.alateen.org e-mail wso@al-anon.org

Chapter 10
Strengthening Our Families

1-   Neihardt, John G., *Black Elk Speaks*, University of Nebraska Press, Lincoln, 1961

2-   Erikson, Erik H., *Childhood and Society*, W.W. Norton, NY, 1950, 1963, 1985

Erikson, Erik H., *Identity and the Life Cycle*, W.W. Norton, NY, 1959, 1980

Evans, Richard I. *Dialogue with Erik Erikson*, Jason Aronson, Inc. , Northvale, N.J., 1964, 1967, 1981, 1995

❖

References

SUGGESTED READINGS

RECOVERY IN GENERAL

Alcoholics Anonymous, Alcoholics Anonymous World Services, Inc., NY, 1939-2002

Twelve Steps and Twelve Traditions, Alcoholics Anonymous World Services, Inc. NY

Al-Anon's Twelve Steps & Twelve Traditions, Al-Anon Family Group Headquarters, Inc., NY

Black, Claudia, PhD, MSW, *Children of Alcoholics*, Ballantine Books, 1981-1991

Friel, John, PhD, and Friel, Linda, MA, *An Adult Child's Guide to "What's Normal"*, Health Communications, Inc., Deerfield Beach, FL, 1990

Friel, John, PhD, and Friel, Linda, MA, *Adult Children: The Secrets of Dysfunctional Families*, Health Communications, Inc., 1988

Friends in Recovery, *The Twelve Steps for Adult Children*, RPI Publishing, Curtis, WA, 1987-1996

Krestan, Jo-Ann, *Bridges to Recovery: Addiction, Family Therapy, and Multicultural Treatment*, The Free Press, New York, 2000

Kritsberg, Wayne, *The Adult Children of Alcoholics Syndrome: A Step by Step Guide to Discovery and Recovery*, Bantam, NY, 1985, 1988

Matsakis, Aphrodite, PhD, *I Can't Get Over It: A Handbook for Trauma Survivors*, 2nd edition, New Harbinger Publications, Oakland, 1996

Monahan, Sister Molly, *Seeds of Grace: Reflections on the Spirituality of Alcoholics Anonymous*, Riverhead Books, NY, 2001

References

Rich, Phil, EdD, MSW and Copans, Stuart A., MD, *The Healing Journey Through Addiction:* Your Journal for Recovery and Self-Renewal, John Wiley and Sons, Inc., NY, 2000

Schaef Anne Wilson, *Meditations for Women Who Do Too Much,* Harper SanFrancisco, 1990

Schaef, Anne Wilson, *When Society Becomes an Addict,* Harper & Row, San Francisco, 1987

NATIVE AMERICAN CULTURE

Arbogast, Doyle, *Wounded Warriors: A Time for Healing,* Little Turtle Publications, Omaha, Nebraska,1995

Axtell, Horace, Aragon, Margo, *A Little Bit of Wisdom,* Confluence Press, 1997

Beck, Peggy V., Walters, A.L., *The Sacred: Ways of Knowledge, Sources of Life,* Navajo Community College, Navajo Nation, 1977

Bopp, Judie, et. al, *The Sacred Tree,* Lotus Light, Wilmot, WI, 1984-1989

Brown, Joseph Epes, *The Sacred Pipe: Black Elk's Account of the Seven Rites of the Oglala Sioux,* University of Oklahoma Press, 1953 1989

Cajete, Gregory, *Look to the Mountain,* Kivaki Press, 1994

Cajete, Gregory, *Native Science: Natural Laws of Interdependence,* Clear Light Publishers, Santa Fe, 2000

Coyhis, Don, *Meditations With Native American Elders,* Coyhis Publishing, Colorado Springs, CO, 1995

Deloria, Vine, Jr., Wildcat, Daniel, R., *Power and Place: Indian Education in America,* Fulcrum Resources, Golden, Colorado, 2001

References

Deloria, Vine, Jr., *God is Red: A Native View of Religion*, (1973) Fulcrum Resources, Golden, Colorado, 1996

Eastman, Charles Alexander (Ohiyesa), *Indian Boyhood*, Fawcett Premier, 1972

Foreman, Grant, *The Five Civilized Tribes*, University of Oklahoma Press, 1934, 1989

Hill, Norbert S., Jr., *Words of Power: Voices From Indian America*, Fulcrum Resources, Golden, Colorado, 1995

Mails, Thomas, E., *Fool's Crow*, University of Nebraska, Bison, Book, Lincoln, Nebraska, 1979, 1990

Neihardt, Hilda, and Utecht, Lori, editors, *Black Elk Lives: Conversations With the Black Elk Family*, University of Nebraska press, 2000

Nerburn, Kent, *The Soul of an Indian: And Other Writings From Ohiyesa*, New World Library, San Rafael, California, 1993

Standing Bear, Luther, *My Indian Boyhood*, Bison Books, Lincoln, Nebraska, 1931-1988

Thomas, Chief Jacob, with Terry Boyle, *Teachings From the Longhouse*, Stoddart Publishing, Toronto, Canada, 1994

White Bison, Inc. *Healing a Nation: Hoop Journey Video*, White Bison, Inc. 2001